Fundamentals of Municipal Bonds

Fourth Edition

by

 **THE BOND MARKET TRADE ASSOCIATION**

New York

Fourth Edition

Copyright © 1981, 1982, 1987, 1990 by the Public Securities Association

First printing 1981
Second edition printing 1982
Third edition printing 1987, 1989
Fourth edition printing 1990

Library of Congress Cataloging in Publication Data
Main entry under title:

Fundamentals of Municipal Bonds/Public Securities Association—Rev. ed.

    p. cm.
    Includes bibliographical references.
    Includes index.
    1. Public Securities Association. 2. Municipal bonds—United States.
    I. Public Securities Association.
HG4952.F86   1990   332.63'233'0973—dc 20   89-39361 CIP
ISBN 0-9605198-2-3

Printed in the United States of America

Table of Contents

Preface

The political philosopher Edmund Burke once said, "Government is a contrivance of human wisdom to provide for human wants."

This book details one relatively little-known aspect of how governments—the 83,200 local and state governments in the United States—attempt to provide for human wants when they have to finance their futures.

These governments satisfy human wants by facilitating movement along streets and sidewalks, by rail or by air; educating the young; taking care of the sick; helping to provide housing; removing and disposing of our wastes; providing water, gas, steam, or electricity; keeping our land, water, and air clean; providing buildings for those who serve the people, courthouses to uphold the law, and jails to confine those who commit wrongs against society.

State and local governments have essentially two budgets—an operations budget, which usually relates to day-by-day expenses, and a capital budget, which is used to build public works. Much of those capital budgets is borrowed money. In fact, since 1900, more than $2.1 trillion has been borrowed by local and state governments by issuing municipal bonds as of 1989.

This book outlines the process by which local and state governments borrow money and how the free-market system operates to facilitate that borrowing. It is a process that for all practical purposes has served the nation well.

It is safe to say that wherever you are, whenever you are reading this book, you have already touched something that was built by bonds.

Fundamentals of Municipal Bonds has long been regarded as a definitive and informative basic text on the municipal securities market. It was first published under the auspices of the Investment Bankers Association of America (IBAA) and later updated and reprinted in 1973 by the Securities Industry Association (SIA) through the efforts of its Public Finance Information and Education Committee. The Public Securities Association (PSA) was established in 1976 to continue the work of the IBAA and the SIA in serving the members of the public securities industry. In 1981, PSA published a revised, updated, and expanded *Fundamentals of Municipal Bonds,* similar in style to the present edition.

PSA is the international organization of banks, dealers, and brokers that underwrite, trade, and sell municipal securities, mortgage-backed securities, money market securities, and U.S. government and federal agency securities. PSA's member firms collectively account for approximately 95 percent of the nation's municipal securities underwriting and trading activity. The membership also includes all primary dealers in government securities, as recognized by the Federal Reserve Bank of New York, all major dealers in mortgage-backed securities, and major money market dealers. PSA currently has approximately 300 member firms, 100 associate member firms, and 21 affiliates.

Because of some new developments in the municipal securities industry in recent years, PSA now offers the present edition as a revision of the third edition of the book. This text is intended to provide a basic understanding of the municipal securities market to:

1. Newcomers to the municipal securities industry who are preparing for a professional qualifications examination.
2. Other securities industry professionals who seek to increase their knowledge of the municipal market to serve their clients and customers better.
3. Individuals engaged in portfolio management for institutional investors.
4. Public officials who wish to better understand the capital-raising mechanism for state and local governments.
5. Individual investors, academicians, and students seeking an overview of the municipal securities market.

Acknowledgments

We would first like to mention that we are deeply indebted to all of those individuals within the municipal securities industry who worked so hard to produce the first 1981 edition of this book for the PSA. We will not acknowledge each of them by name here, but we want to emphasize that their research, their willingness to be interviewed, and their factual contributions during the original writing of the text laid the groundwork for an excellent book and made our work updating this volume that much easier.

For this fourth edition we would like to repeat the acknowledgements that appeared in the third edition, because we retained most of the textual changes that were made for that substantial revision of the book that was published in 1987. The current fourth edition was primarily updated to include a major rewrite of Chapter 9 by R. Thomas Stanton, Esq., Managing Partner, Squire, Sanders & Dempsey and to reflect year-end figures from 1989 in all of the charts and graphs compiled by P. Anders Nybo, Research Analyst, Public Securities Association. In addition to the above, the following individuals from the PSA staff contributed to the preparation and editing of the fourth edition: Caroline M. Benn, Vice President, Public Relations and Member Services; George Brakatselos, Vice President; and Randall E. Clarke, Publications Manager. We would also like to thank Sandi Schroeder, of Schroeder Editorial Services, for her preparation of a new index for this edition.

What follows is a reprint of the acknowledgments that appeared in the third edition with a few changes of title and firm:

For the third edition we would like to recognize the participation of Robert H. Muller, Managing Director of Securities Research, J.P. Morgan Securities Inc., in every phase of the revision process. As Chairman of the Research and Education Committee of the Municipal Securities Division of the Public Securities Association, 1985-1986, Mr. Muller supervised the project. The following industry professionals also deserve our utmost appreciation for having acted as the senior editors reviewing the manuscript and often rewriting sections of the book: George D. Friedlander, Managing Director/Fixed Income Research, Smith Barney, Harris Upham & Co., Inc.; R. Thomas Stanton, Esq., Managing Partner, Squire, Sanders & Dempsey; and Joseph C. Taylor, Vice President, Smith Barney, Harris Upham & Co., Inc. Squire, Sanders & Dempsey also graciously offered its own in-house glossary as the main source for new definitions and terms used to substantially update the glossary of municipal terminology.

The following individuals in the municipal securities market deserve recognition as major contributors to the third edition; they were responsible for updating and often rewriting different chapters or sections of the text that reflect their areas of expertise: Thomas S. Buckmeyer, Vice President, Fixed Income Research Department, Smith Barney, Harris Upham & Co.; Patricia S. Deford, Vice President, Alex. Brown & Sons, Inc.; Angela Desmond, General Counsel, Municipal Securities Rulemaking Board; John B. Esau, Vice President, Marine Midland Bank; Sylvan G. Feldstein, Ph.D., Vice President, Municipal Bond Research, Merrill Lynch Capital Markets; Michael E. Godwin, former Senior Vice President and Director of National Marketing and Municipal Bond Sales, Shearson Lehman Brothers Inc.; Hyman C. Grossman, Managing Director, Standard & Poor's Corporation; Judith A. Harvey, Assistant Vice President, VanKampen Merritt Investment Advisory Corp.; Arthur J. Hausker, Assistant Vice President and Assistant Manager of the Municipal Division, Fitch Investors Service, Inc.; Dee Dee Hegel, Senior Marketing Manager, Chicago Board of Trade; James L. Kochan, Associate Director, Securities Research and Economics, Merrill Lynch Capital Markets; Austin V. Koenen, Managing Director, Morgan Stanley & Co. Incorporated; Charles E. LeCroy, Assistant Vice President, Marine Midland Bank; Peter J. Maguire, Executive Vice President, J.J. Kenny Co., Inc.; Duane

H. Miyagishima, Assistant Vice President, Morgan Guaranty Trust Company of New York; Robert J. Murphy, Vice President, Public Finance Department, Cowen & Company; Jeffrey B. Noss, Vice President, The Bank of New York; Stephen Peters, Senior Vice President, Shearson Lehman Brothers Inc.; Steven P. Rofsky, Vice President, J.P. Morgan Securities, Inc.; Elsie Schuyler Smith, Assistant Vice President, Municipal Credit Analysis Department, Chemical Bank; John F. Thompson, Senior Consultant, Shearson Lehman Brothers Inc.; and Kimberly L. Quinones, Vice President, Public Finance Department, Prudential-Bache Securities, Inc.

We deeply appreciate the expert advice of the following professionals in the municipal securities industry, not mentioned above, who commented on the final manuscript of the third edition: Frank D. Bernardi, Assistant Vice President, Colorado National Bank Denver; Mobley E. Cox, Jr., Senior Vice President, Texas Capital Markets Incorporated; Robert N. Downey, Partner, Goldman, Sachs & Co.; Mark B. Florian, Vice President, Goldman, Sachs & Co.; David E. Hartley, Managing Partner, Stone & Youngberg; Robert M. Kessler, Vice President, Citicorp Investment Bank; Richard F. Kezer, Senior Vice President, Citicorp Investment Bank; John E. Petersen, Senior Director, Government Finance Research Center, Government Finance Officers Association; George Popoff, Vice President, The First Boston Corporation; Heather L. Ruth, President, Public Securities Association; and Karl H. Velde, Jr., Partner, William Blair & Company. In addition to those listed, we would like to acknowledge many individuals, too numerous to mention, who also made valuable contributions by verifying facts and statistics throughout the text.

AUSTIN V. KOENEN
Chairman
Public Securities Association, 1990
Managing Director
Morgan Stanley & Co., Incorporated

Introduction:
An Overview of the
Municipal Securities Industry

The debt of state and local governments has grown rapidly, with only a handful of interruptions, for more than a century and a half. Debt financing became an acceptable means to support the development of the young, vigorous cities in the 1820s. The amount of state and local debt outstanding expanded quickly during the remainder of the century, set back seriously only by the Panic of 1873 and its aftermath. In the year 1900, state and local governments borrowed $175 million from investors, bringing the level of outstanding debt to more than $2 billion.

In the twentieth century, the volume of offerings continued to push upward. Total state and local debt outstanding had reached $5 billion when the Sixteenth Amendment to the United States Constitution established the federal income tax in 1913. Interest on state and local issues was exempted from the new tax, and, as a result, yields fell markedly compared with rates on taxable corporate and U.S. government securities. Only in the last years of the Depression and during World War II did growth in volume stop altogether. By 1950, there was about $24 billion of outstanding *municipal* securities—a term that by convention has come to include all publicly offered state and local debt. In 1966, new issues totaled $17.6 billion and the amount of debt outstanding exceeded $105 billion, and by 1971, the comparable figures were $50.6 billion and $161.8 billion, respectively. (See Figures I-1 and I-2.)

The growth in volume slowed during the first half of the 1970s, first on long-term issues and then, after the default by New York City on its notes in 1975, on short-term issues. Thus by 1976, total new issuance of $55 billion was only slightly higher than the $50.6 billion recorded five years earlier. The growth in volume reaccelerated in the late 1970s and 1980s. (See Figure I-2.)

The municipal market has gone through a series of major changes since the early 1970s which mark the past 20 years as a very different era from the three decades

1

FIGURE I-1. State and Local Debt Outstanding, 1948-1989
($ in billions)

1989	$784.0	1968	$123.2
1988	759.8	1967	113.7
1987	713.2	1966	105.9
1986	679.1	1965	100.3
1985	655.5	1964	92.9
1984	520.0	1963	86.9
1983	469.0	1962	81.2
1982	417.9	1961	75.9
1981	373.7	1960	70.8
1980	350.3	1959	65.5
1979	320.1	1958	59.2
1978	289.7	1957	53.7
1977	261.4	1956	49.5
1976	239.5	1955	45.9
1975	223.8	1954	40.6
1974	207.7	1953	34.5
1973	191.2	1952	30.2
1972	176.5	1951	26.6
1971	161.8	1950	24.4
1970	144.4	1949	21.0
1969	133.1	1948	18.5

SOURCE: Federal Reserve Board

following the Depression of the 1930s. The most far-reaching change in the municipal marketplace has been the rise and eventual domination of the market by revenue bonds. Municipal debt had been issued over the years primarily as a general obligation of the state or local government. General obligation bonds are usually backed by the "full faith and credit" of the issuer—in other words, the full taxing power of the state or local government. Revenue bonds, on the other hand, usually have no claim on the other revenues of the issuer. Rather, they are issued to support a particular project, such as a utility, and they are typically paid for out of the revenues generated by that project. By the end of the 1970s, the volume of new revenue bonds was outpacing traditional general obligation debt by almost a two-to-one margin, a trend which extended into the last half of the 1980s. In the late 1960s, however, general obligation debt comprised some 65 percent of annual new issues. This shift was stimulated in part by the emergence of new types of

Figure 1-2. State and Local Borrowing, 1969-1989

Volume of New Issues of Long- and Short-Term Securities
($ in millions)

Year	Long-Term	Short-Term	Total	Total Number
1989	$122,500.0	$28,400.0	$150,900.0	11,199
1988	116,946.8	23,119.4	140,066.2	10,249
1987	105,729.8	18,684.0	124,413.8	8,855
1986	151,559.8	22,199.3	173,759.1	9,445
1985	222,240.7	23,098.7	245,339.4	12,933
1984	107,983.3	20,818.8	128,802.1	9,095
1983	86,755.7	36,878.3	123,634.0	8,672
1982	79,137.2	44,757.8	123,895.0	9,095
1981	47,814.4	37,444.4	85,258.8	6,652
1980	48,492.5	27,739.4	76,231.9	7,689
1979	43,334.9	21,715.2	65,050.1	6,931
1978	48,349.0	21,383.8	69,732.8	7,063
1977	46,705.9	24,750.9	71,456.8	7,370
1976	35,313.6	20,078.7	55,392.3	7,381
1975	29,326.2	28,972.8	58,299.0	8,107
1974	22,824.0	29,040.7	51,864.7	7,701
1973	22,952.6	24,667.4	47,620.0	8,147
1972	22,940.8	25,221.8	48,162.6	8,420
1971	24,369.5	26,281.5	50,651.0	8,811
1970	17,761.6	17,880.0	35,641.6	7,604
1969	11,460.3	11,783.1	23,243.4	6,395

SOURCE: Public Securities Association Municipal Securities Database, 1969-1985;
IDD Information Services/PSA Municipal Securities Database, 1986-1989;
The Bond Buyer

revenue bonds, but also by the taxpayer revolts of the late 1970s and early 1980s against high property taxes which were the primary source of payment for general obligation bonds. Since revenue bonds did not require the imposition of taxes, they became a favored means of financing during this period.

With revenue bonds, municipalities have been able to expand their uses of tax-exempt borrowing without burdening the taxpayer. Indeed, municipal debt has increasingly been used to support various public purpose projects once financed only by the private sector. In the 1950s, revenue bonds were issued primarily for highways, turnpikes, and public utilities. During the 1970s and 1980s, tax-exempt revenue bonds were being issued to provide financing for housing, hospitals, industrial pollution control equipment, massive public power projects sometimes involving several public and private utilities, sports stadiums, convention centers, airports, and higher education facilities. A hybrid bond of sorts, the moral obligation bond, became popular in the 1970s as a method of financing some state projects. These bonds were secured by revenues from the project. In addition, they were secured by a moral though not binding obligation on the part of the state to make up any shortfall in debt service reserve funds. Their use has been far less prevalent in recent years.

The municipal bond market was also to be tested by major defaults in the 1970s and 1980s. Few occurrences in the history of the municipal securities market were more momentous than New York City's financial difficulties in 1975. After rapidly increasing its outstanding debt for more than a decade, New York City's access to the municipal securities market came to an abrupt halt. The city defaulted on a note issue, and prices of some outstanding city obligations declined substantially. New York City's problems, in turn, cast doubt on the security of various municipal credits throughout the country.

For investors in municipal bonds, the temporary note default by New York City came as a sudden jolt. The rating agencies of Moody's Investors Service, Inc., and Standard & Poor's Corporation had given New York City bonds a respectable rating of A prior to 1975. Municipal issues, whose safety was long considered second only to U.S. government securities, suddenly were viewed as potentially involving an element of serious risk.

In 1983, a second major default, on $2.25 billion of long-term revenue bonds by the Washington Public Power Supply System (WPPSS) Projects 4 and 5, marked the largest such event in market history. Unlike the situation in New York City, default did not occur because participants in the projects were found to be incapable of paying amounts under supply contracts which would be applied to debt service on the bonds. Rather, state courts ruled that the participants were not authorized to enter into the supply contracts, and thus, the participants had no legal obligation to make the payments. As in the case of New York City, both aforementioned rating agencies had at one time rated these bonds A.

The increasing concern among investors, particularly individuals, following New York City's default and later that of WPPSS led to the growth of an entirely new industry, bond insurance and credit guarantees. These enhancements involve a third party guaranteeing the debt service of the issuer in the event of a failure to pay by the issuer. The first bond insurance companies emerged in the early 1970s, but volume as a percentage of the market was low until the early 1980s. In 1983, 15 percent of all new issues sold were insured and in 1989, 25 percent. Commercial banks also entered the guarantee business and began to issue letters of credit to back many different kinds of bonds.

Another change was the emergence of regulation. Until the 1970s, the municipal securities industry had not been subject to any direct federal securities regulation, having been exempted from the Securities Acts of 1933 and 1934, which established regulation for other securities markets. But a number of proceedings initiated by the Securities and Exchange Commission (SEC) in the early 1970s against several dealers in municipal securities captured the attention of Congress, and a demand for some form of regulation arose. In 1975, Congress passed the Securities Acts Amendments, which established the Municipal Securities Rule-making Board (MSRB), composed of industry and public members, to write rules governing the activities of brokers and dealers in the municipal securities market. The 1975 amendments also required all municipal securities dealers and brokers to register with the SEC and the MSRB to establish qualifications examinations for municipal securities professionals.

In recent years, both the MSRB and the SEC have focused on the adequacy of voluntary disclosure practices and the general availability of credit and issue information concerning municipal securities. This focus has resulted in rules governing underwriter activities and increased initiatives by the MSRB to provide mechanisms for the storage and retrieval of municipal securities disclosure documents and related information.

At the Congressional level, concerns over increased use of tax-exempt financing and financing mechanisms have led to continuing efforts to both curtail the issuance of municipal securities and limit the investment advantages of those securities. Such efforts climaxed in 1986 with the passage of a major reform of the tax code. The revised law appears likely to usher in a new era in municipal bonds. Limitations on the supply of and demand for bonds, efforts to tax interest for some categories of investors and bonds, and major reductions in tax rates already are changing the municipal marketplace.

These major changes in recent years require a revision of the basic literature on the municipal securities industry. This updated volume is intended to provide that information. It is a fundamental text for any individual interested in acquiring an understanding of the basics of the municipal securities market and provides a broad and up-to-date summary of all important principles and practices in the industry. Its range is intentionally very wide. Specialists will find it a valuable guide to those areas of the business outside their own fields. The newcomer to the industry will find it an accessible, clear, and accurate primer that covers the important basic information about the securities and the industry. It may be particularly helpful to those preparing for the MSRB qualifications examinations.

The first chapter covers the rudimentary characteristics and technicalities of municipal securities, and defines the various important types of bonds. Chapter 2 outlines the roles of all the major participants in the market, from issuers to investors. The objective is to give the reader an overview of the entire marketplace and the functions performed by the various market participants. Several of the major participants, however, require their own chapters. Chapters 3, 4, and 5 discuss in greater depth the issuers, underwriters, and the secondary market, respectively. The roles of dealers as underwriter and market maker are examined carefully in the latter two chapters.

The major investors are discussed in Chapter 6, as are basic investing strategies and tax matters that affect investors. In Chapter 7, what analysts look for in determining the creditworthiness of general obligation and revenue bonds is examined. The economic, financial, and special market factors that determine the level of municipal interest rates are the subject of Chapter 8. Chapter 9 includes a summary of the current rules of the Municipal Securities Rulemaking Board, as well as a look at other areas of federal oversight and involvement in the municipal securities market. The historical basis for the tax exemption is also discussed. The Appendix on mathematical calculations reviews both the theory and the methods of calculating yields and bids.

The Basics of Municipal Securities

Terminology

"Municipal securities" and, a term used even more frequently, "municipal bonds" refer generically to interest-bearing obligations issued by state and local governmental entities to finance operating or capital costs. As discussed in this chapter, municipal securities have certain common characteristics. However, they also take many forms, are issued for a variety of purposes, and can be payable from different sources. The distinguishing characteristics of municipal securities, as well as municipal securities market practices, have given rise to a specialized terminology. Familiarity with that terminology is very useful, indeed, almost essential, for an understanding of municipal bond fundamentals. To aid that understanding and for reference purposes, a glossary of municipal terminology defining commonly used words and phrases is included as an appendix.

The Federal Tax Exemption

The principal characteristic that has traditionally set municipal securities apart from all other capital market securities is the federal tax exemption: the interest income on municipal bonds has historically been exempt from federal income tax. Evidence of the significance of this characteristic is reflected by the fact that municipal securities are often commonly referred to simply as "tax-exempt bonds." And, as discussed in this and later chapters, the federal tax status of interest and related tax consequences on municipal securities greatly influence the nature, type, and level of investor interest.

As discussed in Chapter 9, the basis of the federal income tax exemption for municipal securities is historical and was originally premised upon Supreme Court decisions predating the ratification of the Sixteenth Amendment to the U.S. Constitution, which authorized Congress to pass federal income tax laws. Since that ratification, all such tax laws, including the Internal Revenue Code of 1986, have provided for the municipal securities exemption. However, as also discussed in Chapter 9, federal tax laws, including particularly the 1986 Code, have increasingly imposed significant restrictions and limitations on the types and amounts of tax-exempt municipal securities that can be issued. In addition, such tax laws as the alternative minimum tax provisions of the 1986 Tax Code and amendments to the Social Security Act enacted in 1983 have reduced the tax exemption applicable to certain types of bonds and to certain taxpayers. In part because of such federal tax limitations and restrictions, a taxable municipal securities market is in an incipient stage of development. To date, that market has remained relatively small in scope and has focused largely on particular financial products.

The savings that the tax exemption affords to state and local issuers became obvious soon after the first federal income tax was initiated. Before 1913, interest rates on municipal securities were about the same as rates on corporate bonds since neither was subject to federal income taxation. After 1913, the rates on tax-exempt municipal securities fell sharply relative to taxable, corporate bond interest rates. That dynamic has persisted: Throughout the 1980s, interest rates on long-term municipal securities averaged about 75 percent of rates on comparable long-term corporate bonds (Figure 1-1).

Investors are willing to accept the lower yields because they, too, gain advantages from the tax exemption; and the higher the investor's tax bracket, the greater the advantage. For example, a high-quality, long-term municipal bond bore an average annual interest rate of 7 percent during 1990. For an investor in the 33 percent federal income tax bracket, that rate, being tax-exempt, represented the equivalent of a 10.45 percent return on a taxable bond, since 33 percent of the earnings of the taxable bond would have been paid out in federal income tax. At the same time, an investor in the 28 percent tax bracket would have had to earn 9.72 percent on a taxable bond to earn the net equivalent of earnings on a 7 percent municipal bond. In fact, during the same period, a corporate bond paid only about 9.56 percent.

The relative advantage of tax-exempt bonds can be even greater for the investor who lives in a state that imposes state and local income taxes, for, frequently, municipal bonds are exempt from these taxes also. However, though laws vary greatly from state to state, many states exempt interest income only on bonds issued within their own boundaries. For example, in 1991 a married couple

FIGURE 1-1. Municipal Bond Yields as a Percentage of Corporate Yields, 1970-1989

Year	Average Aa Municipal Yield* ÷	Average Aa Corporate Yield* =	% Ratio
1970	6.28%	8.32%	75%
1971	5.36	7.78	69
1972	5.19	7.48	69
1973	5.09	7.66	66
1974	6.04	8.84	68
1975	6.77	9.17	74
1976	6.12	8.75	70
1977	5.39	8.24	65
1978	5.68	8.92	64
1979	6.12	9.94	62
1980	8.06	12.50	64
1981	10.89	14.75	74
1982	11.31	14.41	78
1983	9.17	12.39	74
1984	9.88	13.31	74
1985	8.93	11.82	76
1986	7.16	9.47	76
1987	7.39	9.68	76
1988	7.49	9.94	75
1989	7.10	9.46	75

SOURCE: *Moody's Bond Survey.* Percentage calculations prepared by the Public Securities Association.

* Moody's yearly averages of yields on Aa municipal and Aa corporate bonds.

State and local governments achieve considerable interest cost savings in debt financing as a result of the tax-exempt status of municipal bonds. In 1990, interest rates on long-term municipal bonds averaged 25 percent lower than rates on corporate securities from 1/90 to 10/90.

resident in New York City with a combined taxable income of $90,000 will be in the 31 percent federal tax bracket and would be subject to a 7.7 percent state and a 3.86 percent city income tax on their taxable earnings. Note, however, that state and local income tax payments are deductible on the federal tax return under current law. Assuming that this couple itemize deductions, the effect of the state and local taxes must therefore be offset by the amount gained back from the deduction on the federal return. Thus, the total effective income tax rate for the couple is not $31 + 7.7 + 3.86 = 42.56$ percent, but $31 + 7.7 (1 - .31) + 3.86 (1 - .31) = 38.98$ percent. A 7 percent return on a municipal bond issued within the state for that couple, therefore, has the same after-tax benefit as an 11.47 percent taxable bond, since $(11.47) (1 - .3898) = 7$ percent.

The Tax-Exempt/Taxable Yield Equivalent Formula

This formula represents the municipal bond industry's standard way of demonstrating to investors the relative advantages of tax-exempt bonds. The key variable in computing equivalent yields is the investor's marginal tax rate (Figure 1-2). Since federal income tax rates increase with additional dollars earned, the mar-

FIGURE 1-2. Tax-Exempt/Taxable Yield Equivalent Tables

- Select the appropriate return (single or joint return).
- Determine which tax bracket you are in according to the amount of taxable income you have. Taxable income is your income after the appropriate exemptions and deductions are taken. (The tables do not take into account special provisions affecting federal tax rates, especially the alternative minimum tax.)
- The numbers in the column under your tax bracket give you the approximate taxable yield equivalent for each of the tax-exempt yields in the far left column.

Tax-Exempt/Taxable Yield Equivalents for 1990

	(Taxable Income)		
Single Return	$ 0– $19,450	$ 19,451– $ 47,050 or over $109.100	$ 47,051– $109,100
Joint Return	$ 0– $32,450	$ 32,451– $ 78,400 or over $185,730	$ 78,401– $185,730
Tax Bracket	15%	28%	33%*
(Tax-Exempt Yields %)	(Taxable Yield Equivalents %)		
5.0%	5.88%	6.94%	7.46%
6.0	7.06	8.33	8.96
7.0	8.24	9.72	10.45
8.0	9.41	11.11	11.94
9.0	10.59	12.50	13.43
10.0	11.76	13.89	14.93

* This 33% bracket is based on a 5% surtax and a phase-out of the personal exemption amount for certain income ranges. The income ranges listed above assume (i) a single person with no dependents and (ii) a married couple filing jointly with no dependents. If there are dependents, the upper end of the 33% bracket will increase by $11,480 in 1990. Note that once a taxpayer's income exceeds the upper end of the 33% bracket, any income in excess of that amount is taxed at a marginal rate of 28%.

Tax-Exempt/Taxable Yield Equivalents for 1991

	(Taxable Income)		
Single Return	$ 0 – $20,350	$ 20,351 – $ 49,300	$ 49,301 – and over
Joint Return	$ 0 – $34,000	$ 34,001 – $ 82,150	$ 82,151 – and over
Tax Bracket	15%	28%	31%*
(Tax-Exempt Yields %)	(Taxable Yield Equivalents %)		
4.0%	4.71%	5.56%	5.80%
5.0	5.88	6.94	7.25
6.0	7.06	8.33	8.70
7.0	8.24	9.72	10.14
8.0	9.41	11.11	11.59
9.0	10.59	12.50	13.04
10.0	11.76	13.89	14.49
11.0	12.94	15.28	15.94
12.0	14.12	16.67	17.39

* The Internal Revenue Code phases out the personal exemption deduction for taxpayers with adjusted gross income in excess of $150,000 (married filing jointly) and $100,000 (single taxpayers). In addition, certain itemized deductions are reduced for taxpayers with adjusted gross income in excess of $100,000. In general, the limit on itemized deductions will increase the effective marginal tax rate by 1%, and the personal exemption phaseout will increase the effective marginal tax rate by 1/2% for each exemption claimed.

ginal tax rate is that rate which would be applied to any additional income earned. For example, consider a married couple filing a joint return on a taxable income of $90,000 for the 1991 tax year. They would pay taxes at an effective rate of 31 percent on any additional income. Hence, their marginal tax rate is 31 percent, and for every additional $1,000 of taxable income they would have to pay an additional $310 in tax. Thus, this couple would have to earn only $690 in interest on a tax-exempt bond to do as well as they would if they earned $1,000 in interest on a taxable bond. The formula below calculates exactly what a taxable bond would have to yield in order to equal the yield earned on a tax-free municipal bond:

$$\frac{\text{tax-free yield}}{100\% \ - \ \text{marginal tax rate}} \ = \ \text{taxable equivalent yield}$$

Hence, for the couple that earns $90,000 a year and has bought a tax-exempt bond yielding 7 percent, the taxable yield equivalent is 10.14 percent, as follows:

$$\frac{7\%}{100\% \ - \ 31\%} \ = \ \frac{7\%}{69\%} \ = \ 10.14\%$$

Description of a Municipal Bond

Municipal bonds are typically issued in denominations of $5,000 or integral multiples of $5,000, known as the par value or face value amount of the bond. This is the amount, or principal, paid when the bond matures. Up to the 1960s, the conventional denomination was $1,000, and some market terminology is still based on the $1,000 bond. When a dealer says "one bond," the dealer is typically referring to $1,000 par value. "Twenty-five bonds" are $25,000 par value, although there may be only five bond certificates in denominations of $5,000 each. In the past, several municipalities experimented with denominations as small as $100 to try to attract smaller investors, but the practice did not become widespread.

Any particular municipal bond, at least any bearing a fixed rate of interest, is identified by four pieces of information:

Name of issuer. Identification of the issuing body is the first essential piece of information.

Coupon. This is the interest rate stated on the bond and payable to the bondholder. The rate is referred to as "the coupon" whether or not the bond actually has interest coupons physically attached. The dollar amount paid is generally fixed over the life of the bond. Interest on municipal bonds is usually paid semiannually. For example, a $1,000 bond with a coupon rate of 6 percent will pay $60 a year to the bondholder, $30 every six months. In the case of zero-coupon municipal bonds, however, interest accretes semiannually and is not paid to the investor until the bond matures.

Maturity date. This is the date on which the investor will receive payment of principal and the final interest payment. In other words, it is the day, month, and year on which the bondholder will receive the par value of the bond, plus the final interest payment.

Yield (or price). Corporate and U.S. government bonds are generally quoted in terms of price, but municipal bonds are generally quoted in terms of yield because there are so many issues of different maturities. In the case of a variable-rate bond, the interest stated on the coupon changes on a regular basis (daily, monthly, semiannually, etc.), usually based on market conditions but occasionally based on an index or a formula (prime rate, six-month Treasury bill, commercial paper, etc.), in order to keep the yield in line with the market. If the coupon interest payment is fixed, however, the price of the bond itself must change in order to keep the yield in line with other newly issued bonds.

Bond prices are stated as a percentage of the par value. Par value equals 100; a discount bond trades at a price below 100—at 97, say, or at $970 for a bond with a par value of $1,000; a premium bond trades at a price above 100—at 102, say, or $1,020 for a bond with a $1,000 par value.

When the price changes, the yield automatically changes. For example, an investor who pays less than par for a bond with a 6 percent coupon receives, in effect, more than 6 percent in yield; that is, he or she receives $60 of interest each year on an investment of less than $1,000. An investor who pays more than par for the same bond would receive a yield of less than 6 percent. Yields on municipal bonds are usually quoted in increments of .05 percent, or five "basis points"; a basis point is equal to $1/100$ of 1 percent.

Applying these four pieces of information, then, a typical municipal bond quotation would be as follows: "$10,000 City of Minneapolis, Minnesota, 6 percent of February 1, 1993, at 7.5 percent." In this case, a municipal bond dealer would be offering for sale City of Minneapolis bonds with a total par value of $10,000, a coupon of 6 percent, and a maturity date of February 1, 1993. The quotation reflects that the bonds are trading at a price that will yield an interest rate of 7.50 percent, which means the price is approximately $9,157.60.

Municipal bonds fluctuate in yield for the same economic reasons that other bonds do (see Chapter 8). General shifts in interest rates due to Federal Reserve monetary policy or to changing expectations about inflation, for example, affect municipal interest rates as well as other interest rates. Many other factors—short-term swings in the demand for municipal bonds on the part of investors, the perceived creditworthiness of a particular bond issuer, and the total volume of municipal bonds issued, for example—can also cause fluctuations in yield. Moreover, as in all bond markets, yields on older issues rise and fall as yields on new issues with similar maturities and credit characteristics are determined.

The last is an important concept. Consider, for example, a bond issued early in 1979 with a coupon of 6 percent and a 16-year maturity. Eight years later a new bond of similar creditworthiness with a ten-year maturity is issued carrying a coupon of 7 percent. Both bonds are due to mature in ten years—that is, at the same date. Therefore, the bond with the 6 percent coupon must fall in price so that its yield will approximate the yield on the new, 7 percent bond. Ignoring the effects of taxes on pricing, investors would not find a buyer for the older bond until its price fell to 93, because then the yield would be competitive with the yield of the new bond.

Yield to Maturity

Several types of yields can be calculated for different purposes. Current yield, for example, is a quick and simple method of calculating current income on a bond earned from interest payments. The current yield is equal to the coupon interest payment divided by the current price of the bond.

The yield used to describe bonds trading in the market, however, is the yield to maturity, a concept that takes into account the time value of money. If an investor buys a bond at a discount and holds it to maturity, for example, the gain earned at maturity raises the yield to the investor. But the gain received perhaps ten years from the date of purchase will not be worth as much as it would have been if received ten years previously. At the least, it would have earned interest if invested over ten years. The yield-to-maturity concept takes this consideration into account. In simplest terms, it is the annual return, compounded semiannually, that an investor would earn from all interest and principal payments over the life of the bond. (One important assumption in yield-to-maturity calculations is that interest payments are reinvested at the same rate.)

The yield to maturity of a bond with a 6 percent coupon bought at par is 6 percent. If the bond is bought at a discount, or premium, however, the calculation gets more complicated. For example, if that bond were bought at 90 ($900) and were due in ten years, the yield to maturity would be 7.50 percent and the current yield would be 6.67 percent ($60 divided by $900). Another way to look at yield to maturity is to use the analogy of a savings account. If an investor deposits $900 in a savings account and receives $30 every six months in interest, he or she would withdraw $1,000 at the end of ten years. The annual interest return on the account, compounded semiannually, is 7.50 percent—the yield to maturity.

The development of the bond desk calculator has made determining yields to maturity merely a matter of pushing buttons. (See the Appendix of mathematical calculations for a full discussion of the theory and computation of yield to maturity and an alternative calculation of yield to call.) Before the advent of such calculators, however, the quick way to find yields and prices was to look them up in a basis book. An excerpt from a basis book is reproduced in Figure 1-3. If the yield to maturity, the coupon, and the maturity of the bond are known, one can look down the table to find the price. Alternatively, if the price is known, the yield to maturity can be found by looking across the table. As long as any three factors are known, the fourth can be found. For instance, as the figure shows, a bond due in

FIGURE 1-3. Excerpt from a Basis Book

To use the table:

a. If the maturity of the bond, coupon, and yield to maturity are known, read the corresponding price in the intersecting column.

b. If the price is known, to find the yield to maturity, read across to the left to the appropriate bond yield column.

5%				YEARS and MONTHS				
Yield	10-6	11-0	11-6	12-0	12-6	13-0	13-6	14-0
2.00	128.29	129.49	130.68	131.87	133.03	134.19	135.34	136.47
2.20	126.12	127.22	128.31	129.39	130.45	131.51	132.55	133.58
2.40	124.01	125.01	125.99	126.97	127.93	128.89	129.83	130.76
2.60	121.93	122.83	123.72	124.60	125.47	126.33	127.18	128.01
2.80	119.89	120.70	121.50	122.29	123.07	123.83	124.59	125.34
3.00	117.90	118.62	119.33	120.03	120.72	121.40	122.07	122.73
3.20	115.95	116.58	117.20	117.82	118.42	119.02	119.61	120.18
3.40	114.03	114.58	115.12	115.66	116.18	116.70	117.21	117.71
3.60	112.15	112.62	113.09	113.54	113.99	114.43	114.87	115.29
3.80	110.31	110.71	111.10	111.48	111.85	112.22	112.58	112.94
4.00	108.51	108.83	109.15	109.46	109.76	110.06	110.35	110.64
4.20	106.74	106.99	107.24	107.48	107.72	107.95	108.18	108.40
4.40	105.00	105.19	105.37	105.55	105.72	105.89	106.06	106.22
4.60	103.30	103.42	103.54	103.66	103.77	103.88	103.99	104.10
4.80	101.63	101.69	101.75	101.81	101.86	101.92	101.97	102.02
5.00	100.00	100.00	100.00	100.00	100.00	100.00	100.00	100.00
5.10	99.19	99.17	99.14	99.11	99.08	99.06	99.03	99.01
5.20	98.40	98.34	98.29	98.23	98.18	98.13	98.08	98.03
5.30	97.61	97.52	97.44	97.36	97.28	97.21	97.13	97.06
5.40	96.83	96.71	96.61	96.50	96.40	96.30	96.20	96.11
5.50	96.05	95.91	95.78	95.65	95.52	95.40	95.28	95.16
5.60	95.29	95.12	94.96	94.81	94.66	94.51	94.37	94.23
5.70	94.53	94.34	94.15	93.98	93.80	93.63	93.47	93.31
5.80	93.77	93.56	93.35	93.15	92.96	92.77	92.58	92.40
5.90	93.03	92.79	92.56	92.34	92.12	91.91	91.70	91.50
6.00	92.29	92.03	91.78	91.53	91.29	91.06	90.84	90.62
6.10	91.56	91.28	91.00	90.74	90.48	90.22	89.98	89.74
6.20	90.84	90.53	90.24	89.95	89.67	89.40	89.13	88.68
6.30	90.12	89.79	89.48	89.17	88.87	88.58	88.30	88.02
6.40	89.41	89.06	88.73	88.40	88.08	87.77	87.47	87.18
6.50	88.71	88.34	87.98	87.63	87.30	86.97	86.65	86.35
6.60	88.02	87.63	87.25	86.88	86.52	86.18	85.85	85.52
6.70	87.33	86.92	86.52	86.13	85.76	85.40	85.05	84.71
6.80	86.65	86.22	85.80	85.39	85.00	84.63	84.26	83.91
6.90	85.97	85.52	85.09	84.66	84.26	83.86	83.48	83.12
7.00	85.30	84.83	84.38	83.94	83.52	83.11	82.71	82.33
7.10	84.64	84.15	83.68	83.23	82.79	82.36	81.95	81.56
7.20	83.98	83.48	82.99	82.52	82.07	81.63	81.20	80.79
7.30	83.33	82.81	82.31	81.82	81.35	80.90	80.46	80.04
7.40	82.69	82.15	81.63	81.13	80.64	80.18	79.73	79.29
7.50	82.05	81.50	80.96	80.44	79.95	79.47	79.00	78.56
7.60	81.42	80.85	80.30	79.77	79.26	78.76	78.29	77.83
7.70	80.80	80.21	79.64	79.10	78.57	78.07	77.58	77.11
7.80	80.18	79.57	78.99	78.43	77.90	77.38	76.88	76.40
7.90	79.56	78.95	78.35	77.78	77.23	76.70	76.19	75.70
8.00	78.96	78.32	77.71	77.13	76.57	76.03	75.51	75.01
8.10	78.35	77.71	77.09	76.49	75.91	75.36	74.83	74.32
8.20	77.76	77.10	76.46	75.85	75.27	74.70	74.16	73.64
8.30	77.17	76.49	75.85	75.22	74.63	74.05	73.50	72.98
8.40	76.58	75.90	75.24	74.60	74.00	73.41	72.85	72.31
8.50	76.00	75.30	74.63	73.99	73.37	72.78	72.21	71.66
8.60	75.43	74.72	74.03	73.38	72.75	72.15	71.57	71.02
8.70	74.86	74.14	73.44	72.78	72.14	71.53	70.94	70.38
8.80	74.30	73.56	72.86	72.18	71.53	70.91	70.32	69.75
8.90	73.74	72.99	72.28	71.59	70.94	70.31	69.71	69.13
9.00	73.19	72.43	71.70	71.01	70.34	69.71	69.10	68.51
9.20	72.10	71.32	70.57	69.86	69.18	68.53	67.90	67.31
9.40	71.03	70.23	69.47	68.74	68.04	67.37	66.74	66.13
9.60	69.99	69.17	68.38	67.64	66.92	66.24	65.60	64.98
9.80	68.96	68.12	67.32	66.56	65.83	65.14	64.48	63.85
10.00	67.95	67.09	66.28	65.50	64.77	64.06	63.39	62.75

12 years with a 5 percent coupon and trading at a yield to maturity of 6.50 percent will have a price of 87.63.

Under current federal tax laws, any capital gains earned by selling tax-exempt bonds at a price higher than the purchase price, or by redeeming bonds at par that were bought at a discount, are subject to federal income taxes. This will affect both the yield to maturity after taxes and the way the bonds are priced in the market. (Capital gains taxes are addressed more fully in Chapter 8. Chapter 6 covers the tax implications of premium bonds and of bonds sold originally at a discount, which do not produce capital gains subject to tax at maturity.)

Types of Municipal Bonds

The last 15 years have seen the unprecedented development of various types of municipal bonds. More for the sake of convenience than for complete accuracy, municipal bonds are generally broken down into three categories: general obligation bonds, revenue bonds, and hybrids.

The security for the general obligation bonds is the general credit and the taxing power of the state or local government issuing the bonds. Most municipal governments depend largely on *ad valorem* (Latin meaning ''to the value added''), or value-based, property taxes for their revenues. State governments, on the other hand, usually do not levy real estate taxes but rely mostly on sales and income taxes. The full faith and credit backing of a general obligation bond implies that all sources of revenue, unless specifically limited, will be used to pay debt service on the bonds.

Revenue bonds are those that are issued to finance a specific revenue-generating project and, unless backed by a third-party guarantee, are usually secured solely by the revenues from that project. In 1989 revenue bonds accounted for 70 percent of all new long-term municipal issues, compared with only 48 percent in 1975 (Figure 1-4). Occasionally, general obligation bonds are backed by specific revenues of a municipality. These hybrid obligations are called double-barreled bonds.

Other types of municipal securities, which do not fall exactly into these categories, are special tax bonds and moral obligation bonds.

GENERAL OBLIGATION BONDS

Unlimited Tax Bonds

These are general obligation securities that are backed by the full faith and credit of the state or local government. The taxing power of the issuer in support of the payment of the securities is not subject to constitutional or statutory limitations.

FIGURE 1-4. Long-Term New-Issue Volume by Type of Security
($ volume in billions)

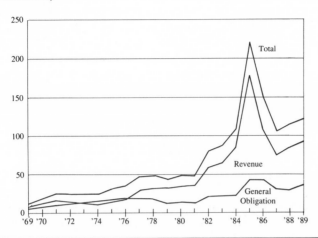

Year	General Obligation Volume ($ Billions)	% GO*	Revenue Volume ($ Billions)	% Revenue*	Total Long-Term Volume ($ Billions)
1970	$11.9	66%	$ 6.2	34%	$ 18.1
1971	15.2	61	9.7	39	24.9
1972	13.3	56	10.4	44	23.7
1973	12.2	51	11.7	49	23.8
1974	13.1	56	10.5	44	23.6
1975	16.0	52	14.7	48	30.7
1976	18.2	51	17.2	49	35.4
1977	18.1	39	28.6	61	46.7
1978	17.8	37	30.8	63	48.6
1979	12.1	28	31.1	72	43.3
1980	14.1	29	34.5	71	48.6
1981	12.7	27	35.2	73	47.9
1982	21.1	27	58.0	73	79.1
1983	21.6	25	65.0	75	86.6
1984	22.7	27	85.4	73	108.1
1985	43.2	19	179.1	81	222.2
1986	42.7	28	108.7	72	151.4
1987	30.5	29	75.2	71	105.7
1988	29.5	25	87.5	75	116.9
1989	36.7	30	85.8	70	122.5

* Percent values are rounded to the nearest whole number.
Note: Totals might not add due to rounding.

SOURCE: IDD/PSA Municipal Securities Database

Revenue bonds have enabled municipalities to expand their uses of debt financing and, in recent years, have accounted for the larger portion of the total volume of long-term securities issued.

Limited Tax Bonds

In some instances, the taxing power of governmental issuers in support of municipal securities is specifically limited by the state constitution or by statutes. The rate of tax on assessed property value, for example, may have a ceiling. Bonds backed by such restricted taxing authority are called limited tax bonds.

REVENUE BONDS

Revenue bonds have enabled state and local governments to finance a wide range of projects. Bridges, airports, water and sewer treatment facilities, health care facilities, and state and local housing projects have been generally financed by revenue bonds. In addition, current law permits certain types of facilities which are owned or used by private entities to be financed by tax-exempt revenue bonds, if they meet specific criteria. Typically, revenue bonds are payable from specific sources of revenues, other than property taxes, and are not backed by the full faith and credit of the issuer. Consequently, they do not usually require electoral approval or constitute "debt" within the meaning of applicable constitutional or statutory limitations. Revenue bonds are typically secured solely by a revenue pledge, by related covenants of the issuer to assure the adequacy of the pledge revenue sources, and sometimes by a mortgage on the facilities financed by the issuance of the revenue bonds. Because the payment sources of revenue bonds are limited, a feasibility study analyzing the projected revenues and operations of the facility being financed is often required to market the bonds.

Revenue bonds are issued by the state or local government, or by an authority, commission, special district, or other unit created for the purpose of issuing the bonds and constructing and operating the project. One common way to classify the variety of revenue bonds is according to the method by which funds are generated to pay the bonds off. Some examples follow.

User fees. Water, sewer, and electricity revenue bonds are among the most commonly issued. The fees charged the users of these services are the sources of payment for the debt and can be varied to meet debt obligations.

Tolls, concessions, and fees. Highway, bridge, airport, dock, and similar projects that are financed by revenue bonds raise funds through tolls, concessions, and direct fees. Restaurants along highways, for example, pay concessions; airlines pay fees for use of space at airports.

Lease-back. The state or local government creates a nonprofit authority or other governmental unit to issue revenue bonds and build a facility such as a school. The local government using the facility will then lease the project from the authority. It makes rental payments under the lease out of tax or other revenues, usually via annual budget appropriations, which may not be counted against the legal debt limit of the state or local governmental unit making the lease payment. The lease payments are used by the issuer to pay out both interest and principal.

Industrial development and other "exempt facility" bonds. Industrial development bonds (IDBs) and municipal securities issued for other types of "exempt facilities" under applicable Internal Revenue Code restrictions (for example, bonds issued to finance privately owned pollution control facilities or airport facilities) are revenue bonds in the sense that the credit and repayment source for such bonds is the private entity for which the facilities are financed. Typically, such municipal securities are issued by a municipality or other governmental unit to finance facilities which are then leased to the private-entity user at a rental equal to debt service on the bonds and for a term equal to the maturity of the securities. Alternatively, in some jurisdictions, the proceeds of the IDBs are loaned by the issuer directly to the private-entity user on repayment terms equal to the terms on the IDBs. The advantage to the private-entity user is to obtain financing at tax-exempt rates in return for making a capital investment which contributes to enumerated public purposes of the issuer, such as job creation, clean air or water, and increasing the tax base.

A description of several of the most popular types of revenue bonds follows. A more detailed discussion of some of these types of bonds can be found in Chapter 7.

Housing Revenue Bonds

Several types of housing revenue bonds exist. These are issued by state or local housing finance agencies or by a unit of the local government and are typically used to support multifamily housing for low- or moderate-income families or single-family housing for first-time home buyers. They are also used to aid in regional redevelopment and in some states to support housing for the aged and for veterans.

State housing agencies are the primary issuers of housing bonds. However, units of local government in certain parts of the country also issue debt for housing purposes.

Housing revenue bonds are structured in a variety of ways. In direct loan programs, bond proceeds are used to make loans directly to a developer or several developers. For single-family issues, mortgages are typically issued through financial intermediaries to home buyers out of the bond proceeds, and the program is often administered by local lending institutions.

Housing revenue bonds are subject to significant restriction and regulation under federal tax laws. Further discussion of these limitations is included in Chapter 9.

Public Utility Bonds

A long-standing use of revenue bonds is to finance electric power, gas, water, and sewer systems that are owned by a governmental unit. Several kinds of public electric utility systems are in existence. They range from self-generation systems with their own plants and distribution systems to systems that simply distribute electricity purchased from a wholesaler. Further, a public utility may supply only part of its own electricity needs, or it may produce enough power to sell to other systems. The fuel source also varies, ranging from coal to hydroelectric and nuclear power. By and large, however, public utility bonds are supported by rates charged to customers. Hence, the economic health and potential growth of the service area are key variables in determining the credit risk of the issues. This is true also of most water, sewer, and gas issues, because the operations are usually monopolies in the areas they serve.

Huge regional power supply systems have been developed that absorb enormous amounts of capital. These systems are among the largest borrowers in the tax-exempt markets. Consequently, joint-action financing has become popular in recent years. These offerings involve two or more communities combining to finance the purchase of generating facilities or to build their own power plants.

Industrial Development and Exempt Facility Bonds

Industrial development bonds, utility bonds, pollution control bonds, and port and airport development bonds have historically represented significant categories of revenue bonds issued in the municipal securities market. The term "exempt facilities" refers to specific types of privately owned or privately used facilities which are permitted to be issued on a tax-exempt basis under the Internal Revenue Code. The Tax Reform Act of 1986 amended prior law to exclude the following types of such facilities from those that can be financed on a tax-exempt basis: sports facilities; convention and trade show facilities; air and water pollution control facilities; privately owned airports, docks, wharves and mass-commuting facilities; and most parking facilities, among others. Principal categories of exempt facilities for which, subject to various restrictions and volume limitations, bonds can be issued under the Tax Reform Act of 1986 include publically owned airports, docks, wharves and mass-commuting facilities, water-furnishing facilities, sewage facilities, certain solid waste disposal facilities, qualified hazardous waste facilities, qualified residential rental projects, facilities for the local furnishing of electric energy or gas, and local district heating or cooling facilities. In addition, small-issue IDBs may be issued to finance manufacturing facilities and farming property.

Hospital and Health Care Revenue Bonds

State legislatures have created state health finance authorities or authorized units of local governments to issue bonds to finance construction for nonprofit hospitals. The debt typically has a first claim on hospital revenues, but the hospitals benefit from the lower cost of the tax-exempt bonds compared with alternative forms of financing. The Tax Reform Act of 1986 imposed new restrictions on bonds issued for nonprofit hospitals and other "501(c)(3)" entities. The designation "501(c)(3)" includes nonprofit hospitals, private higher educational institutions, and other nonprofit organizations.

OTHER

Special Tax Bonds

These bonds have characteristics of both revenue and general obligation bonds. Such bonds, usually issued to finance a particular type of facility, are backed by the pledge of proceeds from a specific tax source—for example, a highway bond issue that is to be paid for out of gasoline taxes.

Short-Term Securities

The issuance of short-term securities (typically called "notes" and usually representing a maturity of one year or less) by state and local governments grew rapidly during the 1960s and early 1970s. After New York City, the largest issuer at the time of notes, defaulted on a note issue in 1975, the use of short-term debt dropped. Beginning in 1979, as interest rates rose and the issuance of project notes (short-term, tax-exempt securities issued to fund housing and urban renewal projects and secured by the project's revenue and the U.S. government) accelerated, short-term debt increased to a new peak of $44.8 billion in 1982. Since then the elimination of project notes by Congress in 1984, a decline in intermediate- and long-term interest rates, and increased use of alternative forms of financing such as variable-rate demand bonds led to another period of reduced issuance of short-term securities. In 1989, issuance of short-term securities had dropped to $28.4 billion.

NOTES

The issuance of notes serves many purposes. State and local governments use short-term financing to bridge the gap between when expenses occur and when revenues are available, in anticipation of incoming tax revenues or new issues of bonds. Interest on notes is usually paid when they mature. Some municipalities, however, issue notes at a discount, much like Treasury bills. The following types of notes are frequently issued by state and local governments:

Tax anticipation notes. TANs are issued in anticipation of tax receipts, and are payable out of those receipts.

Revenue anticipation notes. RANs are issued in anticipation of other sources of future revenue, typically either state or federal aid. (Sometimes notes are issued in anticipation of both tax receipts and other revenues, and they are known as TRANs.)

Bond anticipation notes. BANs are considered the least secure of a municipality's notes. They provide a means of interim financing in anticipation of a future bond offering. Therefore, unless they are otherwise secured, they are dependent upon the local government's ability to issue those bonds.

General obligation notes. Some state and local governments will issue notes for a variety of purposes with the full backing of the issuer. General obligation notes are the equivalent in credit quality of general obligation bonds. They are often used for the same purposes as TANs and BANs.

OTHER SHORT-TERM INSTRUMENTS

As late as 1980, the phrase ''short-term municipal'' referred to notes and short-term municipal bonds. These securities usually had maturities ranging from a few months to a few years, carried fixed interest rates and were issued in anticipation of a bond issue, grant proceeds, or the collection of tax revenues. However, the highly dynamic interest rate movements of the late 1970s and early 1980s and the emergence and growth of tax-exempt money funds fostered one of the most significant developments in the tax-exempt market during that period: a much broader class of short-term municipal securities.

Most of this expansion occurred because of investor and issuer concerns about the effect of interest rates. Investors were concerned about fluctuations in the value of their portfolios, and issuers were concerned about the high cost of borrowing. These ''short-term'' municipal securities were basically new techniques of financings that evolved to meet these issuer and investor concerns. As Figure 1-5 shows, the volume of these ''short-term'' municipals, generically known as demand obligations or variable-rate demand obligations (VRDO), grew enormously during the 1980s. Because these techniques have taken such a prominent role in the municipal market, a separate section later in this chapter covers some of the basic structural features of these securities.

Tax-exempt commercial paper also emerged as a new type of short-term instrument. This is a short-term promissory note issued for periods of up to 270 days and is often used in lieu of BANs, TANs, and RANs because of the greater flexibility offered in both setting maturities and determining rates.

FIGURE 1-5. Financing Volume of Variable-Rate Demand Obligations 1982-1989
($ volume in millions)

Year	Number of Issues	Volume
1982*	102	$ 2,133.9
1983*	115	3,347.7
1984*	822	25,876.5
1985*	1,730	66,855.4
1986	708	29,105.9
1987	682	16,531.6
1988	903	21,622.2
1989	771	14,700.6

* Includes only issues with a par amount greater than $5 million.

SOURCE: IDD Information Services/PSA Municipal Securities Database

Restrictions on Tax-Exempt Bond Issuance

The types of municipal securities, the purposes for which they may be issued, the tax and other sources which may be pledged to their payment, and the manner in which such securities may be issued and sold are subject to state and local law constraints. Consequently, applicable state and local laws must be carefully examined in connection with structuring and issuing municipal securities. In addition, and as covered in Chapter 9, federal tax legislation affects significantly the manner in which and the purposes for which municipal securities may be issued. For example, both the Tax Reform Act of 1984 and the Tax Reform Act of 1986 have curbed significantly the issuance of bonds characterized as "private activity bonds," "exempt facility bonds," and "501(c)(3) bonds," among others.

Financing Techniques

The introduction and refinement of numerous new financing techniques was one of the most important developments in the tax-exempt markets in the early 1980s. As mentioned earlier, the erratic pattern of interest rates during this period led to the invention of these new techniques. Record-high tax-exempt rates and interest rate volatility during the late 1970s and the first half of the 1980s were unprecedented. For example, between October 1979 and January 1982 *The Bond Buyer* 20-Bond Index rose from 7.38 percent to 13.44 percent and then declined again to a low of 6.54 percent in October 1987. Furthermore, the decline in rates was not steady nor did it closely track that of taxables, frequently leaving investors surprised by new wrinkles in the ma. ket. Many of the aberrations in the market resulted from an artificial and temporary oversupply of municipal bonds as issuers rushed into the market to avoid deadlines set by tax legislation and threats of tax legislation in the 1980s.

In response to this prolonged uncertainty about interest rates, participants in the municipal market developed numerous new financing techniques. These techniques answered the concerns of both the investors and the issuers of municipal debt by allowing them access to the short-term municipal market. While investors watched their portfolios decline in value as interest rates rose, issuers watched the cost of borrowing capital increase. Short-term municipal securities offered the investor the assurance of the preservation of principal. Short-term securities also offered the issuer a means of borrowing at substantial savings.

Most of these "short-term" financing techniques are based on a simple idea. A municipal government still issues long-term bonds but they have yields determined or set as if they were short-term notes. The reason that the yields are like those of short-term notes is that the holders of the bonds are entitled to demand purchase of their bonds at par, plus accrued interest on a regular basis. From a bondholder's point of view, a bond subject to such purchase is similar to a bond that matures on the date the bondholder is entitled to demand purchase. Therefore, a bond entitling the holder to demand payment every seven days carries the same yields as if it matured in a week. Similarly, an annual demand bond is priced as if it matured in one year. Although bonds with daily, weekly, or monthly demand periods are the most common, some bonds have quarterly, semiannual, or annual demand periods.

For most of these issues, the coupon rate may change only at a point when the holder can demand interest. Since this market evolved over a several-year period, various names, such as "floaters," "lower floaters," or "put" bonds, may refer to the identical security structure. However, the most widely accepted name for these securities is the variable-rate demand obligation (VRDO). As the market in these securities emerged, certain structures have become more common than others. The structure of these transactions typically has four primary components: (1) the *holder of the security can demand purchase* of his bond at par at predetermined intervals, (2) the *interest rate varies* at predetermined intervals, (3) some kind of *liquidity agreement provides security* that the holder will receive payment of purchase price, and (4) the issuer can *convert the VRDO into a fixed-rate bond* under specified conditions and procedures.

Demand feature. The demand feature of the VRDO is the key element that allows for the short-term interest rate. As the market has developed, a daily, weekly, or monthly demand interval is the most common. The demand feature works in the following way: the holder of a VRDO must give notice to a tender agent in the transaction a few days prior to the date that he will tender his bond for purchase at a price of par plus accrued interest. The tender agent then notifies a remarketing agent (generally a municipal dealer), who will use best efforts to sell tendered bonds to another purchaser. To add even greater flexibility, some VRDO offerings allow the remarketing agent (under specified conditions) to change the demand interval. For example, an issue may have a monthly demand feature, but prevailing market forces might make it more appropriate to shift the demand interval to once a year. Other bond offerings are structured so that only one demand interval is possible.

Interest rate changes. Just as VRDOs have a demand interval, they also periodically reset the interest rate. As a general rule, each time the interest rate is reset, a holder is allowed to tender his bonds for par purchase. The opposite, however, is not true; that is, the interest rate reset may be less frequent than the demand for payment. When this market was in its infancy in the early 1980s, the interest rates offered were often at a fixed percentage of the prime rate or a specific taxable rate, e.g., 60 percent of the 91-day Treasury bill rate. More current structures permit the remarketing agent to determine the new interest rate based upon prevailing market conditions.

Liquidity or credit support. Because these VRDOs allow the holder to demand purchase upon specified notice, the issuer must usually have some form of liquidity or credit support in order to meet a demand. The most common forms of liquidity support are a standby purchase agreement or letter of credit issued by a major commercial bank. In most circumstances, the VRDO holder demanding payment is paid from the remarketing of the security to a new buyer through the efforts of the remarketing agent. However, if a holder demands payment and no new purchases can be arranged by the remarketing agent, then the liquidity support is available to meet the demand.

Conversion to a fixed rate. Most VRDOs allow the issuer to convert the security to a fixed interest rate structure under specified conditions and procedures. If, for example, long-term interest rates decline significantly, then the issuer may want to "lock in" a fixed rate of interest while rates are favorable. In order to "convert" a VRDO to a fixed-rate structure, the trustee notifies all holders of the issuer's intent. The notice generally requires that the holder tender his VRDO as of the specified fixed-rate date or to expressly waive such tender. This "mandatory tender" requirement serves to protect the bondholder against a change in the security of the issue since, commonly, the liquidity or credit support expires at conversion.

Other Features of Municipal Bonds

Several important features and practices distinguish municipal securities from other kinds of securities. Knowledge of these characteristics is necessary to any understanding of the fundamentals of municipal securities. A summary of the most important of them follows.

SERIAL AND TERM BONDS

Unlike most other types of fixed-income securities, municipal bonds traditionally are issued in serial maturities. A typical offering is made up of as many as 20 or more different maturities—the serial bonds. This helps the issuer spread out debt service and stay within financial requirements. The issuance of serial bonds may also be required by state laws dictating that a bond issue contain substantially equal annual maturities. Typically, a certain number of bonds fall due each year from, say, one to 20 years from their date of issue. Generally, the longer the maturity, the higher will be the interest rate offered. A representative maturity schedule for a $746.2 million issue of bonds for the North Carolina Eastern Municipal Power Agency is shown in Figure 1-6.

In this example, $115,885,000 of serial bonds and $630,315,000 of term bonds are included in the issue. In recent years with the growth of revenue bonds, term bonds have become increasingly popular; they come due at only one maturity; and they usually carry a sinking fund requirement—reserves set aside by the issuer to redeem term bonds—to provide for their retirement. Except for being tax-exempt, term bonds are very similar to traditional corporate debt. Like corporate bonds, they are usually quoted by price rather than by yield, and are therefore called dollar bonds.

BEARER BONDS VERSUS REGISTERED BONDS

Until the early 1980s, it was traditional for most municipalities to issue bearer bonds, which are negotiable by anyone who holds them and can prove ownership. Attached to bearer bonds are coupons representing interest due, which the bondholder must clip and deposit in a bank for collection from the issuer's paying agent. Some bearer bonds are still outstanding and are available on the secondary market.

However, under federal tax laws enacted in 1982 and with limited exceptions, all municipal bonds issued on and after July 1, 1983, are required to be registered as to principal and interest. If the investor purchases a fully registered bond, he or she will receive the interest payments without having to clip coupons, as well as the principal when due. This method of payment is also used for corporate and federal government fixed-income securities. Registered bonds can be transferred to another party only with the proper endorsement.

FIGURE 1-6. Maturity Schedule

$115,885,000 Serial Bonds			
Year	Amount	Interest Rate	Price
1998	$ 8,380,000	7.30%	100%
1999	18,140,000	7.40	100
2000	27,725,000	7.50	100
2001	29,745,000	7.60	100
2002	31,895,000	7.70	100

$ 65,895,000 7¾% Term Bonds due January 1, 2004—Price 99.75%
$439,420,000 7¾% Term Bonds due January 1, 2015—Price 99.25%
$ 75,000,000 5 % Term Bonds due January 1, 2017—Price 69 %
$ 50,000,000 4 % Term Bonds due January 1, 2018—Price 57.50%
(accrued interest to be added)

SOURCE: Official Statement, North Carolina Eastern Municipal Power Agency

Serial maturities are often used to spread out debt service and help the issuer stay within financial requirements. Term bonds come due at one maturity.

The use of registered bonds has led to the development of so-called book-entry securities, for which the change in ownership does not require the transfer of a certificate. Rather, ownership is identified through a data entry at a central clearinghouse.

COLLECTING THE INTEREST

As stated above, interest on fixed-rate municipal bonds is generally paid semiannually, usually on the first or fifteenth of the designated month. The last interest payment is made on the day the principal is due. Holders of bearer bonds must clip each coupon, which is numbered and dated, and present it to the issuer (usually a bank that serves as the agent) in order to receive the interest. Holders of registered bonds, as noted above, receive their interest payments without any requirement of presentation.

The bondholder is entitled to accrued interest, beginning at a specified date on the bonds, known as the "dated date," although the bonds are often actually sold or delivered at a different date. A so-called short coupon results when the time between the dated date and the first coupon date is less than six months. A long coupon results when the first coupon date is more than six months away from the dated date.

TRADING PLUS ACCRUED INTEREST

Because most trading of municipal bonds takes place between interest payment dates, it is necessary to allocate interest between buyers and sellers. The investor who sells bonds is entitled to the interest due since the last interest payment date. The convention in the municipal bond business is that the buyer of the bonds must pay the seller any interest due when he or she buys the bonds. If the settlement date for an investor's bond sale is March 1, for example, and the last coupon date was January 1, the seller is entitled to two months' interest from the buyer. Municipal bonds, then, trade "plus accrued interest." That is, the interest due is added to the price of the bonds. The buyer, in turn, will collect and keep the full six months of interest due on the next interest payment date.

OFFICIAL STATEMENT

Most publicly offered new issues of corporate securities are subject to registration and other regulatory requirements under the federal securities laws. Under those laws issuers are required to file a prospectus with the SEC that discloses all "material" information about the offering and the corporation. The SEC reviews the prospectus prior to issuance. The municipal issuer's equivalent of the prospectus is the official statement, although until recently there was no federal requirement that one be prepared and it is not reviewed by any federal agency. However, underwriters are required to send official statements, if they are prepared by an issuer, to all investors in new-issue securities, according to the Municipal Securities Rulemaking Board's (MSRB) rule G-32. Moreover, as discussed in Chapter 9, Rule 15c2-12 as enacted by the SEC requires underwriters of a municipal securities offering of $1 million or more in aggregate principal amount to obtain and review an official statement before bidding on or purchasing the offering, unless the offering qualifies for specific exemption from the requirements. Although the rule places a direct burden on underwriters it also requires issuers to provide official statements in order to permit underwriter compliance.

In addition, according to MSRB Rule G-36, underwriters are required to send copies of official statements to the MSRB.

A sample of an official statement is included in a separate section in Chapter 3.

LEGAL OPINION

One of the most important characteristics unique to municipal bonds is the bond counsel opinion. In order to be marketable, municipal bonds must be accompanied by a legal opinion. The opinion addresses two principal areas: first, that the bonds are legal and binding obligations of the issuer under applicable state and local laws; and, second, that the interest on the bonds is exempt under applicable federal and state tax laws.

The opinion requirement grew out of widespread defaults on municipal bonds in the late nineteenth century which had been issued to finance railroad construction.

When such defaults occurred, some issuers successfully avoided their payment obligation on the basis that the bonds had not been duly authorized or properly issued under applicable laws. In order to restore marketplace confidence, issuers and underwriters commenced the practice of obtaining bond counsel opinions at the time bonds were initially issued, and this practice has continued to the present day. The increased complexity of financial structures and of federal tax restrictions has further resulted in a broadening of the traditional bond counsel role (see Chapter 2).

Special Characteristics of the Municipal Market

The municipal secondary market, or after-market, is distinct from the corporate securities secondary market in several important ways. One major distinguishing characteristic of the municipal market is that all trading is done "over the counter." There are no organized exchanges for municipal securities as there are for corporate securities.

Almost all trades in municipal securities are made on a so-called dealer basis. That is, the dealers who trade municipal securities for investors own, if only temporarily, the securities they buy from one investor and sell to another or keep for their own inventory. Their profit is the difference between the price for which they can sell the securities and the price at which they bought them. This traditional business mark-up is known as the spread.

Also, the municipal secondary market is significantly different from other markets because of the sheer number and variety of issues. While overall a great deal of trading is done, trading in any one individual municipal issue may be infrequent. Although no precise data are available, the volume of trading in the municipal secondary markets has been estimated by many in the industry to be one to two times as large as the new-issue market in any given year. The daily Blue List, a service of Standard & Poor's Corporation, lists those issues that dealers are publicly offering for sale. While not an indication of the trading that actually takes place, the Blue List typically lists some $2 billion to $3 billion of bonds available for sale each day. Dealers estimate that the Blue List accounts for only 30 to 40 percent of municipal securities available in the national market.

CALL PROVISIONS

Call provisions have become a basic feature of most sizable tax-exempt issues. They give the issuer the option to retire all or a portion of the bonds, before the stated maturity date, at a set price—usually at a premium to par. The call provisions are described in the bond resolution and official statement and are set forth in the bonds. The call privilege, as it is sometimes referred to, is a benefit to the issuer. It gives the issuer the flexibility to retire an outstanding bond issue prior to its stated maturity date and reduce debt costs. It can be particularly useful when interest rates have fallen since the original bond offering. The issuer can refund the older, high-interest issue and offer a new issue at lower rates.

Call provisions vary widely. A typical provision used for many years allows the issuer to retire bonds beginning ten years from the date of issue at a premium above par. In such a case, a series of call dates are specified for a period after the initial ten years, at descending prices. Thus, bonds might be callable ten years from the date of issue at, for example, 103 percent of par. In the eleventh year, they would be callable at a lower price, and at later dates at prices declining to par. The earliest possible call is known as the first call.

Changes have evolved in call features to accommodate the needs of particular types of bond issues. For example, single-family housing revenue bonds typically contain a provision allowing the issuer to call the bonds at par at any time, using funds from unexpended bond proceeds or prepayments. This provision clearly benefits the issuer: if all the mortgage money is not loaned to mortgagees (perhaps because the interest rate was not competitive with that of less restrictive, conventional financing, or because there were fewer mortgage applicants than predicted), the bonds can be called at par in as little as one year from date of issue. Also, if considerable mortgage prepayments are made, due to a decline in conventional mortgage rates, a par call can be made at any time.

Even if an issue carries conventional call features such as the ten-year optional call protection, however, the potential for capital gains is limited, and if the bonds are called, the investor is usually left with the principal to be reinvested at a lower interest rate. A yield to call, therefore, is commonly computed for callable bonds, especially those selling at a premium. It is simply the yield to maturity calculated to the call price and first call date. (The calculation is described in the Appendix.) When buying and selling these bonds, dealers will customarily tell investors both the yield to call and the yield to maturity. The MSRB has adopted a rule requiring in a transaction effected on a yield basis that the dollar price be calculated to the lower of price to call or price to maturity disclosed in confirmations of transactions to investors and other dealers.

SINKING FUNDS

Sinking funds are reserves set aside yearly by the issuer to redeem term bonds over a specified period prior to the stated maturity date. Just as serial maturities help issuers spread their financial charges evenly, so do sinking funds help even out payments on term bonds. Instead of paying off the entire issue at maturity, the issuer pays a set amount annually into a sinking fund from which bonds are redeemed on a set schedule. Sinking funds, therefore, add a measure of security to the bonds.

Sinking fund retirements can be optional or mandatory. A provision might require or permit the issuer to redeem a certain principal amount of bonds beginning in ten years, or to buy bonds in that principal amount in the open market. If the bonds are redeemed, the price is always at par or higher, though sometimes the bonds can be bought below par in the open market. If interest rates have risen over the period, creating a downward pressure on bond prices, the possibility of early redemption by operation of the sinking fund will tend to keep the price of the bonds up. On the other hand, if falling interest rates tend to push prices above par, the sinking fund provisions can keep a lid on prices. The bonds to be retired are usually chosen at random, by lot. The procedure should be spelled out clearly in the official statement (see Chapter 3 for further discussion of this).

A "super sinker" is a fund that functions much like a conventional sinking fund. Super sinkers are attached to single-family, mortgage revenue bond issues. These bonds have a specifically identified maturity date, and all mortgage prepayments are applied to the fund so that bonds can be retired before maturity. Such bonds typically carry a long-term maturity date (20 to 30 years, for example), but have a much shorter actual life (usually between four and six years), depending on the issuer's prepayment expectations.

CUSIP

In the mid-1960s, a committee of the American Bankers Association was formed to develop a uniform method of identifying all corporate, U.S. government, and municipal securities. It was called the Committee on Uniform Security Identification Procedures, or CUSIP. The goal was to assign each security its own identification number and keep all these numbers on file.

Standard & Poor's Corporation was chosen to administer the service. The firm assigns CUSIP numbers to most municipal issues. Standard & Poor's provides to subscribers a two-volume master directory of all its CUSIP listings. Currently, more than 1.3 million municipal issues are listed in the directory.

2

The Municipal
Bond Industry

Like most industries, the municipal bond industry enlists the various skills of
many participants. Distinct parts are played in the market by brokers, bankers,
salesmen, traders, underwriters, analysts, lawyers, financial advisors, accountants, state and local government treasurers and directors of finance, federal regulators, and institutional and individual investors. But all are employed to one end:
to raise money and to support a secondary market for debt securities of state and
local governmental units. Their roles can best be understood by tracing how each
participant contributes to the process.

In 1989, $150.9 billion was raised for state and local governments, compared
with a little over $3.7 billion in 1950. Long-term debt issues alone, in 1989,
amounted to $122.5 billion, compared to the long-term debt and equity raised by
corporations of $455.8 billion. In contrast, in 1985, when long-term state and
local debt issues amounted to $222.2 billion, the long-term debt and equity raised
by corporations totaled $191.7 billion (see Figure 2-1).

The size, diversity, and local characteristics of the municipal securities market
provide opportunities for both large and small dealers and specialists in many
areas. Figure 2-2 diagrams the flow of funds through the new-issue market. As the
figure shows, all underwriting is done through dealers and dealer banks. The
issuer's debt is sold by the underwriters to institutional and individual investors.
Both interest and principal are paid directly to investors when due, usually through
a bank acting as the paying agent.

The secondary market supports the new-issue market and provides liquidity to
investors. The secondary market is a term that indicates all trading in securities

**FIGURE 2-1. New Issues of Municipal and Corporate
Capital Securities**

Selected Years 1950 to 1989, by Type of Instrument

($ in billions)

| | Municipal Bonds | | | Corporate Capital Securities | | | |
| | | | | Bonds | | | |
	General Obligation	Revenue	Total	Public	Private Place-ment	Equities	Total
1950	$ 3.1	$ .6	$ 3.7	$ 2.4	$ 2.6	$ 1.5	$ 6.7
1960	5.0	2.2	7.2	4.8	3.3	2.1	10.2
1970	11.9	6.2	18.1	25.4	4.8	8.3	38.5
1975	16.0	14.7	30.7	31.5	10.2	10.9	52.6
1980	14.1	34.5	48.6	41.6	14.5	13.3	69.4
1985	54.1	168.1	222.2	104.9	61.7*	25.1	191.7
1989	36.7	85.8	122.5	278.4	139.8*	30.7	448.9

* Increase may be due in part to increased complete reporting from the investment banks.

SOURCE: Public Securities Association Municipal Securities Database; IDD Information
           Services/PSA Municipal Securities Database; *The Bond Buyer;* Securities and
           Exchange Commission, ''Statistical Bulletin;'' IDD Information Service

**The volume of capital raised in the municipal bond market has increased dramatically
since 1950.**

after they have been sold as new issues. Investors are more likely to buy a security
if they know they can resell that security at a fair market price prior to maturity.
Most underwriters of municipal securities have trading departments that make
secondary markets in outstanding bond issues.

The Issuers

The starting point for any municipal security is, of course, the issuer (see Figure
2-2). Municipal securities are issued by state and local governmental units and
Washington, D.C. United States territories and possessions—American Samoa,
the Commonwealth of Puerto Rico, Guam, the Northern Mariana Islands, and the
U.S. Virgin Islands—can also issue tax-exempt bonds, the interest on which is
exempt from federal, state, and local taxes.

Municipal securities are issued pursuant to express state and local laws
authorizing their issuance. Many authorizing and related laws impose restrictions
on the size and financial structure of the debt. Moreover, each new issue usually

FIGURE 2-2. The New-Issue Market for Municipal Securities: Flow of Funds

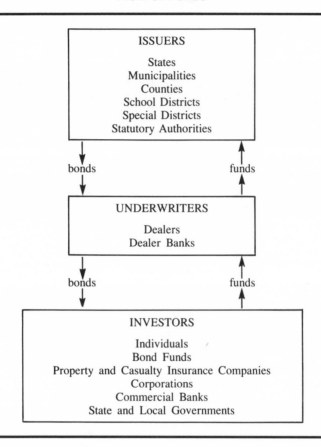

requires the approval of the legislative body of the issuer. Such approval may require an ordinance or resolution. In the case of general obligation bonds, approval by voter referendum is often required.

With the advent of many kinds of revenue bonds, state and local governments have established many new governmental units to issue bonds. Transportation authorities were among the first of this kind of municipal issuer, but public power and state and local housing authorities are now among the most common of these new entities. Nonprofit corporations have also been established to administer projects and finance them with tax-exempt debt.

THE ROLE OF BOND COUNSEL

As noted in Chapter 1, essentially every municipal security issued is accompanied by an opinion of bond counsel (see Figure 2-3). That opinion addresses the main legal issues: that the bonds constitute legal, valid, and binding obligations of the issuer and that interest on the bonds is exempt from federal income taxation under applicable tax laws. In rendering the opinion, bond counsel undertakes a review and examination of all applicable laws authorizing the issuance of securities, ascertains that all required procedural steps have been completed to assure proper authorization and issuance of the securities, and determines that all federal tax law requirements governing the issuance of the bonds have been complied with. In connection with their review of laws and procedure, bond counsel assembles all relevant documentation into a "transcript of proceedings." A copy of the transcript is delivered to the underwriter in connection with the original sale of the bonds. The transcript, thus, serves as a permanent record and reference of the steps taken to issue the bonds and the underlying payment and security arrangements.

FINANCIAL ADVISORS

State and local governments may often seek the advice of a financial advisor or other professional experts. Financial advisors perform a variety of tasks: analyze the financing needs of the community, construct an issue, help choose an underwriter or organize a competitive sale, deal with the rating agencies, and advise on other matters of importance. The scope of the advisors' work overlaps that of the

FIGURE 2-3. Sample Bond Counsel Opinion

We have examined the transcript of proceedings relating to the issuance by the City of Bedford Heights, Ohio, of its $191,000 Perkins Road Improvement Bonds, being a series of Bonds dated as of August 1, 1987, bearing interest at the rate of 7 3/4 percent per annum, maturing serially on December 1 from 1988 through 2007, and issued in anticipation of the collection of special assessments heretofore levied to pay the property owners' portion of the cost of improving Perkins Road between certain termini by widening, grading, draining, curbing, paving, constructing sanitary and storm sewer connections, where necessary, and water mains and acquiring real estate and interests therein in connection therewith, all together with the necessary appurtenances thereto. We have also examined a signed and authenticated Bond of the first maturity.

Based on this examination we are of the opinion that, under existing law:

1. The Bonds constitute valid and legal general obligations of the City and the

principal of and interest on the Bonds, unless paid from other sources and subject to the provisions of federal bankruptcy law and other laws affecting creditors' rights, are to be paid from the proceeds of the levy of ad valorem taxes, within the 8 mill limitation provided by the Charter of the City, on all property subject to ad valorem taxes levied by the City.

2. The interest on the Bonds is excluded from gross income for federal income tax purposes under Section 103(a) of the Internal Revenue Code of 1986, as amended (the Code), is not treated as an item of tax preference under Section 57 of the Code for purposes of the alternative minimum tax imposed on individuals and corporations, is exempt from the Ohio personal income tax and excluded from the net income base of the Ohio corporate franchise tax so long as that interest is excluded from gross income for federal income tax purposes. The Bonds are "private activity bonds" as defined in Section 141(a) of the Code and are "qualified tax-exempt obligations" as defined in Section 265(b)(3) of the Code. We express no opinion as to any other tax consequences regarding the Bonds.

In giving the foregoing opinions with respect to the treatment of the interest on the Bonds and the status of the Bonds under the tax laws, we have assumed and relied upon compliance with the City's covenants and the accuracy, which we have not independently verified, of the City's representations and certifications, contained in the transcript. The accuracy of those representations and certifications, and the City's compliance with those covenants may be necessary for interest to be and remain excluded from gross income for federal income tax purposes and for other tax effects stated above. Failure to comply with certain requirements subsequent to issuance of the Bonds could cause the interest to be included in gross income for federal income tax purposes and to be subject to Ohio personal income tax and included in the net income base of the Ohio corporate franchise tax retroactively to the date of issuance of the Bonds.

Portions of the interest earned by corporations (as defined for federal income tax purposes) may be subject to a corporate alternative minimum tax under the Code. In addition, under the Code, that interest may be subject to an environmental tax imposed on corporations for certain taxable years, to a branch profits tax imposed on certain foreign corporations doing business in the United States, and to a tax imposed on excess net passive income of certain S corporations.

Obligations such as the Bonds that have been designated as "qualified tax-exempt obligations" and that are acquired by a financial institution after August 7, 1986, are treated as obligations acquired on August 7, 1986, for purposes of determining the amount of that institution's interest deduction under Section 265(b) of the Code.

Respectfully submitted,

SOURCE: Squire, Sanders & Dempsey

The legal opinion is virtually a requirement for any significant municipal offering. Counsel must attest that the bonds have been issued legally, according to state and local law, and that the interest is exempt from income tax according to federal law.

underwriters. Indeed, a financial advisor can act as the underwriter for an issue, although this practice is becoming increasingly rare for large issues. The Municipal Securities Rulemaking Board (MSRB) has adopted rule G-23 to cover possible conflicts of interest between advisors and underwriters (see Chapter 4). Financial advisors are usually paid for their services on a fee basis.

Community projects that are backed by bond issues often require the advice of specialists other than financial experts. Some firms, for example, advise solely on the financial, engineering, and architectural aspects of airports; other specialists evaluate transportation facilities and public utilities. The opinions of such consultants are often important not only for establishing the merits of a particular project but also for attracting voter approval of it and promoting investor acceptance of bonds backed by the project's revenues.

The Investors

Three classes of investors dominate the municipal marketplace: (1) retail, consisting of individuals acting directly or through the agency of trust companies and investment counsel; (2) retail proxies, that is, bond funds consisting of managed closed-end funds, open-end funds, and unit investment trusts; and (3) institutional, particularly commercial banks and property and casualty insurance companies. The principal characteristic of all buyers of municipal bonds is that they are in a sufficiently high tax bracket that they can benefit from the tax exemption.

From the early 1960s through 1980, commercial banks buying for their own portfolios were among the leading buyers of municipal bonds. A rapid growth in bank assets—stimulated partly by liberalized limits on interest rates on savings deposits and CDs and partly by profitable operations—made tax-exempt municipals an attractive investment. By 1980, commercial banks owned 42.5 percent of all outstanding municipal bond issues. However, commercial banks have shown a decreased demand for tax-exempt bonds, partly because of the availability of competing forms of tax shelters and, more recently, because of changes in the tax law. At the close of 1989 commercial banks' holdings of outstanding municipal securities had decreased to 16.5 percent.

Until 1980, property and casualty insurance companies were also major purchasers of municipal bonds, with their share of the market reaching about 23 percent. Their net income was subject to the full corporate tax rate, so long-term tax-exempt investment was attractive. But these companies too, due to their own earnings cycle, added volatility to the municipal bond market: while inflation increased the size of insurance settlements and awards, insurance rates periodically lagged, awaiting action by regulators. Then, after a rise in rates, a more profitable period would ensue.

In the early 1980s, the unprofitable phase of this cycle had been quite prolonged because rates had been held down by sharp competition. Hence, insurance companies' tax-exempt investments declined. Beginning in 1985, property and casualty insurance companies' strong profitability influenced their decision to purchase tax-exempts once again and by the end of 1989, they held 19.1 percent of the outstanding supply of municipal securities.

In the 1980s, individuals have accounted for a larger share of the market, and bond funds—which are really intermediaries for individuals—have become major buyers, particularly in the long-term tax-exempt market. At the end of 1989, individuals (or "households") and the funds together owned 58.8 percent of outstanding tax-exempt issues.

Provisions of the Tax Reform Act of 1986 affected the activity of certain traditional investors in municipal securities. For example, under the Act, with limited exceptions for certain small issuers, financial institutions are prohibited from deducting the amount of interest attributable to purchasing or carrying municipal securities acquired after August 7, 1986.

The Dealers

The enormous task of underwriting, marketing, and trading municipal securities is undertaken by the dealer departments of commercial banks and securities firms. Most major stock brokerage firms have municipal bond departments that underwrite and trade state and local government securities. Similarly, many major commercial banks have such departments. A further class of dealer operates solely in the municipal market. Some of the latter firms specialize only in underwriting and financial advice, sometimes solely in one type of security such as housing bonds. Others do mostly "retail" business, that is, trade with investors, often individual investors. Still other firms trade only for dealers; these are the municipal bond brokers, or "brokers' brokers." At the end of May 1990, approximately 2,700 securities firms and banks had paid a Municipal Securities Rulemaking Board fee and were authorized to perform transactions in the municipal market, although only about one-fourth were actively involved in the market.

General obligation bonds are, with some important exceptions, the only type of municipal security that commercial banks can underwrite. The Glass-Steagall Act of 1933 prohibited commercial banks from participating in the underwriting and trading of both municipal revenue bond issues and corporate securities. However, subsequent legislation and the rulings of federal bank regulatory authorities have allowed commercial banks to underwrite certain types of revenue bond issues, such as housing and education revenue bonds and moral obligation bonds. Such bonds are known as "bank-eligible" bonds. In 1989, these types of revenue bonds represented about 30 percent of all revenue bonds issued. A proposal to permit banks to underwrite all types of revenue bonds has been under continuing legislative consideration for some time. Moreover, some banks have established securities subsidiaries that can underwrite revenue bonds in specified circumstances.

COMPETITIVE VERSUS NEGOTIATED UNDERWRITING

General obligation bond issues are frequently underwritten by means of competitive sales except in the case of refunding bonds. Two or more groups of underwriters bid for an issue, each trying to offer the lowest bid to the issuer. The issuer chooses the group that offers to buy the bonds for the lowest interest cost. The underwriters must then pay that price for the bonds no matter how successful they are later in selling those bonds to investors. Dealers and dealer banks alike compete in this market.

Revenue bonds, on the other hand, are often underwritten on a negotiated basis. The municipality or other authority chooses one underwriter or group of underwriters to sell the bonds, often after formal presentations from many applicants. The underwriters try to produce the lowest interest rates on the issue that the market will bear, but they also perform many other services for the issuer.

To facilitate the underwriting of all but the smallest issues, several dealers form underwriting groups called syndicates. The leader or leaders of the syndicate are called managers or co-managers. They perform most of the underwriting and selling. One or two senior or lead managers perform the administrative and organizational work, for which the client pays a management fee as part of the underwriting spread.

Dealers often make markets in securities they have underwritten after the sales have taken place. Many dealers, of course, also trade actively in other municipal securities, and secondary market trading is one of the key activities of most major dealers.

A typical municipal securities department in a commercial bank or securities firm has six distinct functions. A brief description of the activities of each follows (see Figure 2-4).

FIGURE 2-4. Typical Municipal Securities Department

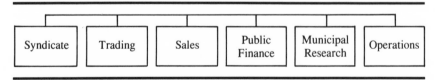

| Syndicate | Trading | Sales | Public Finance | Municipal Research | Operations |

UNDERWRITING (SYNDICATE)

A typical department employs one or more individuals whose full-time responsibility it is to work on competitive and negotiated underwritings. These individuals are primarily responsible for setting prices and yields on the new issues their firm underwrites each week. That requires attending price meetings—a tradition largely limited to New York City—or working over the phone with dealers in other parts of the country. Some large bank dealers, notably in Chicago and the West Coast, maintain underwriting and trading offices in New York that have responsibility for making decisions to commit the bank's funds. Underwriters work closely with traders and salesmen to determine the marketability and appropriate yields for an issue.

TRADING

Traders maintain the secondary market for securities by actively buying bonds and selling them to other dealers and investors in the secondary market. This requires a large inventory of bonds to service clients, because there are so many kinds of issues. An effective trader should be familiar at all times with the bonds that are available for sale or purchase in the market.

Many trading departments have several traders. Typically, one may specialize in term bonds or dollar bonds (bonds that are quoted and traded in dollar prices rather than in terms of yield); another might specialize in notes; another in general obligation bond issues, and so on.

SALES

Dealer firms frequently employ a large staff of salespeople who are responsible for making direct contact with investors. They often sit at the trading desk with the underwriters and traders and attempt to arrange sales of securities during the underwriting of a new issue. The sales staff's responsibilities are organized in various ways. Often, they divide the territory among themselves geographically; other firms divide the sales force according to the clients each salesperson has developed over the years.

Securities firms with many individual investors often have a sales liaison force. The sales liaison staff sits close to the trading desk and works with the account executives in the branch offices. The branch offices contact the sales liaison staff at the trading desk when there is an order, and the liaison staff passes the order to the traders. Several large securities firms have regional trading areas that duplicate their main office trading operation on a smaller scale. The sales force and liaison staff in these regional offices work in much the same way as they do in the main office.

Typically, traders, underwriters, and salespeople sit in a large trading room close to one another, with telephone consoles connecting them with clients, other dealers, and their branch offices. In addition, most larger trading operations have one group assigned to perform computations for underwriting bids.

PUBLIC FINANCE

This is the group that seeks new negotiated underwriting business for the dealer firm or bank. In many cases, they are the primary source of the new products which have changed the form in which municipal bond issuers sell their debt. Usually, this same group also performs financial advisory work for a fee. Commercial banks, which do not fully participate in negotiated underwritings because of the restrictions of the Glass-Steagall Act, often have a financial advisory group as part of their municipal bond department. However, some commercial banks do have active public finance departments which concentrate on bank-eligible revenue bonds.

MUNICIPAL RESEARCH

The increased awareness in recent years of the potential for municipal governments to experience financial difficulties and the growing complexity of the municipal market have led dealers to place greater emphasis on research into the creditworthiness of municipal issuers. At one time, the rating agencies were far and away the most prominent sources of credit information on municipal bonds. These days, dealers as well as investors are expanding their own efforts. Research staffs at bank dealers, securities firms, and insurance companies have grown by multiples of two and three. The research department in an underwriting firm usually prepares a short opinion on important competitive or negotiated issues coming to market that the firm might bid on. This helps the underwriters and traders set yields on the issues.

Many dealer firms also provide such research to institutions and individuals. The general principles of this research are discussed in Chapter 7.

OPERATIONS

This function has become more complex and important in recent years. Operations involves processing securities and payments, as well as performing accounting for the municipal securities department—essentially, the traditional back-office activities. The MSRB's adoption of industrywide requirements for orders, record keeping, and confirmations has significantly standardized the functions of the operations group. Its duties include processing orders and payments, checking and delivering securities, issuing confirmations, and maintaining customer accounts and other required documentation. The operations rules of the MSRB are discussed in greater detail in Chapters 4, 5, and 9.

Bond Brokers

The bond brokers, or brokers' brokers, play a very important part in the workings of the municipal market. Municipal bond brokers trade only for municipal bond dealers and dealer banks; that is, they do not work directly with either institutional or individual investors. Essentially, dealers use brokers to facilitate a trade if they cannot make it more efficiently themselves. For example, dealers often try to sell bonds in their inventories through brokers. They can ask a broker to seek bids on the bonds from other dealers. This is known as the "bid-wanted" business. On the other hand, a dealer may be looking for particular bonds for a customer and may tell the bond broker that he or she would be willing to buy them at a specified yield or price. In this instance, the broker will seek these bonds from other dealers. There are about 14 active municipal bond brokers in the country, most of them located in New York City.

The Rating Agencies

Because of the large number of different issues in the marketplace, bond ratings (or debt ratings) often play a greater role in the municipal securities market than in the corporate market. A rating ranks each security according to what the rating agencies believe is its creditworthiness; such a rating is considered obligatory for the sale of any major issue. However, smaller issues often can be marketed on a nonrated basis.

The two dominant agencies in the ratings field are Moody's Investors Service, Inc., and Standard & Poor's Corporation. Fitch Investors Service, Inc., also rates bonds and was pioneering in health care bonds. All three are located in New York City. Moody's has been rating municipal bonds since 1918 and Standard & Poor's started rating municipal bonds in 1940. In 1989, Moody's had about 40,000 outstanding municipal bond ratings and currently assigns a rating to approximately 6,000 new issues a year. Standard & Poor's had about 23,000 municipal bond ratings outstanding in 1989, and it assigns a rating to a further 3,800 or so new issues each year. Fitch has been rating bonds since 1923. All three now rate short-term notes, commercial paper, and obligations secured by insurance, bank, and other credit enhancements.

The rating agencies charge fees for their bond ratings based on the size of the issue and the amount of analysis needed. Most major issuers communicate regularly with the agencies, and underwriters are often involved in making presentations to the agencies on behalf of issuers. The rating agencies review their ratings periodically and request updated information. In addition, they provide a review process for municipalities seeking to improve their ratings. The municipal securities ratings assigned by Moody's, Standard & Poor's, and Fitch are described in Figure 2-5.

FIGURE 2-5. Guide to the Municipal Bond Ratings of Moody's Investors Service, Inc., Standard & Poor's Corporation, and Fitch Investors Service, Inc.

KEY TO STANDARD & POOR's DEBT RATINGS CRITERIA
Long-Term Debt

AAA Debt rated "AAA" has the highest rating assigned by Standard & Poor's. Capacity to pay interest and repay principal is extremely strong.

AA Debt rated "AA" has a very strong capacity to pay interest and repay principal and differs from the highest-rated issues only in small degree.

A Debt rated "A" has a strong capacity to pay interest and repay principal although it is somewhat more susceptible to the adverse effects of changes in circumstances and economic conditions than debt in higher-rated categories.

BBB Debt rated "BBB" is regarded as having an adequate capacity to pay interest and repay principal. Whereas it normally exhibits adequate protection parameters, adverse economic conditions or changing circumstances are more likely to lead to a weakened capacity to pay interest and repay principal for debt in this category than in higher-rated categories.

BB
B Debt rated "BB," "B," "CCC," or "CC" is regarded, on balance, as predominantly speculative with respect to capacity to pay interest and repay
CCC principal in accordance with the terms of the obligation. "BB" indicates the
CC lowest degree of speculation and "CC" the highest degree of speculation. While such debt will likely have some quality and protective characteristics, these are outweighed by large uncertainties or major risk exposures to adverse conditions.

C This rating is reserved for income bonds on which no interest is being paid.

D Debt rated "D" is in default, and payment of interest and/or repayment of principal is in arrears.

Plus (+) or Minus (−): The ratings from "AA" to "B" may be modified by the addition of a plus or minus sign to show relative standing within the major rating categories.

Provisional Ratings: The letter "p" indicates that the rating is provisional. A provisional rating assumes the successful completion of the project being financed by the debt being rated and indicates that payment of debt service requirements is largely or entirely dependent upon the successful and timely completion of the project. This rating, however, while addressing credit quality subsequent to completion of the project, makes no comment on the likelihood of, or the risk of default upon failure of, such completion. The investor should exercise judgment with respect to such likelihood and risk.

L The letter "L" indicates that the rating pertains to the principal amount of those bonds where the underlying deposit collateral is fully insured by the Federal Savings & Loan Insurance Corp. or the Federal Deposit Insurance Corp.

* Continuance of the rating is contingent upon S&P's receipt of an executed copy of the escrow agreement or closing documentation confirming investments and cash flow.

NR Indicates no rating has been requested, that there is insufficient information on which to base a rating, or that S&P does not rate a particular type of obligation as a matter of policy.

Notes

A Standard & Poor's note rating reflects the liquidity concerns and market access risks unique to notes. Notes due in 3 years or less will likely receive a note rating. Notes maturing beyond 3 years will most likely receive a long-term debt rating. The following criteria will be used in making that assessment:

Amortization schedule (the larger the final maturity relative to other maturities, the more likely it will be treated as a note).

Source of payment (the more dependent the issue is on the market for its refinancing, the more likely it will be treated as a note).

SP-1 Very strong or strong capacity to pay principal and interest. Those issues determined to possess overwhelming safety characteristics will be given a plus (+) designation.

SP-2 Satisfactory capacity to pay principal and interest.

SP-3 Speculative capacity to pay principal and interest.

Tax-Exempt Commercial Paper

A Issues assigned this highest rating are regarded as having the greatest capacity for timely payment. Issues in this category are delineated with the numbers 1,2, and 3 to indicate the relative degree of safety.

A-1 This designation indicates that the degree of safety regarding timely payment is either overwhelming or very strong. Those issues determined to possess overwhelming safety characteristics are denoted with a plus (+) sign designation.

A-2 Capacity for timely payment on issues with this designation is strong. However, the relative degree of safety is not as high as for issues designated "A-1."

A-3 Issues carrying this designation have a satisfactory capacity for timely payment. They are, however, somewhat more vulnerable to the adverse effects of changes in circumstances than obligations carrying the higher designations.

B Issues rated "B" are regarded as having only an adequate capacity for timely payment. However, such capacity may be damaged by changing conditions or short-term adversities.

C This rating is assigned to short-term debt obligations with a doubtful capacity for payment.

D This rating indicates that the issue either is in default or is expected to be in default upon maturity.

Variable-Rate Demand Bonds

Standard & Poor's assigns "dual" ratings to all long-term debt issues that have as part of their provisions a variable-rate demand or double feature.

The first rating addresses the likelihood of repayment of principal and interest as due, and the second rating addresses only the demand feature. The long-term debt rating symbols are used for bonds to denote the long-term maturity and the commercial paper rating symbols are used to denote the put option (for example, "AAA/A-1+") or if the nominal maturity is short, a rating of "SP-1+/AAA" is assigned.

KEY TO MOODY'S MUNICIPAL RATINGS

There are nine basic rating categories for long-term obligations. They range from **Aaa** (highest quality) to **C** (lowest quality). Bonds in the **Aa, A, Baa, Ba** and **B** groups which Moody's believes possess the strongest investment attributes are designated by the symbols **Aa1, A1, Baa1, Ba1** and **B1.**

There are four rating categories for short-term obligations, all of which define an investment-grade situation. These are designated Moody's Investment Grade as **MIG 1** through **MIG 4.**

In the case of variable-rate demand obligations (VRDOs), two ratings are assigned; one representing an evaluation of the degree of risk associated with scheduled principal and interest payments, and the other representing an evaluation of the degree of risk associated with the demand feature. The short-term rating assigned to the demand feature of VRDOs is designated as **VMIG** (pronounced **vee MIG**). When no rating is applied to the long- or short-term aspect of a VRDO, it will be designated **NR.**

Definitions of Bond Ratings

Aaa Bonds which are rated **Aaa** are judged to be of the best quality. They carry the smallest degree of investment risk and are generally referred to as "gilt edge." Interest payments are protected by a large or by an exceptionally stable margin and principal is secure. While the various protective elements are likely to change, such changes as can be visualized are most unlikely to impair the fundamentally strong position of such issues.

Aa Bonds which are rated **Aa** are judged to be of high quality by all standards. Together with the **Aaa** group they comprise what are generally known as high-grade bonds. They are rated lower than the best bonds because margins of protection may not be as large as in **Aaa** securities or fluctuation of protective elements may be of greater amplitude or there may be other elements present which make the long-term risks appear somewhat larger than in **Aaa** securities.

A Bonds which are rated **A** possess many favorable investment attributes and are to be considered as upper-medium-grade obligations. Factors giving security to principal and interest are considered adequate, but elements may be present which suggest a susceptibility to impairment some time in the future.

Baa Bonds which are rated **Baa** are considered as medium-grade obligations; i.e., they are neither highly protected nor poorly secured. Interest payments and principal security appear adequate for the present but certain protective elements may be lacking or may be characteristically unreliable over any great length of time. Such bonds lack outstanding investment characteristics and in fact have speculative characteristics as well.

Ba Bonds which are rated **Ba** are judged to have speculative elements; their future cannot be considered as well assured. Often the protection of interest and principal payments may be very moderate, and thereby not well safeguarded during both good and bad times over the future. Uncertainty of position characterizes bonds in this class.

B Bonds which are rated **B** generally lack characteristics of the desirable investment. Assurance of interest and principal payments or maintenance of other terms of the contract over any long period of time may be small.

Caa Bonds which are rated **Caa** are of poor standing. Such issues may be in default or there may be present elements of danger with respect to principal or interest.

Ca Bonds which are rated **Ca** represent obligations which are speculative in a high degree. Such issues are often in default or have other marked shortcomings.

C Bonds which are rated **C** are the lowest-rated class of bonds, and issues so rated can be regarded as having extremely poor prospects of ever attaining any real investment standing.

Con.(...) Bonds for which the security depends upon the completion of some act or the fulfillment of some condition are rated conditionally. These are bonds secured by: (a) earnings of projects under construction, (b) earnings of projects unseasoned in operating experience, (c) rentals which begin when facilities are completed, or (d) payments to which some other limiting condition attaches. Parenthetical rating denotes probable credit stature upon completion of construction or elimination of basis of condition.

Definitions of Short-Term Loan Ratings

Issues or the features associated with **MIG** or **VMIG** ratings are identified by date of issue, date of maturity or maturities or rating expiration date and description to distinguish each rating from other ratings. Each rating designation is unique with no implication as to any other similar issue of the same obligor. **MIG** ratings terminate at the retirement of the obligation while **VMIG** rating expiration will be a function of each issue's specific structural or credit features.

MIG 1/ This designation denotes best quality. There is present strong protection by
VMIG 1 established cash flows, superior liquidity support, or demonstrated broad-based access to the market for refinancing.

MIG 2/ This designation denotes high quality. Margins of protection are ample al-
VMIG 2 though not so large as in the preceding group.

MIG 3/ This designation denotes favorable quality. All security elements are ac-
VMIG 3 counted for but there is lacking the undeniable strength of the preceding grades. Liquidity and cash flow protection may be narrow and market access for refinancing is likely to be less well established.

MIG 4/ This designation denotes adequate quality. Protection commonly regarded as
VMIG 4 required of an investment security is present and although not distinctly or predominantly speculative, there is specific risk.

Tax-Exempt Commercial Paper Ratings

Moody's Short-Term Debt Ratings are opinions of the ability of issuers to repay punctually senior debt obligations which have an original maturity not exceeding one year. Tax-exempt commercial paper is among the obligations covered. Moody's employs the following three designations, all judged to be investment grade, to indicate the relative repayment ability of rated issuers:

Prime-1 Issuers rated **Prime-1** (or supporting institutions) have a superior ability for repayment of senior short-term debt obligations. **Prime-1** repayment ability will often be evidenced by many of the following characteristics:
— Leading market positions in well-established industries.
— High rates of return on funds employed.
— Conservative capitalization structures with moderate reliance on debt and ample asset protection.
— Broad margins in earnings coverage of fixed financial charges and high internal cash generation.
— Well-established access to a range of financial markets and assured sources of alternate liquidity.

Prime-2 Issuers rated **Prime-2** (or supporting institutions) have a strong ability for repayment of senior short-term debt obligations. This will normally be evidenced by many of the characteristics cited above but to a lesser degree. Earnings trends and coverage ratios, while sound, may be more subject to variation. Capitalization characteristics, while still appropriate, may be more affected by external conditions. Ample alternate liquidity is maintained.

Prime-3 Issuers rated **Prime-3** (or supporting institutions) have an acceptable ability for repayment of senior short-term debt obligations. The effect of industry characteristics and market composition may be more pronounced. Variability in earnings and profitability may result in changes in the level of debt protection measurements and may require relatively high financial leverage. Adequate alternate liquidity is maintained.

Not
Prime Issuers rated **Not Prime** do not fall within any of the Prime rating categories.

KEY TO FITCH'S MUNICIPAL RATINGS
Bond Rating Symbols

AAA rated bonds are considered to be investment grade and of the highest quality. The obligor has an extraordinary ability to pay interest and repay principal, which is unlikely to be affected by reasonably foreseeable events.

AA rated bonds are considered to be investment grade and of high quality. The obligor's ability to pay interest and repay principal, while very strong, is somewhat less than for AAA rated securities or more subject to possible change over the term of the issue.

A rated bonds are considered to be investment grade and of good quality. The obligor's ability to pay interest and repay principal is considered to be strong, but may be more vulnerable to adverse changes in economic conditions and circumstances than bonds with higher ratings.

BBB rated bonds are considered to be investment grade and of satisfactory quality. The obligor's ability to pay interest and repay principal is considered to be adequate. Adverse changes in economic conditions and circumstances, however, are more likely to weaken this ability than bonds with higher ratings.

BB rated bonds are considered speculative and of low investment grade. The obligor's ability to pay interest and repay principal is not strong and is considered likely to be affected over time by adverse economic changes.

B rated bonds are considered highly speculative. Bonds in this class are lightly protected as to the obligor's ability to pay interest over the life of the issue and repay principal when due.

CCC rated bonds may have certain characteristics which, with the passing of time, could lead to the possibility of default on either principal or interest payments.

CC rated bonds are minimally protected. Default in payment of interest and/or principal seems probable.

C rated bonds are in actual or imminent default in payment of interest or principal.

DDD, rated bonds are in default and in arrears in interest and/or principal payments.
DD, D Such bonds are extremely speculative and should be valued only on the basis of their value in liquidation or reorganization of the obligor.

Plus(+) or Minus(−) Signs: These signs are used after a rating symbol to designate the relative position of a credit within the rating grade. The + and − signs are carried in ratings from ''AA'' to ''B.''

Note Ratings

These symbols are assigned to Bond Anticipation Notes, Revenue or Tax Anticipation Notes, plain Notes or less frequently seen notes such as Grant Anticipation Notes.

FIN-1 Notes assigned this rating are regarded as having the strongest degree of assurance for timely payment.

FIN-2 Notes assigned this rating reflect a degree of assurance for timely payment only slightly less in degree than the highest category.

FIN-3 Notes with this rating have a satisfactory degree of assurance for timely payment, but the margin of safety is not as great as in the two highest categories.

FIN-4 Notes with this rating have speculative characteristics which suggest that the degree of assurance for timely payment is minimal and is susceptible to near-term adverse change.

A plus(+) symbol may be used in the three highest categories to indicate relative standing.

Tax-Exempt Commercial Paper Ratings

Tax-exempt commercial paper ratings are assigned to obligations issued as commercial paper, or as notes issued under a commercial paper program, with an original maturity of up to a year.

So-called Floating-Rate Demand Notes may allow the investor to require the issuer (or a trustee) to purchase the notes at the demand of the investor, thus giving the notes some of the characteristics of commercial paper insofar as liquidity is concerned. In this case a commercial paper rating may be assigned. Fitch commercial paper ratings are grouped into four categories as defined below:

Fitch-1 (Highest Grade) Commercial paper assigned this rating is regarded as having the strongest degree of assurance for timely payment.

Fitch-2 (Very Good Grade) Issues assigned this rating reflect an assurance of timely payment only slightly less in degree than the strongest issues.

Fitch-3 (Good Grade) Commercial paper carrying this rating has a satisfactory degree of assurance for timely payment but the margin of safety is not as great as the two higher categories.

Fitch-4 (Poor Grade) Issues carrying this rating have characteristics suggesting that the degree of assurance for timely payment is minimal and is susceptible to near-term adverse change due to less favorable financial or economic conditions.

Plus (+) This sign is used after a rating symbol in the first three rating categories to designate the relative position of an issuer within the rating category.

LOC The symbol (LOC) following any of the above four grades indicates that a letter of credit issued by a commercial bank is attached to the commercial paper note. The note holder is the direct beneficiary of the bank's obligation to use its own funds to pay the full amount of the note at maturity at the time such action is required by the terms of the letter of credit.

Other commercial paper programs supported by a bank letter of credit but where the letter of credit is not attached to the commercial paper note do not carry this designation.

SOURCE: Moody's Investors Service, Inc., Standard & Poor's Corporation, and Fitch Investors Service, Inc.

The Qualifications Examinations

One of the first rules the MSRB adopted requires that all persons involved with "any transaction" in municipal securities must pass a qualifying examination. The exams are administered by the National Association of Securities Dealers (NASD).

The Board has established four distinct classes of municipal securities employees, according to rule G-3, and has developed a different qualifying exam for each class. The great majority of employees are termed municipal securities representatives. They include anyone who underwrites, trades, or sells municipal securities, does research or offers investment advice, provides financial or advisory services to issuers, or is involved in "any activities other than those specifically enumerated above which involve communication, directly or indirectly, with public investors in municipal securities." Clerical personnel are not, in general, included in this group.

There are two important exemptions from the qualifications test for representatives. First, anyone who performed these activities from December 1, 1975, through July 14, 1978, does not have to take the examination. Second, anyone who has already passed the NASD examination for general securities representative need not take the municipal securities exam. New employees of securities firms may take the general securities exam in lieu of the municipal securities exam. In addition to taking the qualifying exam, all new municipal securities representatives must serve a minimum apprenticeship of 90 days on the job before they can transact any business. The passing score for the exam is set by the MSRB. An apprentice must pass the exam before the end of a 180-day time limit or cease to perform the functions of a municipal securities professional.

The three other classes of municipal securities employees are the municipal securities principals, the municipal securities sales principals, and the financial and operations principals. The municipal securities principal has a supervisory role, and each firm must have at least one municipal securities principal; many firms have more. A municipal securities sales principal may supervise only sales to customers for a securities firm, and is usually a branch manager. The financial and operations principal is the person designated to be in charge of preparing and filing financial reports to the SEC or any other regulatory agency for a securities firm. There are separate exams for municipal securities principals, municipal securities sales principals, and financial and operations principals. Those financial and operations principals who are qualified as such under the NASD examination are also exempted.

3

The Issuers

According to U.S. Census Bureau figures for 1987, there are approximately 83,200 state and local governments in this country, about 50,000 of which have issued municipal securities. In addition, several thousand special-purpose authorities exist. These are entities like housing, transportation, hospital, public power, water, sewer, industrial development, and education authorities. Unlike the federal, state, or local governments, these authorities exist solely in order to provide and supervise specific projects, for which they may issue municipal securities.

The municipal securities market differs from the market for corporate debt securities in that the former consists largely of smaller issues. The Public Securities Association estimates that, from 1980 to 1988, an average of about 22 percent of municipal bond issues were for $1 million or less and that, on average, 62 percent of all issues were for $5 million or less. The bulk of the dollar volume of new issues has been concentrated in the larger issues. Most large issues have amounted to between $100 million and $500 million, and the New Jersey Turnpike Authority has come to market for as much as $2 billion at one time.

The history of municipal debt predates that of corporate debt by several centuries: during the Renaissance, Italian city-states were borrowing money from the major merchant banking families. Careful records of U.S. municipal bond issues, however, were begun only in 1843, although borrowing by some U.S. cities dates back to the seventeenth century. By the 1840s, many U.S. cities were in the debt market, and by 1843 cities had about $25 million of debt outstanding. The following two decades of rapid urban development saw a correspondingly explosive growth in municipal debt used to finance both urban improvements and a burgeoning system of free public education.

53

For a few years after the Civil War, a great deal of local debt was issued to build the railroads. Because railroads were private corporations, these bond issues were very similar to today's industrial revenue bonds. However, the 1873 Panic and the several years of depression that followed put an abrupt, if temporary, halt to the rapid growth of municipal debt. Widespread defaults jolted the municipal bond market; new state statutes were passed that restricted the issuance of local debt; and some states wrote these restrictions into their constitutions. The legality of the railroad bonds was widely challenged, giving rise to the marketwide demand for an opinion of bond counsel to accompany each new issue.

Once the economy started to move forward, municipal debt resumed its momentum, which it maintained well into the early part of this century. The Great Depression of the 1930s halted its growth, though defaults were not as severe as in the 1870s. The amount of municipal debt outstanding then fell during World War II as resources were devoted to the war effort. After the war, municipal debt burst into a new period of rapid growth for an ever-increasing variety of uses. Just after World War II, municipal debt per capita was $145. By 1988, per capita debt had risen to $2,990.

The Theory of Municipal Debt: Pay-as-You-Use Versus Pay-as-You-Acquire

Corporations borrow in order to build facilities or to make other investments that will improve their returns. The profits from their investments are used to pay back the debt. Lacking such a profit motive, municipalities justify borrowing by reference to the purposes of borrowing. Deciding who will pay for the debt, and in what way, tends to depend on the political and economic climate.

Proponents of the liberal use of debt financing argue that new facilities should be paid for over time by the people who are benefiting from them—the pay-as-you-use approach. According to this argument, a community that pays for a new water system immediately is assuming a burden that should be shared by future taxpayers who will also benefit from the water system. Furthermore, it is argued, a growing city will be better able to afford the debt payments over time—and new projects today may be necessary for the municipality's growth tomorrow. With this in mind, policymakers often want the repayment schedule for any municipal debt raised to finance a project to coincide with the minimum expected life of that project.

The theory behind municipal revenue bonds is, in part, an extension of this pay-as-you-use philosophy. Revenue bonds are paid off from revenues generated by the particular project being financed. The beneficiaries of the project—the customers or users—are paying off the debt, not the community as a whole.

At a time when debt financing has become a way of life for corporations, municipalities, and consumers alike, theoretical justifications for borrowing may seem unnecessary. In the past, however, whenever the economy has taken a downturn, the pay-as-you-use approach has come under heavy criticism. In periods of economic stringency, such as the 1930s, state and local officials have favored a pay-as-you-acquire philosophy. Simply put, this means that new projects should be paid for immediately.

Political as well as economic circumstances can also affect the issuance of municipal debt. In 1978, for example, Proposition 13 amended the California state constitution by limiting the property tax to 1 percent of full value. While no direct action was taken to limit debt, one result of the amendment was that the issuance of general obligation debt in the state slowed substantially. More recently, however, local authorities in California have substantially readjusted to the tax limitation and are issuing more municipal debt. It is safe to conclude, therefore, that the accepted view of fiscal probity for state and local governments will fluctuate both with the health of the national economy and with the political climate of the times.

The Uses of Municipal Debt

Everyday operating expenses of state and local governments are paid for out of current tax and other revenues. Municipal debt is used generally to finance capital projects.

The major purposes for which municipal debt has been issued for selected years are shown in Figure 3-1. In 1970, transportation, education, and water and sewer systems were the major uses of debt. In 1976, housing and public power facilities became more important. This trend continued in 1982 with an increasing share of debt issuance occurring on behalf of housing, hospitals and public power. The major use of debt in 1989 was predominantly education facilities. Education has remained a major user of municipal debt, with an increasing emphasis on college education, as the baby boom generation has aged.

The 1980s also saw the continued dominance of revenue bond financing. The popularity of the revenue bond, which puts no direct strain on a municipality's finances, has given state and local governments more latitude than ever before in financing public-purpose projects. The Tax Reform Act of 1986 placed further limitations on the purposes for which tax-exempt debt may be issued in the future.

FIGURE 3-1. Major Uses of Municipal Debt, Selected Years, as a Percentage of Total Long-Term Borrowing*

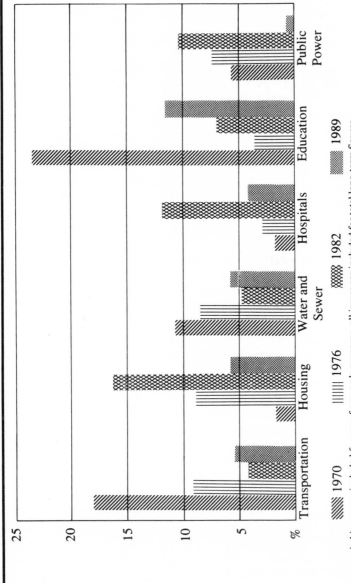

*Only new capital issues are included for use of proceeds purposes, all issues are included for total long-term figures.

SOURCE: IDD Information Services/PSA Municipal Securities Database.

Changes in the major uses of debt financing over the years reflect both the evolution of new financing techniques and the demand for government-provided services.

AUTHORITIES AND SPECIAL DISTRICTS

In the early part of this century, state and local governments began to create new debt-issuing entities called authorities and special districts. Sometimes they were formed to administer a geographical area that encompassed or crossed several political boundaries; sometimes they were formed in order to administer and raise money for a single project whose purpose and use was not necessarily limited to one state, county, or city. Two prominent early authorities were the Port of New York Authority (now the Port Authority of New York and New Jersey) and the Triborough Bridge Authority (now the Triborough Bridge and Tunnel Authority). The debt issues of such authorities are exempt from federal taxes and are backed by conservative bond covenants and ample reserve funds.

Today, authorities and special districts of all kinds are found across the country. The majority of states, for example, have housing authorities, and special district bonds are commonly issued to finance water, sewer, and utility services where user charges are involved. Indeed, bond-issuing authorities have been created to finance and construct an increasing variety of public projects: transportation facilities, including roads, airports, docking facilities, and mass transit systems; sports arenas and convention centers; and resource recovery systems, educational facilities, and hospitals. Thus, the relative importance of statutory authorities as issuers of municipal securities has increased dramatically during the 1970s and 1980s (see Figure 3-2).

Figure 3-2. Municipal Borrowing by Type of Issuer, Selected Years, 1970-1989.

As a Percentage of Total Long-Term Borrowing.

	1970	1976	1982	1989
States	26.8%	20.4%	11.2%	9.3%
Counties	9.3	8.9	11.8	8.6
Municipalities	21.7	18.7	13.3	19.6
School Districts	11.7	8.0	3.5	6.7
Special Districts	5.9	7.5	3.9	4.0
Statutory Authorities	24.6	36.5	56.3	51.8
				100.0%

SOURCE: IDD Information Services/PSA Municipal Securities Database.

The relative importance of statutory authorities as issuers of municipal securities has increased dramatically during the last two decades.

THE FINANCING DECISION

Borrowing has become an important management tool for many state and local governments, a tool which has endowed them with flexibility in arranging finances. In particular, the advent of the revenue bond has given state and local governments a range of financing methods that neither require a voter referendum nor add any debt to the community's balance sheet, while the use of short-term debt to bridge gaps in longer-term financing has also increased the municipalities' financial options.

A complete analysis of the political, economic, and financial factors involved in municipal fiscal management is beyond the scope of this volume. However, Chapter 7 discusses the key considerations for municipal borrowing: the debt burden a community can tolerate, the economic maturity of and prospects for the local economy, and the legal restrictions on borrowing. Some basic financial considerations for issuers are summarized below.

DEBT REPAYMENT SCHEDULES

The arrangement of serial bond schedules can provide great flexibility to financial officers to meet annual budget considerations: serial maturities of issues can be constructed to dovetail with expected revenues and outlays; interest and principal payments can be set up to produce a near-level debt service year after year; term maturities with all principal payments coming due 15 to 30 years after issue can provide a useful financing option whose marketability is enhanced if a mandatory sinking fund schedule is included in the debt repayment structure (see Figure 3-3).

Marketability is an important factor in the choice of maturities. A diversity of maturities will usually broaden the appeal of an issue, attracting a variety of investors. The level of interest rates will also influence decisions concerning maturities. For example, if short-term interest rates are considered to be unusually low or if demand for short-term issues is strong, an issue weighted more heavily toward shorter-maturity serial bonds can be constructed.

CALL PROVISIONS

The cost to an issuer of having a call privilege can be a higher interest rate on the issue. Investors will often demand a higher yield for a security with a call provision because the potential for capital gain on a callable bond is limited. Also, if the issuer calls the bonds before they mature, the investor may be left with his or her principal to be reinvested at a lower interest rate. The question the issuer must consider, therefore, is whether the advantages of the call privilege outweigh the higher interest rate that must be offered to investors. When interest rates in general are high and volatile, a call provision is clearly most desirable as it enables the issuer to refund an issue and raise money again when interest rates are lower.

Thirty days before bonds are due to be called, the issuer usually notifies investors through an advertisement in a financial publication. The advertisement will state which bonds are being redeemed and how the bondholder will receive payment. The call provision normally states in which order bonds will be called—usually in a randomly selected order. Investors with unregistered bonds who have not seen or been notified of the call often lose six months' interest as, typically, they are notified of the call by the paying agent when they send in a coupon for payment six months later, not when they return the coupon payable when the bonds are called. Since July 1983, all new bonds are registered, thereby eliminating this problem for bonds issued since that date.

NEGOTIATED VERSUS COMPETITIVE SALES

In many instances, certain types of municipal securities, particularly general obligation bonds, are required by law to be sold pursuant to competitive bidding. Where not required, the advantage to the issuer of competitive bidding is the competition on the open market. For lesser-known issuers or for complicated offerings, a negotiated sale may offer a better alternative. In negotiated sales, the dealers' salespeople have more time to prepare the sale and will expend more effort in advance because they know they will have the right to sell the issue. Dealers also have the advantage of more flexibility in timing negotiated offerings as well as in developing a sales package that suits current market conditions. Novel and complicated issues can especially benefit from close work with the underwriters.

NET INTEREST COST VERSUS TRUE INTEREST COST

The issuer must also decide on what basis competing syndicates will calculate their bids for the bonds. The traditional method is an arithmetic calculation known as the net interest cost (NIC). There have been some attempts in recent years, however, to adopt a different calculation known as the true interest cost (TIC). This method of calculation takes into account the time value of money to produce what proponents argue is a more accurate indication of the true interest cost of an issue. However, virtually all bids are still based on the net interest cost, though bidding constraints have been devised to help insure that the costs of bids thus calculated are consistent with the true interest cost of the issue. A full discussion of NIC, TIC, and these rules can be found in the Appendix.

FIGURE 3-3. Maturity Schedule and Debt Service Schedule of a Level Debt Service Issue

$746,200,000
North Carolina Eastern Municipal Power Agency
Power System Revenue Bonds, Refunding Series 1986 A
Maturity Schedule

Dated: April 1, 1986   Due: January 1, as shown below

The 1986 A Bonds are issuable as fully registered bonds in the denomination of $5,000 or any integral multiple thereof. Principal will be payable at the principal corporate trust office of The Chase Manhattan Bank (National Association), New York, New York, Bond Fund Trustee and Bond Registrar. Interest on the 1986 A Bonds is payable semiannually on each January 1 and July 1, commencing July 1, 1986 (three months' interest), to the registered owner as of the close of business on the 15th day of the next preceding calendar month by check mailed to the address appearing on the books of registry.

The 1986 A Bonds are subject to redemption prior to maturity as described herein.

Year	Principal Amount	Interest Rate	Price
1998	$ 8,380,000	7.30%	100%
1999	18,140,000	7.40	100
2000	27,725,000	7.50	100
2001	29,745,000	7.60	100
2002	31,895,000	7.70	100
2004	65,895,000	7.75	99.75
2015	439,420,000	7.75	99.25
2017	75,000,000	5.00	69
2018	50,000,000	4.00	57.50

Serial maturities provide issuers with a flexible tool for meeting governmental budget requirements. In the debt service schedule following, interest and principal payments have been set up to produce a nearly level debt service each year for the life of the bonds.

Debt Service Requirements

The following table shows the annual accrued debt service requirements for the outstanding Bonds and the 1986 A Bonds. Power Agency's plan of financing incorporates an overall debt structure based on amortization schedules initially designed to result in level debt service with respect to all Bonds allocated to each of the six Joint Units over the estimated useful life of each such Joint Unit. Debt service on refunding Bonds (including the 1986 A Bonds) has been structured such that debt service on each issue of refunding Bonds is lower in the earlier years and no higher in any year than was debt service on the Bonds refunded with proceeds of such refunding Bonds.

1986 A Bonds

Year Ending January 1	Outstanding Bonds Debt Service[1]	Sinking Fund Installments	Interest	Debt Service	Total Debt Service
1987	$186,877,724		$40,246,442	$40,246,442	$227,124,166
1988	186,870,774		53,661,923	53,661,923	240,532,697
1989	187,593,533		53,661,923	53,661,923	241,255,456
1990	192,176,933		53,661,923	53,661,923	245,838,856
1991	193,147,833		53,661,923	53,661,923	246,809,756
1992	193,336,428		53,661,923	53,661,923	246,998,351
1993	193,516,688		53,661,923	53,661,923	247,178,611
1994	193,962,813		53,661,923	53,661,923	247,624,736
1995	195,655,323		53,661,923	53,661,923	249,317,246
1996	191,003,163		53,661,923	53,661,923	244,665,086
1997	191,224,135		53,661,923	53,661,923	244,886,058
1998	183,082,908	$ 8,380,000	53,661,923	62,041,923	245,124,831
1999	183,388,868	18,140,000	53,050,183	71,190,183	254,579,051
2000	183,865,888	27,725,000	51,707,823	79,432,823	263,298,711
2001	187,043,188	29,745,000	49,628,448	79,373,448	266,416,636
2002	191,988,794	31,895,000	47,367,828	79,262,828	271,251,622
2003	192,973,531	34,270,000	44,911,913	79,181,913	272,155,444
2004	204,467,538	31,625,000	42,255,988	73,880,988	278,348,526
2005	205,579,213	34,065,000	39,805,050	73,870,050	279,449,263
2006	204,586,850	36,670,000	37,165,013	73,835,013	278,421,863
2007	203,766,931	39,470,000	34,323,088	73,793,088	277,560,019
2008	204,443,000	42,500,000	31,264,163	73,764,163	278,207,163
2009	211,467,006	45,750,000	27,970,413	73,720,413	285,187,419
2010	143,116,069	32,430,000	24,424,788	56,854,788	199,970,857
2011	144,919,725	34,080,000	21,911,463	55,991,463	200,911,188
2012	146,614,942	36,700,000	19,270,263	55,970,263	202,585,205
2013	148,772,485	39,510,000	16,426,013	55,936,013	204,708,498
2014	173,071,090	54,505,000	13,363,988	67,868,988	240,940,078
2015	154,328,069	54,030,000	9,139,850	63,169,850	217,497,919
2016	160,936,804	48,190,000	5,235,500	53,425,500	214,362,304
2017	149,528,981	41,335,000	2,826,000	44,161,000	193,689,981
2018	186,629,350	25,185,000	1,007,400	26,192,400	212,821,750
2019	174,212,075				174,212,075
2020	15,798,500				15,798,500
2021	16,008,937				16,008,937
2022	16,012,812				16,012,812
2023	16,103,875				16,103,875
2024	16,507,500				16,507,500

[1]Excluding debt service on refunded Bonds and $150,000,000 Security Bonds issued to the Collateral Agent in connection with Power Agency's TECP program (see "PLAN OF FINANCING — Plan of Future Financing"). Interest payable on the $100,000,000 1985 B Bonds and $100,000,000 1985 C Bonds maturing in 2018 and on the $100,000,000 1985 F Bonds and $100,000,000 1985 G Bonds maturing in 2016 is based upon the actual respective rates to the next Adjustment Dates (February 27, 1987, September 1, 1987, June 1, 1987, and December 1, 1987, respectively) and an assumed Adjusted Rate of 6½% thereafter. The 1985 B, C, F and G Bonds will each be payable at par at the option of the holders of each Series on each Adjustment Date for such Series of Bonds prior to the Fixed Rate Date for such Series. On the Fixed Rate Date for a particular Series of Bonds, such Bonds will become subject to mandatory redemption or purchase in lieu thereof unless the registered owners thereof exercise an election not to have their Bonds redeemed or purchased.

State and Local Governmental Accounting

Governmental accounting necessarily differs in several important ways from business accounting. Business accounting is ultimately concerned with the profits of the owners; governments have no such clear-cut measure of success. Businesses must match sales to the expenses incurred in making those sales; governments must be certain that resources are sufficient to meet outlays. Businesses try to maximize profits; governments must meet the annual budget. To the owner of a business, the consolidation of all business expenses and revenues, no matter how diversified, makes sense; sources of revenue for certain governmental services, however, often have little to do with revenues raised for other purposes, so that segregated accounts are usually more appropriate as well as, frequently, legally mandated.

Such differences have resulted in a separate set of accounting principles for government, originally developed by the National Council on Governmental Accounting. The NCGA started to formulate these principles in 1934. In 1984, through an agreement between the Financial Accounting Foundation, which sets business accounting standards, the American Institute of Certified Public Accountants, and the NCGA, the latter was replaced by the Government Accounting Standards Board (GASB), which now sets standards of accounting and financial reporting for state and local governments.

FUND ACCOUNTING

To account for the diverse activities of state and local governments, accounts are divided into separate funds. As noted above, statutes and regulations often require that government resources and expenditures must be accounted for separately, by area of expenditure. This is called fund accounting, which, government officials argue, makes good sense anyway because it gives a clearer picture of how the government's various sources of revenue are used to finance different kinds of expenditures.

Each fund includes a set of accounts to record the revenues, expenditures (or expenses), assets, liabilities, and fund balances (or equity) of the activities of that fund. The GASB specifies eight major types of funds, falling into three categories (governmental, proprietary, and fiduciary). A governmental unit may require one or several funds of a single type or, on the other hand, may require fewer than eight funds. Six of the eight types of funds are described below. The other two funds are the special assessment fund and the internal service fund, categorized as, respectively, governmental and proprietary types of funds.

Governmental Funds

Most typical government functions are financed through these funds:

The general fund. This is normally the largest of the funds. It essentially accounts for all financial resources other than those accounted for in any other fund. Most current operations of the government are recorded here. Such taxes as property, income, and sales taxes will typically be recorded in the general fund.

Special revenue fund. This fund records proceeds from specific sources that are usually earmarked for special use, such as the care of parks, museums, or highways. Special assessments, major capital projects, and expendable trusts are recorded in other funds.

Capital projects fund. Any resources used for the acquisition and construction of capital facilities are accounted for here. Exceptions are those projects financed by the special assessment and enterprise funds. Formerly called the bonds fund, the capital projects fund was created because so many capital projects are no longer funded with bonds but funded from other sources such as direct revenues and grants. Separate capital projects funds are commonly set up for individual projects.

Debt service fund. This fund records the payment of interest and principal on long-term general obligation debt, as well as the accumulation of resources to pay off the debt.

Proprietary Funds

These funds account for governmental operations that are similar to those of business. The accounting principles for such funds are generally the same as those for business.

Enterprise fund. This is essentially the fund in which ongoing activities operated like those of a business are recorded. Public utilities financed by user charges are one example of such activities. Proceeds from revenue bond issues and their disposition are usually accounted for here.

Fiduciary Funds

These are *trust and agency funds.* They account for money or property that is being held by the governmental unit as a trustee, guardian, or agent for individuals, governmental entities, or nonpublic organizations. For example, pension funds are recorded here.

CASH VERSUS ACCRUAL BASIS OF ACCOUNTING

One of the major sources of controversy in governmental accounting is the question of when to record expenditures and revenues. Businesses do their accounting on an accrual basis—that is, revenues are recorded when they are earned, not when the cash comes in; and expenses are recorded when they are incurred, not simply when they are paid for. Some municipalities follow a different system, recording revenues when the cash comes in and expenditures when the cash goes out—some states even require this. However, this pure-cash type of accounting has been criticized for being confusing at best and misleading at worst.

The GASB requires a modified accrual basis for governmental accounting, which is known as GAAP—generally accepted accounting principles. Because a government is not trying to measure expenses against sales as a business does, GAAP requires that revenues be recognized only when they are available and measurable, while expenditures should be recognized when incurred. However, according to GAAP, interest and principal payments on debt should be recorded only when the payment is due.

BUDGETING

Budgeting is the primary means of financial management and control for governments. All 50 states require that operating budgets be in balance, and the GASB requires that budgets be drawn up annually for all government funds. The GASB also requires that comparisons between actual and budgeted revenues and expenditures be provided along with the financial statements.

FINANCIAL REPORTING

The GASB requires that governmental units should prepare both a comprehensive annual financial report and a more limited set of general-purpose financial statements. The GASB states that the latter are adequate for official statements, as well as for widespread distribution to those not interested in greater detail. The comprehensive annual financial report, however, is the official annual report. The GASB also requires that independent audits be undertaken of all state and local government financial statements.

The GASB's required set of general-purpose financial statements includes the following:

1. Combined balance sheet of all types of funds and accounts.
2. Combined statement of revenues, expenditures, and changes in balances of all governmental funds.
3. Combined statement of revenues, expenditures, and changes in fund balances—both budgeted and actual—of general and special revenue funds and of similar governmental funds for which annual budgets have been legally adopted.

4. Combined statement of revenues, expenses, and changes in retained earnings (or equity) of all proprietary fund types.
5. Combined statement of changes in financial position of all proprietary funds.
6. Notes to the financial statements.

The GASB requires that the comprehensive annual financial report contain all these statements, as well as considerably more detail. It lists in detail the material it recommends for both the comprehensive report and the general purpose statements in *Codification of Governmental Accounting and Financial Reporting Standards,* published jointly by the GASB and the Government Finance Officers Association (GFOA).

Official Statement

The GFOA has actively encouraged state and local governments to adopt, voluntarily, guidelines for municipal disclosure in official statements that accompany new offerings. Basically, the GFOA believes the official statement should contain all information that could be pertinent to prospective investors. This includes the terms, features, and characteristics of the bonds; the legal authority for the bonds; the use of proceeds; and the financial health of the government in question or of the projects being financed. The financial information about a city would include outstanding debt, revenues, expenditures, budgets, and other liabilities such as pension funds. A revenue issue would ideally include a detailed description of the finances of the project, as well as a listing and explanation of the protective covenants.

The cover page of an official statement gives a summary of the terms and features of the securities. A sample cover page is shown in Figure 3-4. It should include the following information (with appropriate cross-references to more complete discussions in the body of the official statement), as recommended by the GFOA (in its pamphlet, *Disclosure Guidelines for Offerings of Securities by State and Local Governments)*:

1. The total principal amount of the securities being offered.
2. The name of the issuer (with appropriate identification), the title of the issue, and the date of the official statement as of which it speaks.
3. The type of issue being offered (e.g., general obligation, water revenue, etc.).
4. The dates of the obligations, interest payment dates, the date from which interest is paid and identification of any special interest payment features (e.g., zero coupon, limited interest, variable rate, etc.)

5. The denominations in which the securities are being offered.
6. A brief statement of the security or other source of payment.
7. Names and cities of the principal offices of the trustee, registrar and paying agents.
8. Identification of mandatory, optional and extraordinary redemption or prepayment features and put or tender features.
9. Maturity date and principal amount by maturity in columnar form.
10. Statement of the tax status of interest on the securities being offered (including alternative minimum tax, original issue discount, bank qualification, etc.).
11. Reference to any credit enhancement.

FIGURE 3-4. Sample Cover Page from an Official Statement

NEW ISSUE

⑩ In the opinion of Wood Dawson Smith & Hellman, New York, New York, the interest on the Bonds is exempt from taxation by the United States of America under existing laws and regulations, except as described under "TAX EXEMPTION" herein, and, under the existing laws of the State of Tennessee, the bonds and the interest thereon shall at all times be free from taxation by the State or any county, municipality or taxing district of the State, except for inheritance, transfer and estate taxes, and except to the extent such interest may be included within the measure of corporate privilege taxes imposed pursuant to state law.

OFFICIAL STATEMENT

① **$113,075,000**

② **STATE OF TENNESSEE**

③ **General Purpose Bonds**

Dated: February 15, 1987   Due: March 1, as shown below

MATURITIES, AMOUNTS, INTEREST RATES AND YIELDS OR PRICES

⑨

Due	Amount	Interest Rate	Yield or Price	Due	Amount	Interest Rate	Yield or Price
1988	$5,752,000	5.40%	3.50%	1998	$5,621,000	5.50%	5.35%
1989	5,752,000	5.40	3.80	1999	5,621,000	5.60	5.45
1990	5,752,000	5.40	4.10	2000	5,621,000	5.60	5.55
1991	5,752,000	5.50	4.30	2001	5,621,000	5.50	5.65
1992	5,752,000	5.50	4.50	2002	5,621,000	5.60	5.75
1993	5,621,000	5.50	4.70	2003	5,621,000	5.60	5.85
1994	5,621,000	5.50	4.85	2004	5,621,000	5.60	5.95
1995	5,621,000	5.50	5.00	2005	5,621,000	5.60	6.00
1996	5,621,000	5.50	5.15	2006	5,621,000	5.60	6.05
1997	5,621,000	5.50	5.25	2007	5,621,000	5.60	6.05

Plus Accrued Interest from February 15, 1987

(6) The Bonds are direct general obligations of the State of Tennessee for the payment of which as to both principal and interest the full faith and credit of the State of Tennessee is pledged. The Bonds are being issued to finance the costs of capital improvements of the State.

The Bonds will be issued in fully registered form without coupons in the name of Cede
(7) & Co. as nominee of The Depository Trust Company, New York, New York, to which principal and interest payments on any of the Bonds will be made. Individual purchases
(5) will be made in book-entry form only in the principal amount of $1,000 or any integral multiple thereof. Beneficial owners of the Bonds will not receive physical delivery of
(4) bond certificates. Interest on the Bonds is payable September 1, 1987, and semi-annually each March 1 and September 1 thereafter as more fully described herein. The Bonds are
(8) subject to redemption prior to their stated maturities as more fully described herein.

The Bonds are offered when, as and if issued and are subject to the approving opinions of Wood Dawson Smith & Hellman, New York, New York, and the Attorney General and Reporter of the State of Tennessee, Nashville, Tennessee. It is expected that delivery of the Bonds will be made within thirty days from the date of sale.

(2) Dated: February 24, 1987

Additional information often set forth on the cover page or in the introductory section includes:

12. Indication if the securities are in book-entry form or eligible for custodial deposit with a registered securities depository, identifying the depository.
13. Identification of counsel.
14. Statement, if applicable, that the securities are offered when, as and if issued and subject to satisfaction of certain conditions.
15. Ratings by the various rating agencies.
16. Designation as a new issue.
17. Brief statement of the authority for issuance.
18. Anticipated date, manner and place of delivery.
19. Registration and exchange features.
20. Purpose of the issue.

By reason of the efforts of GFOA in the publication of its *Disclosure Guidelines*, the involvement of bond counsel and other municipal market participants in assessing market practices and investor demand for information, disclosure practices in the municipal securities area are under continued review and change. A related area of increased interest and current activity is an examination of measures to improve the distribution of disclosure documents and to create more centralized sources of issuer information. In this connection, the SEC's promulgation of Rule 15c2-12, discussed in Chapter 9, serves to establish certain under-writer review and distribution requirements and both the SEC and the MSRB have stimulated industry-wide discussions concerning the nature and utility of one or more central repositories providing access to municipal securities disclosure doc-umentation. MSRB Rule G-36 requires underwriters to send copies of official statements to the MSRB.

Insurance

Bond insurance typically represents a legal commitment by a third party (in this case, an insurance company) to make timely payments of principal and interest in the event that the issuer of the debt is unable to do so. Generally, such payments will be made as originally scheduled, and the principal will not be accelerated.

The role of municipal bond insurance in the tax-exempt market is threefold: to reduce interest costs to issuers, to provide a high level of security to investors, and to furnish improved secondary-market liquidity and price support. From 1971 to 1988, approximately $200 billion of new-issue municipal bonds was insured, and in 1985, approximately 25 percent—almost $50 billion—of new issues was insured. In 1989, 25 percent, or $30.6 billion, of new issues was insured. In the earlier years of municipal bond insurance, most of the new, insured issues were general obligation bonds. Today, many different kinds of bonds—including hos-pital, housing, and public power bonds—are routinely insured. Of the approxi-mately $450 billion of insured principal and interest outstanding, about 35 percent consists of general obligation bonds and the remainder of revenue bonds. The interest savings to issuers that have sold insured bonds since the beginning of municipal insurance in 1971 is estimated at $5 billion.

Currently, four major insurers are actively involved in the insurance of new-issue municipal bonds. Also insured are municipal unit investment trusts, private portfolios, and, most recently, bonds traded in the secondary market, which trade subsequent to the new issue. The major insurers of municipal bonds are the Municipal Bond Investors Assurance Corporation (MBIA Corporation), succes-sor to the Municipal Bond Insurance Association founded in 1974, with $64 billion par value insured; the American Municipal Bond Assurance Corporation (AMBAC), founded in 1971, with $49 billion par value insured; the Financial Guaranty Insurance Company (FGIC), founded in 1983, with $44 billion par value insured; and the Capital Guaranty Insurance Company, founded in 1986, with $3.2 billion par value insured.

In total, these four municipal bond insurance companies bring together a com-bined policy holders' surplus of nearly $3.5 billion. Standard & Poor's rates all bonds insured by these four companies AAA, and Moody's rates bonds insured by all four as Aaa.

While bond insurance provides significant additional security for those issues insured, investors should be aware that the issuers are still the first source to look to for payment of principal and interest on their bonds. For that reason (and for other, technical and tax-related considerations), all insured bonds do not carry identical rates of return. The perceived strength of the insurer by the marketplace is a major determinant of that insurer's trading value. It is anticipated that the insured segment of the bond market will continue at a significant level, although the percentage of bonds insured may vary as the relative interest rates of higher- and lower-quality municipals fluctuate and as the impact of the Tax Reform Act of 1986 is fully absorbed.

4

How the Underwriter Works

The vast number of new municipal offerings each year, from every region of the country, has given rise to a large underwriter industry. At the end of May 1990, approximately 2,700 securities firms and banks had paid a Municipal Securities Rulemaking Board fee and were authorized to perform transactions in the municipal market, although only about one-fourth were actively involved in the market. Many of the dealers are small local underwriters that handle their communities' business, but in some states local underwriters handle most major issues.

Nevertheless, as issues have grown larger and more complex, major securities dealers and bank dealers in New York, Chicago, and on the West Coast have come to take the largest share of the business. The 25 leading underwriting firms, for example, managed about 75 percent of the total volume of all new long-term issues in 1989, according to statistics compiled by IDD Information Services/PSA Municipal Securities Data Base. Over the last ten years municipal underwriting has been one of the two or three fastest-growing areas for some large securities firms.

In principle, the underwriter's task is very straightforward. In a competitive offering, the underwriters bid against one another to buy the issuer's bonds and then reoffer them to investors. The profit is the difference, or spread, between what the underwriters paid for the bonds and the price at which they sell them. In a negotiated offering, there is no bidding; the underwriter is chosen beforehand. In both cases, however, underwriters assume complete risk and responsibility for selling the bonds, although the underwriter's risk will be somewhat less in a negotiated offering than in a competitive offering.

Successful underwriting depends on trading and sales personnel who know the market well and who can reach prospective buyers quickly. Successful underwriters also generally have enough capital to carry their positions during the selling period if the issue is selling slowly. For most sizable issues, however, negotiated or competitive, underwriters join together in a syndicate in order to spread the risk of the sale and to gain wider access to potential investors. Typically, several underwriting syndicates bid against one another on competitive issues.

The composition of syndicates varies from issue to issue. One syndicate co-manager might be a major national dealer or dealer bank, while the other might be a smaller dealer with a strong marketing organization in the region or state of the issuer. Another team might combine one manager specializing in institutional sales and a so-called wire house—that is, a firm with several branch offices and a broad clientele of individual investors.

The procedures, rules, and technicalities involved in underwriting an issue are intricate and the pace is often very fast. Major underwriting firms may bid on ten or twelve issues a day and purchase ten or more issues a week. The professionals in the business become adept at preparing bids quickly and making very fast market decisions. Each underwriting generally involves the entire trading and sales operation of the firm.

The Notice of Sale

Usually with the help of a financial advisor or investment banker, the issuer decides how, when, and in what amount to issue bonds. The laws of most states require that general obligation bonds be sold on a competitive basis. Sales of revenue issues are often negotiated.

Bond issuers who employ professional financial consultants will initiate underwriting procedures by getting expert opinion as to the size, terms, and timing of an offering from their financial advisors. These financial advisors will also prepare or assist in the preparation of the necessary notices of sale and official statement, act as liaison between the issuer and the municipal bond attorneys providing the necessary legal documents for the closing, and assist the local officials in making their presentations to the rating agencies.

Financial advisors occasionally act as underwriters of an issue for which they are advisors, but this practice is becoming rare for large issues. The Municipal Securities Rulemaking Board (MSRB) has adopted rule G-23 to address potential conflicts of interest in such relationships. This rule requires that a financial advisor must terminate the advisory relationship or disclose possible conflicts of interest and compensation to be earned before acting as underwriter on a negotiated issue. In competitive issues, the issuer must consent to the financial advisor also being a bidder for the issue.

If the issuer decides to sell the bonds on a negotiated basis, arrangements for the sale are made with the underwriters selected by the issuer. In competitive sales, the issuer places an announcement of the proposed sale—that is, an official notice of sale—in local and national newspapers and in trade publications. An advertisement in the industry's national trade paper, *The Bond Buyer,* is virtually a requirement for any significant issue, and industry members also recommend advertisements in local publications, including the municipal bond publications found in some states. Active issuers usually send the notice of sale directly to prospective bidders, together with a copy of the preliminary official statement, in addition to placing the notice in such publications.

The notice of sale typically includes the following information:
1. Date, time, and place of sale.
2. Amount of issue, maturity schedule, and call features.
3. Authorization for the bond sale.
4. Type of bond (general obligation or revenue bond).
5. Interest payment dates.
6. Limitation on coupon rates.
7. Denominations of the bonds.
8. Total amount of the bid at par or better (or discount allowed).
9. Required amount of good-faith check.
10. Names of the bond counsel and statement of legality.
11. Basis for bidding and method of award.
12. Method, approximate date, and place of settlement for the bonds.
13. Dating of the issue.
14. Statement of purpose of bonds and security for them.
15. Bearer of printing, legal, and other expenses.
16. Statement of municipality's right to reject any or all bids.
17. Form of bond (registered, book-entry).
18. Depository eligibility, if any.
19. Name(s) of financial consultant or advisor.

Underwriting departments keep close track of new issues coming to market. *The Bond Buyer* lists most significant negotiated and competitive issues in one of three of its sections: Proposed New Issues, Invitation for Bids, and Official Municipal Bond Notices. *The Bond Buyer* also offers a separate service that provides specific information about major new offerings, as well as worksheets that have become accepted throughout the industry to work out yields and prices for an issue. The service is available on a subscription basis and is called the *New Issue Worksheet and Record Service.* It also provides information on the offering yields of the other issues that have recently come to market. Kenny Information Systems, Inc. also provides *K-sheets* with pre-sale and post-sale worksheets including extensive economic data on all competitive issues of $1 million or more.

Research and Sales

Underwriters usually solicit an opinion from their own in-house research staff as to the relative creditworthiness of an offering. If their own research staff is particularly confident about the financial health of a municipality, the underwriters may make a more aggressive bid for the offering. If the firm's municipal analysts feel that the disclosure is inadequate or that the credit is weak, the firm may not bid at all.

An underwriting firm informs its sales force each week about the upcoming bond issues in which the firm expects to participate. A typical procedure is to hold a Monday morning meeting with sales personnel or managers to review each new issue on the week's calendar. The in-house research concerning the issues is discussed, together with the underwriters' and traders' sense of the trend of the market and how issues to be underwritten may trade in that environment. A preliminary strategy is then established, and the sales force seeks prospective buyers. Underwriters report that their salespeople work far more energetically on a negotiated issue in which they are a senior or joint manager because they are certain that their firm will underwrite it and that they will probably have the bonds to sell.

The Syndicate

For small issues, a single dealer may underwrite the entire offering. For larger issues, however, underwriters usually form bidding syndicates. In most cases, the composition of the syndicate is clear-cut in advance: traditionally, underwriters stay with the group with which their firms bid on the last occasion that the issuer came to market. Further, the same managers usually retain their positions within the syndicate. The composition of a syndicate can change, of course. Firms go out of business; new firms are started; and some firms may simply want to drop out of the syndicate for a particular offering.

Syndicates in municipal bonds can have as few as two members or as many as 100 or more members. There may be one manager or several co-managers, although only one of them—the senior or lead manager—actually "runs the books of the account," that is, keeps track of sales and of the availability of the bonds.

The syndicate members are bound together on any issue by the syndicate letter or contract. The letter contains the terms under which the account will be managed, including the obligations of all the members. The manager sends the letter to each member of the account—typically two weeks before the issue is to be sold. Each member must sign and return to the manager a copy of the syndicate letter, indicating the member's acceptance of the terms. The letters vary, but they generally include the following:

1. Preliminary amount of bonds to be underwritten by each member (that is, the participations).
2. Duration of the account.
3. Acknowledgment that the bid and offering terms will be set by the majority of the members.
4. Obligations of members as to expenses, good-faith deposit, and liability for any unsold bonds.
5. Appointment of the manager as agent for the account.
6. Granting of rights to the syndicate manager, including rights to borrow, advertise, pledge securities, and make the bid.
7. Granting of unspecified authority to the manager where necessary for the proper performance of management functions.
8. A provision that no liability is assumed by the manager except for lack of good faith.
9. Priority of orders (MSRB requirement).

EASTERN AND WESTERN ACCOUNTS

Two types of syndicate accounts exist. The Eastern account is generally used in the major financial centers of the East and West Coasts, while the Western account is used more frequently in the central part of the country. Use of the Western account has declined substantially in recent years.

The Eastern account is undivided as to sales and liability. This means that the members of these accounts pool the bonds they have to sell as well as the liability for any unsold bonds. "Undivided as to sales" means that syndicate members can sell any of the bonds in an account as long as they are available. However, the syndicate profits are divided according to the participations agreed upon before the sale, no matter how many bonds any individual member sells. "Undivided as to liability" means that, if any bonds cannot be sold, all members are liable for a proportionate share of those bonds according to the same participations.

For example, a member might have a 10 percent participation in an account but sell only 5 percent of the bonds. In this case, the member is still entitled to 10 percent of the syndicate's net underwriting profits. On the other hand, a member may sell more than 10 percent of the bonds, while the syndicate as a whole is unable to sell the entire issue. In this case, the member is still liable for 10 percent of the unsold bonds, despite its own sales record, and will still receive only 10 percent of the net underwriting profits—or be assessed for 10 percent of the net underwriting losses. Syndicate managers usually take the largest participations; other members take varying amounts of participation.

Western, or divided, accounts are predominantly found in the center of the country. In this type of account, members are assigned a portion of each of several groups of bonds. The bonds, for example, might be broken down into several categories (or brackets) of different maturities. However, the account is divided only as to liability, not as to sales. Thus, as in the Eastern account, a member firm can sell any of the bonds in the issue, according to a priority that is discussed later in this chapter. However, a member is liable for unsold bonds only if it has not sold its full participation in each bracket. Sometimes, certain maturities in a given offering are sold on a completely undivided basis, while others are sold on a divided basis.

It should be emphasized that net underwriting profits are by no means the only revenues that the members of a syndicate can earn through participation in an underwriting. They receive discounts, known as concessions and takedowns, on bonds they sell or take for their own inventory; and if a member can sell a bond for its offering price or at a smaller discount than the member's price, the remainder can be kept as the firm's revenues. This is discussed more fully later in this chapter.

SELLING GROUPS

In recent years, some underwriters and syndicate managers have formed selling groups to participate in the initial distribution of municipal securities. Members of a selling group are brokers and dealers that are permitted by a syndicate manager to acquire underwritten municipal securities for resale on the same terms offered to syndicate members. However, selling group members do not share in the syndicate's net underwriting profits; they also do not assume pro rata liability for any underwriting loss or for the purchase of any unsold securities. In some instances, particularly on smaller offerings, selling groups are formed by a managing underwriter in lieu of the formation of a syndicate.

Competitive Sales

Once the syndicate is formed, the requirements are in place to make the bid. Typically, one day before the bid must be placed, syndicate members hold a preliminary price meeting. In New York and several other large cities, the members usually meet at the senior manager's office. Throughout the rest of the country, price meetings with the various account members are usually set up by the manager over the phone. When syndicates are very large, managers often use the Munifacts wire, a service of *The Bond Buyer,* or the Dalcomp wire, another private syndicate service, to transmit information to members. Munifacts is the principal news wire that serves the municipal bond industry, but it also has a service that can communicate information only to specified clients, if desired. Most dealers subscribe to the wire.

The preliminary meetings are comparatively relaxed. Dealers are usually represented by one of the two or three members of their syndicate personnel. This member consults with the firm's traders and salespeople on the day of the meeting to see what potential there is in the market, how other comparable issues have sold, and so on. He or she will typically enter the proposed prices or yield for each maturity of the issue (called the reoffering scale) onto worksheets for distribution to salespeople and traders.

Syndicate managers run the preliminary pricing meetings. They ask for each member's proposed scale, reading off their own preliminary ideas as well. Possibly, they will also discuss the spread for the underwriters. There is seldom much argument at the preliminary meetings, and a consensus is often reached easily. The goal is to come up with the highest bid to the issuer (that is, the lowest interest rate) and still be confident of selling the bonds at a profitable spread. A preliminary scale is set and salespeople at the member firms solicit orders. Frequently, some orders for the bonds are already lined up by the day of the bid.

The manager must also send the municipality a "good-faith check" in advance of the bid. The good-faith check is a security deposit, which the issuer retains as compensation in the event that the winning bidder fails to pay for the bonds or notes on the delivery date, as agreed upon in the contract. The amount of the good-faith requirement is established by the issuer and is stated in the notice of sale. The winning syndicate's good-faith deposit is subtracted from the final payment for the issue at the time of delivery and final settlement. The good-faith requirement may range from 1 to 5 percent of the par value of the bonds or notes and is normally about 2 percent. The good-faith checks of the losing syndicates are returned to their managing underwriters after the bid award has been made.

FINAL PRICE MEETING

The final price meeting usually begins with the manager announcing the proposed pricing scale, and perhaps suggesting the size of the spread. If any sales have been made or lined up already, they are announced at this time. These final price meetings can be very tense, for the bid usually must be placed within about an hour, and the high bidder will often be known immediately at the time of sale.

During the final price meeting, the manager might also inform members of the latest developments in the marketplace. The yields on other issues for sale that day are watched closely as benchmarks for determining yields on the issue being underwritten. The manager then polls the members for their opinions about the scales and the spread.

As the members discuss their feelings on the issue, disagreements often arise. They tend to center on the yields for particular maturities or on the size of the spread. A member can drop out of the syndicate at any time before the bid is placed.

During a typical final price meeting, pre-sale orders are still coming in. The trading and sales departments of the member firms are working to line up sales, and they call their representatives at the meeting immediately on receiving an order. In an offering that is going well, some maturities may sell out before the meeting is over. As orders come in, the members can start to raise their bids by lowering the yields on some maturities. If few orders come in, the group may become more cautious and raise yields.

As the price meeting continues, an idea of where demand is strong or weak develops and the scale falls into place. Sometimes, the members decide the spread is too small, and they try to get the manager to widen it. Occasionally, a compromise is reached, where the spread is widened while yields on some maturities are reduced. Generally, the manager wields the most influence at the price meetings, but a big order from a member can force a sudden adjustment in the scale. The order period is also set at the final price meeting. The order period usually runs for one or two hours. A few minutes before the deadline, the final scale and bid are calculated.

The manager has already set up the procedure for delivering the sealed bid by the deadline. The deadline is very strictly adhered to, and most bids must be delivered by hand. Therefore, the syndicate manager usually arranges for a local dealer or bank to send someone to the municipality with the bid. (See the Appendix for the various alternative computations.) The bid is then telephoned to the person who is to deliver it to the municipality. When the high bidder is determined, the syndicate members work immediately to sell the balance of the issue.

Negotiated Sales

Usually, a preliminary pricing is made three or more days prior to purchase date, which may be revised upward or downward depending on the degree of success of the pre-sale order period. Final prices are set by the managers on the day of sale. Negotiated sales usually entail significantly less market risk than competitive sales.

Another difference between negotiated and competitive offerings is in the degree of involvement of the public finance department. In negotiated sales, it is the public finance group that usually maintains contact with the issuer. As the number of negotiated offerings has grown in recent years, the size of the public finance departments of municipal dealers and dealer banks has also grown. The syndicate department usually is still in charge of pricing the issue.

Types of Orders

A complete understanding of the several types of orders and their pricing is important. The highest-priced order is sold to investors "at the net," that is, at the price or yield actually shown in the reoffering scale. These prices are always the ones agreed to by the syndicate. The underwriting group retains the full spread.

However, an underwriting group will generally give up part of its spread to get orders from dealers who are not in the syndicate. These dealers are offered what is known as a concession, which works as follows. A typical spread might be $10 per $1,000 bond (one point). The concession might be $2.50 (¼ point), so that a nonsyndicate dealer with a municipal bond department would be entitled to a $2.50 discount, enabling it to buy the bonds for $997.50 and to sell them to a customer for the full $1,000, retaining the $2.50. The bonds are said to be bought "at the concession."

Individual members of a syndicate can buy the bonds "at the takedown" for their own accounts, for sale to another dealer, or for sale directly to an investor. The takedown might amount to an additional $2.50, the total takedown coming to $5.00. Hence, a syndicate member could buy the bonds at $995 and sell them to a dealer outside the group for $997.50; the dealer, in turn, could sell them for $1,000. In this case, the member would keep only the $2.50 for compensation. If the bonds are sold at the net price to an investor, the syndicate member would keep the full $5.00 takedown.

The prices and priorities of the several types of orders are a critical part of an underwriting. If an offering is oversubscribed, low-priority orders may not be filled. According to MSRB's rule G-11, the priority of orders must be furnished in writing to all syndicate members. The traditional types of orders, in order of priority, are as follows (pre-sale orders occur before the order period; orders 2 through 5 occur during the order period):

1. *Pre-sale orders.* These are orders submitted before the syndicate actually offers the bonds. These orders may be taken at a net price, concession, or takedown.

2. *Group net orders.* These are orders taken at the net reoffering price. The spread is retained by the whole syndicate as part of its profit.

3. *Group orders less the concession.* These are purchases made by nonmembers

of the syndicate at the concession. The remainder of the spread accrues to the whole syndicate.

4. *Designated orders.* These are sales made to investors at the net or concession price, where a commission is designated by the investor to be retained by two or more members of the account.

5. *Member orders.* These are purchases made by members at the takedown price, for their own account or for sale to another dealer or investor.

Should the offering be oversubscribed, the first orders to be filled are the presale net orders and group net orders. The last orders to be filled are the member orders. Investors might prefer to enter group orders rather than designated or member orders to be more certain that they will receive their bonds. An order is seldom confirmed until the order period is over.

Order Procedures

If the issue or certain maturities of the issue are indeed oversubscribed, allotments will be made according to the priority of orders, as stated earlier. If a given level of priority bonds is oversubscribed, bonds are fairly allotted to members of the syndicate by the senior manager.

MSRB's rule G-11 requires that the procedure for changing the priority of orders—and any permission for the syndicate manager to allot orders in any way other than by the agreed-upon priority—be furnished in writing by the manager to syndicate members prior to the first offer of securities by the syndicate. In addition, the manager must inform members, in writing, of any changes in priority not previously agreed upon. If orders may be confirmed prior to the end of the order period, that information too must be furnished in writing to members beforehand. According to rule G-11(g), the senior syndicate manager must, within two business days from the date of sale, give the other members of the syndicate a written summary of the allocation of securities to orders which, under the priority provision, are entitled to a higher priority than a member's takedown order.

MSRB's rule G-8 regarding record keeping requires the manager of the syndicate to maintain the records of the account. The records must include the following: a description of the bonds and a statement of their aggregate par value, the name and percentage participation of each member of the syndicate, the terms and conditions governing the syndicate, a list of all orders received for securities from the syndicate, a statement of all allotments of securities and their prices, the date and amount of the good-faith deposit, the date of settlement and of the account closing, and a reconciliation of profits and expenses.

Orders are usually confirmed by telephone by the manager of the account when the order period is over. However, only issues in the greatest demand are typically sold out within the one or two hours of the order period. Subsequently, orders are taken from members on a first-come, first-served basis, regardless of the type of order. When the issue is sold out, the syndicate is disbanded.

Most syndicate accounts are set up to run for 30 days. They can then be renewed by the members if necessary, but very few new offerings are held open for that long. When an issue proves difficult to sell, the terms of the offering are often revised. Changing the terms usually requires the majority consent of the members, with votes weighted by their respective participations.

If the issue still cannot be sold, the bonds may be distributed among the members to try to sell, or they may be given to a bond broker. All the remaining bonds may be given to one broker, or they may be split up in groups—according to maturity, for example—and given to one broker or several brokers. The broker then "puts the bonds out for the bid." Members also have the right to bid for the bonds, as may any other dealer. Whoever produces the best bid for the group of bonds will win them, although the manager always retains the right to reject all bids. Brokers usually get ¹/₈ of a point ($1.25 per $1,000 par value) as a commission for the transaction.

After the Sale

After the issue is sold, the manager of the syndicate must undertake a number of procedures to confirm orders, deliver and pay for the bonds, and meet legal requirements. MSRB's rule G-12 (the Board's Uniform Practice Code) describes the procedures for confirming orders to members in an underwriting. All sales of new issues are made on a "when, as, and if issued" basis. Written confirmations for "when, as, and if issued" orders must generally be sent within two business days after the trade date, according to MSRB rule G-12(c)(iii). Rule G-12(c)(v) sets forth the information requirements for interdealer confirmations. Rule G-15(a) establishes the requirements for confirmations to a customer. The requirements are listed in Chapter 5.

Just after the purchase of the issue by the underwriters, the senior manager sends a letter to all members of the account, stating the terms for the issue. The letter sets forth the reoffering terms of the issue, including the spread, takedown, and concession, and confirms the price to be paid to the issuer. It also announces whether and how the issue will be advertised in the financial press, lists the participations of the members in a competitive sale, and can include other information as well. The members must sign and return the letter. In most advertisements, the members of the account are listed in the order of the size of their participations.

MSRB's rule G-32 requires that before or at the time that customers are sent their final written confirmations, the underwriter must send each customer a copy of the final official statement for the issue, if one is being prepared, by settlement of the transaction. In negotiated sales, information on underwriting spreads, fees, and the offering price for each maturity must also be sent to customers. The rule requires dealers to promptly provide copies of official statements to dealers that have purchased the new-issue securities, upon request. It also places other requirements on managers and financial advisors to facilitate distribution of these important disclosure documents.

It usually takes about one month from the sale date for the bonds to be actually ready to be delivered to investors. This allows time for printing the bonds and for the bond counsel to prepare the final opinion and transcript of proceedings. Up to that point, bond counsel has given only a preliminary opinion, and the sale of bonds is conditional on the final opinion. The opinion is usually printed on the back of the bonds. The transcript typically includes a certificate stating that there is no litigation pending against the bonds and a guarantee of the signatures of the officials who signed the bonds.

The bonds must be paid for by the senior manager when they are available for delivery. The manager will borrow the money to finance the purchase of the bonds. The payment made is the bid price less the amount of the good-faith check. In turn, the bonds are delivered to the members of the account according to the allotments. The members then pay for their shares of the sales. As the payments come in, the manager pays off the loan, usually within a few days. According to MSRB rule G-12(c)(iii), the manager must furnish a written confirmation of orders as well as notification of the settlement date to members six business days before the settlement date. The settlement date is the date on which the bonds are delivered and paid for.

Once the bonds are paid for and expenses totaled, the senior manager will distribute the profits to members of the account. If there was a loss on the underwriting, the members are assessed for their share. The distribution is accompanied by a final statement of the member participations and the expenses and profits of the syndicate. Rule G-11(h) requires that the manager disclose to account members all expenses and a summary statement concerning all allocations of securities sold from the account. Rule G-12(j) requires syndicate accounts to be settled within 60 days after bonds have been delivered.

Because it generally takes a month for the bonds to be delivered, investors are not entitled to the full six months' interest for the first payment period. They have not put up their money on the date when interest first starts accruing—the dated date—nor have the municipalities had use of the proceeds. As pointed out in Chapter 1, the investor must pay the accrued interest to the seller—in this case, the issuer. The investor then receives the full six months' interest on the interest payment date. Dealers will simply add on the accrued interest to the price of the bonds.

5

The Secondary Market

Few markets for new issues of securities can function well without the support of a secondary market where securities can be traded after they are first sold. Investors will pay a higher price for a new issue if they know that the security can be readily sold at a fair price before its maturity. The best-known secondary markets are for corporate equities—and for good reason. Because stocks are not redeemable at a specific date, investors need a secondary market in order to convert their investments to cash. Bondholders can expect to receive their principal in cash when their bonds mature, but they still want the option of selling their securities before maturity.

In addition to supporting the primary market, a thriving secondary market also serves investors by providing them with an array of different types of securities to suit their needs, as well as a way to buy and sell quickly when necessary. This makes possible a variety of investing strategies of varying risks and maturities.

The size of the secondary market in municipal securities is hard to determine. Unlike the case for corporate securities, almost no secondary trading in municipals is done on any exchange. Nor is there a computerized marketplace designed to capture at least a significant number of the trades. The Blue List—Standard & Poor's daily listing of securities being offered by dealers—typically lists 16,000 to 17,000 municipal issues a day, with an average face value of over $1.4 billion; but not all the bonds are traded every day. Observers generally estimate that secondary market trading comes to between two and three times the volume of trading in the primary market. More than $150.0 billion in new bond and note issues came to market in 1989; the secondary market may, therefore, have traded more than $400 billion of securities.

Investors sell municipal securities before maturity for many reasons. Individual or institutional investors may need cash; new heirs may want to sell; the outlook for interest rates may vary; investors' perceptions of the credit quality of securities may change; the profitability of other investments may increase; tax laws may change the relative yield relationships between municipals and fully taxable issues; or investors may simply see better opportunities elsewhere in the marketplace.

When they do sell, investors may get more or less for the bonds than they originally paid, depending on two major factors: market risk and credit risk.

Market risk is the term given to the potential price fluctuations in a bond due to changes in the general level of municipal interest rates. If the general level of municipal interest rates has changed since the date on which the bonds were bought, the resale value of those bonds will reflect that shift. Thus, if interest rates are currently higher than they were when the investor bought the bonds, the bonds may be worth less; if interest rates have declined, bond prices generally will rise and the bonds in question may be worth more.

The second factor, credit risk, is associated with the individual issue and issuer. If the credit standing of the issuer improves, the bonds may be worth more in the market. If the issuer's credit standing weakens, the bonds may fall in value. In an extreme case, some New York City issues fell in price by 300 to 400 basis points (3 to 4 percent) and more in the wake of the city's financial crisis of 1975. However, generally smaller shifts in price can be anticipated as a result of changes in the perceived creditworthiness of an issuer.

Municipal bond traders of dealer firms and dealer banks are the principal market makers in the secondary market. Working at telephone consoles throughout each day, with the aid of computers, they buy from and sell to other dealers and investors and for their own inventories. Municipal traders must have a sense of what kind of bonds clients might want. They must not get caught with an inventory that is hard to sell, especially when interest rates are rising. It is a fast-paced and risky business.

Securities dealers. The municipal trading departments of full-service securities firms typically provide services to both investors and dealers. Traders at these firms make markets and maintain large inventories in a variety of securities. In firms with many branch offices, the sales liaison staff also plays an important role. These employees are usually located near the traders and are assigned to specific sales offices. Sales account executives place their orders through the liaison staff.

Dealer banks. Commercial banks that actively underwrite municipal bonds also generally maintain sizable trading operations. However, such dealer banks can— with some important exceptions—neither underwrite revenue bonds nor trade them as principals in the secondary market, although they may buy and sell revenue bonds on an agency basis upon specific orders from a customer. Dealer banks actively make markets in general obligation bonds. A dealer bank's trading department may not, however, act as principal in executing transactions for its trust department when that trust department is purchasing bonds or notes for the bank's individual trust accounts. (It is normal for large commercial bank trust departments to maintain their own trading operations and thus avoid any possible conflict of interest which could arise from purchases or sales through the dealer department.) In the case of an underwriting where the bank's dealer department is in the syndicate, most associated trust departments are prohibited from purchasing bonds from that syndicate until the syndicate account is closed.

Brokers' brokers. The bond brokers' brokers play a very significant role in the diverse secondary market for municipal bonds, although they act only for registered dealers and dealer banks. The relatively small number of brokers in municipal bonds are mostly located in New York City. Some of them maintain elaborate trading operations; others specialize in certain types of securities. They act as agents, not as principals. They do not carry inventories of bonds, and they charge a broker's commission.

When dealers cannot or do not wish to obtain bids directly for bonds they want to sell, they may give them to a broker who will obtain bids from other dealers. "Bid-wanted" business is one type of transaction for the broker.

Brokers also provide other services. For instance, if a dealer has an inquiry for specific bonds or types of bonds, a dealer can ask a broker to help him find them. Part of the brokers' role is to identify specific buyers in the market. If a dealer has an offering which he doesn't want the whole dealer community to see, a broker should be able to identify a buyer after a limited number of calls. As noted in Chapter 4, bond brokers are also occasionally called on to obtain bids for the balance of an underwriting. Brokers generally do not release the identity of the dealers involved in any transactions without permission.

The advantage that bond brokers have is their continuous communication with dealers. The brokers track closely who owns what and who might want to sell or buy bonds. They have what is known as a "picture" of the market. The anonymity they guarantee to dealers makes the latter more willing to give bond brokers information, and, often, bond brokers have access to more information than do dealers. Brokers are paid a commission only when they trade bonds and it varies among brokers but is usually determined by the size of the trade.

Municipal Bond Trading

Municipal bond trading has several characteristics that differentiate it from trading in other securities: most municipal bonds are traded on the basis of yield; all trades are done over the counter; and there are no set trading hours. Moreover, as noted in Chapter 1, almost all transactions are principal or dealer transactions. This means that firms generally do not act as brokers between two parties trading municipal securities—which is the way corporate stocks are often traded. Rather, municipal bonds are usually sold out of a firm's inventory. The revenues to the firm (assuming no intervening change in the price level) is the markup above the cost to the dealer.

A typical dealer trading department employs people who specialize in various kinds of bonds. Almost all trading operations of any size have one trader who specializes in dollar bonds (bonds traded by dollar price, rather than by yield). Some of the more active and competitive trading occurs in these securities, because the issues are usually large and create considerable institutional investor interest. Firms also frequently maintain a specialist in the trading of notes and other short-term paper such as variable-rate demand obligations (VRDOs) and tax-exempt commercial paper. Here again, trading in such short-term paper is more active than in other types of municipal securities. Notes, VRDOs, and commercial paper appeal principally to financial institutions and to money market funds, which typically trade in large denominations and desire liquidity.

Trading departments can vary in their emphasis. Some firms have specialists in "odd lots" of bonds—usually trades of $25,000 or less. (A "round lot" in municipal trading is generally worth $100,000, although some firms consider it to be higher.) Local issues are often the province of one trader on the desk. Sometimes, for example, dealers have one person trading in issues of New York State municipalities. Trading operations with broader geographical territories may divide their trading staff by region. With the rise in the number of housing revenue and health care issues, some traders have begun to specialize in these areas also. Some large securities dealers also maintain small trading staffs in various regional sales offices where municipal bond trading is particularly active. For most issues, trading decisions in these offices are often made independently of headquarters, although some firms refer very large trades to the main office. A handful of Chicago and West Coast banks keep their underwriting and trading operations offices in New York City.

Probably the most significant characteristic of municipal bond trading is the vast number of issues of which dealers must keep track. The inevitable result of this is a thin market for many smaller issues. These smaller issues generally trade at wider bid-offer spreads than do larger blocks.

The large number of issues also significantly handicaps municipal traders relative to their counterparts in other markets. To reduce risk and to be able to shift strategies quickly, traders of most other kinds of securities are able to maintain short positions—that is, they borrow and then sell securities that they do not own, either in anticipation of a decline in prices or to hedge against a long position in other securities. If prices do fall, then the trader can buy at a lower price the securities which were sold short, return the securities to the lender with interest, and earn a profit. By going short, these dealers are able to hedge against a loss in their inventory position due to a rise in interest rates (and a decline in prices).

Because there are so many municipal issues, many of which have small amounts of serial maturities, it is often difficult to find owners willing to lend the specific securities needed. As a result, municipal traders can seldom go short to the same degree as can traders in other securities. (See the next section, on municipal futures.)

Probably the most important sources of information to the bond trader are personal contacts and those of the sales staff. Traders will develop a knowledge of who has what bonds and at what price they may be willing to sell them. They will develop a sense of demand for bonds and of potential supply. Trading desks and bond brokers frequently keep records of the amounts held by customers in certain actively traded issues.

The goal of the trading department is to turn over its inventory quickly and profitably. Carrying inventory for too long is expensive because it ties up capital that could be used elsewhere. Dealers usually borrow to finance their inventories. Furthermore, holding securities always has an inherent risk of loss should interest rates move upward quickly, since prices must then be marked down. To spread risk, dealers often take large positions in conjunction with other dealers. Through the use of the "joint account," dealers are able to service large investors without being locked into inordinately large positions, although these joint accounts frequently limit flexibility.

Trading conforms to the normal bid-and-offer procedure followed in most over-the-counter markets. The listing of the yield by dealers is always the offered side of the market. Investors, however, may not care to buy the bonds at that yield and may therefore bid for them at a higher yield—that is, at a lower price. A bid yield of 6.40 percent and an offered yield of 6.25 percent means that a dealer is willing to buy the bonds at 6.40 percent and to sell them at 6.25 percent.

Typically, the description of bonds in a verbal transaction includes the following: the agreed yield or dollar price; concession, if any; the par value of the bonds; the name of the bonds; the coupon rate; the maturity date; and the CUSIP number. If bonds are callable, the call date, price, and whether the bonds are priced to maturity or call date must be made known to the buyer. Traders often go over the terms of a trade twice, and it is common for traders to call back immediately if there is any doubt over the terms agreed upon.

Sometimes, offerings are made on an "all or none basis." These are known as AON offerings, where the offerer agrees to sell the bonds only if all the bonds he has available will be bought. "Multiples of" offerings are also common, where, for example, sellers offer bonds only in lots of 25, 50, 100, or 200 bonds of $1,000 each.

A frequent practice in the industry is the option to buy, and—unlike the case for most securities—this option is free. The seller is asked to make a firm offering to the prospective buyer which will hold good for a stated time (usually from 30 minutes to an hour). The bonds are then said to be "out firm," and the prospective buyer has the option to get back to the seller and buy the bonds at the agreed-upon yield within the set time. If the buyer does not do so, the dealer can sell the bonds elsewhere. As a rule, the option is accompanied by a recall privilege, which gives the seller the right to recall the "firm" bonds in a shorter time period. The amount of time is agreed upon beforehand.

Municipal Futures

The Commodities Futures Trading Commission approved the trading of municipal bond index futures contracts on the Chicago Board of Trade (CBOT). Trading in municipal futures began on Tuesday, June 11, 1985. In order to understand the muni bond futures contract, one must understand the makeup of the underlying index as well as the basics of the futures market.

The contract is based on *The Bond Buyer* 40-Bond Index of 40 general obligation and revenue bonds. This index, composed of long-term, investment-grade issues was expressly designed to track the broader municipal bond market.

In order to qualify for inclusion in the index, bonds must fulfill specific criteria. For example, all bonds must:

1. Be rated A − or better by Standard & Poor's or A or better by Moody's.
2. Equal or exceed $50 million in size ($75 million for housing issues).
3. Have a remaining maturity of at least 19 years.
4. Be callable prior to maturity, with first call between seven and 16 years from date of inclusion in the index.
5. Have a fixed coupon with semiannual interest payments.
6. Be reoffered, out of syndicate, at prices ranging from 95 to 105.

Bonds subject to the alternative minimum tax will continue to be included in the index. Private placement bonds are not eligible for index inclusion, nor are bonds with certain unusual or extraordinary features. Taxable municipal bonds will not be included in the index either.

The bonds in the index are subject to change every two weeks—on the 15th and the last day of each month. At that time, new bonds fulfilling the inclusion criteria are added to the index and bonds which no longer fit these criteria or which are the least actively traded are deleted.

The index is evaluated daily and reported at approximately 2:30 PM, Chicago time, over the Munifacts wire. (During the contract settlement months of March, June, September, and December, the index is evaluated twice daily and reported at about 11:30 AM and 2:30 PM Chicago time.)

Evaluations are performed by six dealer-to-dealer municipal bond brokers. The brokers assess the price at which $100,000 face value of each bond will trade and submit their prices to *The Bond Buyer.*

The Bond Buyer uses these evaluations in an averaging and conversion process which produces the final index reading for the day.

The futures contract based on this index was devised for use as a hedging instrument and as an alternative to trading in the cash market. As a hedging instrument, the contract can be used to protect the value of a portfolio of municipals. For example, an owner of municipal bonds might want to short futures so that when prices in the market decline they could produce a profit in their futures position which would offset the loss of value in their cash portfolio.

As a trading vehicle, the contract established its worth on March 19, 1986, when Senator Robert Packwood (R-Oregon) proposed to tax interest earned on all municipal bonds. Although cash market activity came to a near standstill as a result of this announcement, trading in municipal futures continued, proving that the municipal futures market provides a liquid alternative to the cash market.

As in all futures contracts, certain features of the Municipal Bond contract are standardized. For example, each contract represents an underlying par value of $100,000. Contracts are quoted in points and 32nds of a point. Each 32nd is equal to $31.25. The daily price change limit is two points ($^{64}/_{32}$, or $2,000). Contracts have quarterly settlement cycles, with settlements occurring in March, June, September, and December.

CBOT Municipal Bond Index futures differ from traditional bond futures in that, on the delivery date, no physical bonds change hands. Instead, the contract is settled in cash.

For example, assume you are long one Municipal Bond Index futures contract for September settlement and that you intend to maintain this position until the last day of trading for the September contract. On that day, the closing September index futures value is automatically set to equal the cash index value for that day. Your account would be marked-to-market one final time—that is, gains or losses since the previous day's September futures close would be credited or debited from your account, representing the final settlement for your September futures position.

Bids and offers on futures contracts are made openly by public competitive outcry in the CBOT muni bond futures trading pit. Thus, while the futures contract is based on *The Bond Buyer* 40-Bond Index, the daily closing value of the contract does not necessarily coincide with that of the index until the last day of trading for each quarterly contract settlement. On this day, the settlement value for the futures contract is set to equal the index value for that day.

For example, if the Bond Buyer Index (BBI) has a value of 95-05 (95 $^5/_{32}$) on the close of the last day of trading, the futures contract has an underlying value of $1,000 times the index, or $95,156.25. (Note that each 32nd is equal to $31.25.)

Before that day, the price of the futures contract is established in the marketplace.

It should be noted that an investment in a Municipal Bond Index futures contract is not an investment in a municipal bond. Profits or losses derived from transactions in Municipal Bond Index futures contracts are subject to federal tax treatment different from interest income derived from municipal bonds, which is generally free from federal income taxation.

Although the BBI is heavily weighted with many revenue bonds which are ineligible for dealer banks to trade, the regulatory authorities have opined that, since there is no specific security or commodity for delivery, municipal futures contracts are not ineligible under the Glass-Steagall restrictions, and may therefore be held and traded by dealer banks.

Internal control procedures for dealers in municipal futures contracts should conform to the accounting and reporting requirements outlined in Statement No. 80 of the Financial Accounting Standards Board (FASB), "Accounting for Interest Rate Futures."

In order to meet these requirements and conform to the policy statements of the regulatory authorities, trading by dealer banks for the bank's own account must be limited to an amount which can be justified as genuine hedging against interest rate risks on the municipal investment portfolio and on the dealer's bond and note position. Both the regulatory authorities and FASB-80 recommend that the authority to engage in futures trading be subject to specific written policies and procedures endorsed by the board of directors or executive committee of the dealer firm. Moreover, record-keeping systems must be sufficiently detailed to permit internal auditors and examiners to determine whether operating personnel have acted in accordance with the authorized objective (noted above) in using futures, forward, and standby commitments in this manner.

Sources of Information

In addition to the municipal bond traders' own contacts with the marketplace, several important sources of information are available to them.

THE BLUE LIST

Perhaps the most widely available trading information in the municipal market, and one of the oldest, is the Blue List. Distributed nationally every morning by Standard & Poor's, it lists securities and yields or prices of bonds and notes being offered by dealers. The Blue List has been computerized, enabling participating dealers to retrieve current information throughout the day. Dealers do not have to wait until the next morning to see what offerings have been added to or deleted from the list. The changes appear immediately on a computer screen—the Blue List Ticker—for subscribers to the service.

MUNICIPAL DEALER OFFERING SHEETS

Many municipal bond dealers publish a list of bonds and notes held in their inventory, along with offering yields or prices, which they are currently seeking to sell. Such lists are usually made available to other dealers and to the firm's investors. Typically, these dealers publish a list weekly.

MUNIFACTS WIRE

Apart from the regular news and underwriting services, Munifacts, run by *The Bond Buyer,* carries offerings on the wire of securities with yields and concessions. Dealers phone in their offerings, which then appear on the subscriber's wire frequently throughout each day. The wire has been computerized in a form which is called "Munifacts Plus."

BID-WANTED WIRES

J.J. Kenny Co., Inc., a municipal bond broker, has developed a computerized wire service that reaches more than 700 dealers. While it carries other information on the wire, its primary activity is to list bonds for which bids are being sought by dealers. A competitive wire, called the C-Wire, was started in 1978 by Chapdelaine & Co.

ACTIVE MARKET COMPUTER SCREENS

Following is a brief description of the two most widely used computer screens displaying the active municipal market. J.J. Kenny Drake, Inc. provides a computer based Kenny Drake Screen that displays current prices of active issues, bid-wanteds, offerings by region and market, analytic information from other sources, and Dow Jones provided municipal bond market news. The user can also access a range of more detailed information. Titus & Donnelly Inc., another municipal bond broker, also provides a screen that reports the active bid-wanteds and offerings. The Titus screen is dedicated primarily to the New York markets.

THE BOND BUYER PLACEMENT RATIO AND VISIBLE SUPPLY

The Bond Buyer publishes daily two measures of the demand for bonds that are widely followed in the industry. These are the Placement Ratio and the Visible Supply.

Although these are indicators of the primary market, they are bellwethers of the demand for municipal bonds in general and good indicators of secondary market demand, since a sizable inventory of unsold new issues in the primary market depresses the secondary market, while unsatisfied demand for new issues will improve the secondary market.

The Bond Buyer Placement Ratio

The Bond Buyer Placement Ratio is compiled weekly from data as of the close of business on Friday and is reported on Monday. Since 1973, the ratio has reflected only the sales from competitively bid issues. The ratio represents the dollar amount of competitive bond sales of new issues greater than $5 million and the par values of those issues sold by the syndicates (see Figure 5-1). Prior to January 20, 1984, the ratio was based on sales of $1 million or more.

Since 1973, the highest percentage of competitive offerings placed was recorded at 100 percent on December 30, 1983, and July 6, 1984, and the lowest percentage was 0.0 percent on January 3, 1986, and January 2, 1987 and 1988. (There were no bond sales in those weeks.) Previously, the lowest percentage recorded since the initiation of the ratio was 29.2 percent on November 23, 1960, when the ratio was based on combined competitive and negotiated sales.

FIGURE 5-1. Placement Ratio

The Bond Buyer Placement Ratio is compiled weekly, on Fridays. The ratio represents the dollar amount of competitive bonds brought to market over $5 million and the dollar amount of what sold during the week.

Since the competitive ratio has been reported separately in 1973, the highest percentage was recorded on 12/30/83 at 100% and the lowest percentage was 0% on 1/3/86, 1/2/87 and 1/2/88. The highs and lows for the previous years are based on sales of $1 million or more.

Starting on Jan. 20. 1984, *The Bond Buyer* highs and lows are based on sales on $5 million and over.

Date	Number of New Accounts	Total Amount New Accounts ($000)	Sales From New Accounts ($000)	Placement Ratio %
1988				
Dec. 30	0	0	0	N/A
Dec. 16	19	$ 388,759	$ 269,844	69.4%
Nov. 25	9	355,948	284,205	79.8
Nov. 11	6	53,290	39,175	73.5
Oct. 28	18	838,550	723,280	86.3
Oct. 14	9	135,925	91,387	67.2
Sept. 30	9	193,850	152,225	78.5
Sept. 16	15	520,556	406,591	78.1
Aug. 26	15	699,865	542,155	77.5
Aug. 12	11	202,958	155,493	76.6
July 29	11	179,844	100,869	56.1

(continued onto next page)

Date	Number of New Accounts	Total Amount New Accounts ($000)	Sales From New Accounts ($000)	Placement Ratio %
July 15	17	$ 292,430	$ 199,390	68.2%
June 24	11	323,570	218,230	67.4
June 10	10	269,520	232,725	86.3
May 27	27	525,639	438,194	83.4
May 13	16	488,985	417,925	85.5
Apr. 29	8	235,845	143,930	61.0
Apr. 15	16	506,575	431,030	85.1
Mar. 31	8	464,280	443,550	95.5
Mar. 18	22	602,162	479,319	79.6
Feb. 26	12	207,685	155,720	75.0
Feb. 12	17	690,490	541,035	78.4
Jan. 29	12	456,110	420,170	92.1
Jan. 15	7	215,965	209,590	97.0
1987				
Dec. 31	1	7,065	4,633	65.6
Nov. 27	8	135,780	91,080	67.1
Oct. 30	9	136,935	128,790	94.1
Sept. 25	12	399,505	300,940	75.3
Aug. 28	12	340,678	211,938	62.2
July 31	12	582,760	460,885	79.1
June 26	20	919,712	653,412	71.0
May 29	12	289,585	258,146	89.1
Apr. 24	14	284,527	239,427	84.1
Mar. 27	8	231,290	184,300	79.7
Feb. 27	11	562,435	314,430	55.9
Jan. 30	9	177,205	100,690	56.8

	High	Date	Low	Date
1988	97.0%	1/15	0.0%	1/2
1987	99.8%	10/23	0.0%	1/2
1986	95.3%	2/28	0.0%	1/3
1985	96.6%	4/12	56.1%	5/24
1984	100.0%	7/6	57.3%	2/24
1983	100.0%	12/30	55.5%	1/21
1982	99.0%	12/31	59.7%	5/14

SOURCE: *The Bond Buyer*

Visible Supply of Municipals

The 30-day Visible Supply is a list compiled each day from *The Bond Buyer's* columns "Sealed Bids Invited for Competitive Issues" and "Proposed Bond Issues for Negotiated Offerings," which appear in *The Bond Buyer* on a daily basis. (In the negotiated sector this indicator frequently understates prospective issuance.) It reflects the total dollar volume of bonds and notes with maturities of 12 months or more, announced for probable sale over the following 30 days. It is an indication of expected supply in the new-issue market. *The Bond Buyer* indicates which of these are competitive and which are negotiated issues.

The 30-day Visible Supply of competitive bond sales has been reported since 1927. It has ranged from a low of $928,000 on March 3, 1943, to a high of $3,215,699,069 on May 19, 1986. The 30-day Visible Supply of negotiated issues has been reported since 1971, and has ranged from a low of zero on January 4, 1971, to a high of $6,696,987,000 on November 13, 1985.

Figure 5-2a lists Visible Supply figures for every other Friday in 1988. Monthly averages of the daily Visible Supply figures are also reported. Shown in another chart are the highs and lows for 1988 and for the prior ten years (see Figure 5-2b).

FIGURE 5-2a. Visible Supply of Municipals

The 30-day Visible Supply is compiled each day from *The Bond Buyer's* columns, Sealed Bids Invited and Proposed Negotiated Offerings, and it reflects the total dollar volume of bonds expected to reach the market over the next 30 days. Notes with maturities of 13 months or more are included.

The 30-day Visible Supply of competitive bond sales has been reported since 1927, ranging from a low of $928,000 on March 3, 1943, to a high of $3,215,699,069 on May 19, 1986. The Visible Supply of negotiated issues has been reported since 1971, ranging from a low of zero on Jan. 4, 1971, to a high of $6,696,987,000 on Nov. 13, 1985.

The table includes Visible Supply figures on the last two Fridays for each month in 1988. Also included are average Visible Supply figures for each month in 1988.

1988	Competitive	Negotiated	Total
12/30	$ 615,402	$ 727,665	$1,343,067
12/16	804,478	665,980	1,470,458
11/25	1,143,348	1,130,340	2,273,688
11/11	1,179,518	1,239,898	2,419,416
10/28	819,995	454,530	1,274,525
10/14	1,332,002	1,647,110	2,979,112
09/30	883,061	777,740	1,660,801
09/16	1,040,680	680,292	1,720,972
08/26	547,995	237,639	785,634
08/12	924,021	975,008	1,899,029
07/29	1,029,353	120,410	1,149,763
07/15	1,090,140	820,500	1,910,640
06/24	807,328	238,810	1,046,138
06/10	1,749,657	486,730	2,236,387
05/27	2,086,150	769,800	2,855,950
05/13	1,475,060	396,260	1,871,320
04/29	1,156,165	1,044,768	2,200,933
04/15	976,544	606,689	1,583,233
03/31	1,268,040	1,402,180	2,670,220
03/18	1,149,522	1,758,120	2,907,642
02/26	956,428	507,510	1,463,938
02/12	855,214	1,261,796	2,117,010
01/29	1,599,570	671,630	2,271,200
01/15	1,157,374	389,215	1,546,589

(continued onto next page)

1988	Competitive	Negotiated	Total
	Monthly Average		
Dec.	$ 657,944	$ 1,070,596	$ 1,728,540
Nov.	1,030,599	1,253,231	2,283,829
Oct.	1,109,033	1,694,515	2,803,547
Sept.	935,021	988,009	1,923,029
Aug.	792,793	661,138	1,453,931
July	970,216	1,129,120	2,099,336
June	1,162,810	821,885	1,984,695
May	1,687,055	918,606	2,605,661
Apr.	959,761	996,996	1,956,757
Mar.	1,281,122	1,756,716	3,037,838
Feb.	1,021,159	1,113,857	2,135,015
Jan.	1,136,658	594,274	1,730,932

SOURCE: *The Bond Buyer*

BOND INDEXES

The most widely watched municipal bond indexes are compiled by *The Bond Buyer*. The 20-Bond Index is composed of dealers' estimates, gathered weekly by *The Bond Buyer*, of the yield that a hypothetical 20-year bond would have to offer if that issue came to market during the week. The 20-Bond Index includes bonds of 20 actual issuers. The average of the ratings of these issuers falls midway between Moody's top four rating categories (Aaa-Baa). The 11-Bond Index is composed of bonds of 11 of the 20 issuers in the first average, but the quality rating averages a solid Aa from Moody's.

On September 20, 1979, *The Bond Buyer* began to compute a separate index based on 30-year revenue bonds. The Revenue Bond Index includes bonds of 25 issuers of revenue bonds covering a variety of purposes, including housing, transportation, hospitals, and pollution control. The ratings on the bonds included in the index range from Moody's Aaa to Baa-1, and from Standard & Poor's AAA to A. Highs and lows for the 20-Bond GO, 11-Bond GO, and 25 Revenue Bond Indexes in recent years have been as shown in Figure 5-3.

Since April 2, 1985, *The Bond Buyer* has been compiling its 40-Bond Index, used as the basis for Municipal Futures contracts. This index is heavily weighted with revenue bonds. It is priced daily and reported in *The Bond Buyer* (see discussion of Municipal Futures above).

The Wall Street Journal also publishes weekly indexes based on 500 issues which represent a broad cross section. The indexes are compiled by Merrill Lynch and Kenny Information Systems, Inc.

FIGURE 5-2b. Visible Supply — High and Low Volume in Recent Years
($ in millions)

Year	Visible Supply Highs		Visible Supply Lows	
	Competitive	Negotiated	Competitive	Negotiated
1988	$2,402.4 (5/23)*	$3,032.3	$285.3 (8/25)*	$120.4
1987	1,879.9 (6/22)	4,696.2	261.7 (1/7)	122.2
1986	3,215.7 (5/19)	5,478.1	123.7 (12/22)	-0-
1985	2,812.2 (11/29)	6,696.6	204.0 (12/19)	120.7
1984	1,818.8 (5/14)	3,840.6	241.5 (12/19)	538.9
1983	2,302.2 (3/28)	4,395.8	228.3 (6/16)	673.3
1982	2,732.8 (11/08)	5,286.8	98.7 (12/16)	323.6
1981	1,526.6 (3/24)	2,105.7	197.7 (12/16)	325.1
1980	1,824.7 (5/23)	1,825.8	361.2 (12/23)	192.2
1979	2,037.5 (10/08)	1,593.2	189.0 (12/20)	17.1
1978	1,752.0 (4/24)	1,867.6	311.7 (8/22)	40.1

*Dates included for competitive offerings only.

SOURCE: *The Bond Buyer*

FIGURE 5-3. *Bond Buyer* **Indexes, Highs and Lows**

20-Bond G.O.	—1990*—		—1989—		—1988—		—1987—	
High...	7.54	5/3	7.72	3/22	7.97	5/19	9.17	10/15
Low...	7.03	1/11	6.86	8/3	7.33	11/3	6.54	3/5
Record High:	13.44%	1/14/82			Record Low:	1.29%	2/14/46	
11-Bond G.O.	—1990*—		—1989—		—1988—		—1987—	
High...	7.40	5/3	7.62	3/22	7.85	5/19	9.05	10/15
Low...	6.89	1/4	6.75	8/3	7.22	11/3	6.40	3/5
Record High:	13.05%	1/14/82			Record Low:	1.04%	2/21/46	
25 Revenue	—1990*—		—1989—		—1988—		—1987—	
High...	7.79	5/3	7.95	3/22	8.34	5/19	9.59	10/15
Low...	7.35	1/11	7.19	8/3	7.64	11/3	6.92	1/22
Record High:	14.32%	1/14/82			Record Low:	6.92%	1/22/87	

SOURCE: *The Bond Buyer*   *As of 5/18/90

MSRB Record-Keeping Rules

The MSRB has established several rules governing record keeping for holding securities and for transactions with customers. Rule G-8 is the basic record-keeping rule of the MSRB. Rule G-8(a)(iii) requires that records be kept to show the following for each security: all long and short positions carried by a municipal securities broker or dealer for its own account or for the account of a customer; the current location of all such securities held in the long position and the offsetting position to all such securities sold short; and the name or other designation of the account in which each position is carried. The securities records should also show any movement of the securities, such as whether securities have been sent out for validation or transfer.

Rule G-8(a)(ii) requires every municipal securities broker and dealer to maintain account records for each customer, showing "all purchases and sales, all receipts and deliveries of securities, all receipts and disbursements of cash, and all other debits and credits to such account."

Also, records of each transaction, whether undertaken as a principal or agent, must be maintained according to rules G-8(a)(vi) and (vii). Trading tickets will suffice for such records. They must show such information as the price and amount of the order, as well as the time of the execution "to the extent feasible." Other areas covered by rule G-8 include the types of information to be obtained from customers, customer complaints, records for put options and repurchase agreements, and several other categories. By and large, the record-keeping regulations do not apply to dealers or brokers that do not do their own clearing, but rule

G-8 does provide that the non-clearing dealers and brokers remain responsible for accurate maintenance and preservation of the books and records.

Uniform Practices and Confirmation of Transactions

The MSRB has written rule G-12 to establish uniform practices among municipal securities dealers and rule G-15 to establish procedures for confirmation, clearance, and settlement of transactions with customers. Many provisions of the rules are codifications of traditional practices and industry standards that were in existence prior to the establishment of the MSRB. The Board also has written into the rules new standards and procedures to expedite the processing of transactions. For example, the rules require clearance and settlement of most interdealer transactions and most transactions with institutional customers to occur through automated systems operated by clearing agencies and depositories registered with the Securities and Exchange Commission.

The rules allow the settlement date of a transaction—the date used for computing yields and price—generally to be subject to agreement by the parties to the transaction. The rules specify, however, that for "cash" transactions the settlement date will be the day of trade and, for "regular way" trades, five business days after trade date. For "when, as, and if issued" transactions, between dealers the settlement date may not be earlier than five business days after the confirmation containing the final settlement date is sent (six days for syndicate members), or, if cleared in an automated comparison system, five days after the notice of the settlement date is provided to the registered clearing agency by the managing underwriter.

For interdealer transactions not cleared and settled through automated systems, rule G-12 provides standards for the contents of confirmations and procedures for verifying confirmations sent between dealers. The rule requires confirmations to be sent on the business day after trade date and to contain certain items of information; dealers receiving confirmations with incorrect information or describing trades that they do not recognize must take specific steps to resolve the discrepancies or trades. Similarly, rule G-15 requires certain information to be on each customer confirmation and requires the confirmation to be provided prior to the completion of the transaction (if the transaction is a delivery versus payment or receipt versus payment transaction, the confirmation must be sent within a business day of the trade date). Information required to be on an interdealer or customer confirmation includes certain items which provide evidence of the contract, a description of the securities and, in the case of customer transactions, certain other items that the Board has deemed necessary for disclosure to customers. The items required to be on a customer confirmation are:

1. Name, address, and telephone number of the broker, dealer, or municipal securities dealer.
2. Name of customer.
3. Designation whether the transaction was a purchase from sale or sale to the customer.
4. Par value of the securities.
5. Description of the securities, including the issue name, interest rate, maturity date, whether securities are limited-tax, subject to redemption prior to maturity, whether the securities are revenue bonds, type of revenue if necessary for a materially complete description of the securities, and the names of any obligors of the bonds.
6. CUSIP number.
7. Trade date and time of execution, or a statement that the time of execution will be furnished upon request.
8. Settlement date.
9. Yield and dollar price at which transaction was effected. (If the yield or dollar price is calculated to a call date, this must be stated along with the call date and the price used. The computed dollar price [or yield] must be the lower of price [or yield] to call or to maturity.)
10. Amount of accrued interest.
11. Extended principal amount.
12. Total dollar amount of transaction.
13. Whether the broker or dealer acted as a principal for its own account, an agent for the customer, an agent for someone else, or an agent for both the customer and another party. (If the broker or dealer is acting for another party, the name or a promise to provide the name of the party is required, as is the amount of the remuneration to be received.)
14. Dated date if it affects yield or price computations.
15. Whether the securities are fully registered, registered as to principal, or in bearer form.
15a. Whether the securities are identified as subject to federal taxation.
15b. Whether the securities are identified as subject to alternative minimum tax.
16. Whether the securities are called or prerefunded and, if so, the date of maturity set by the call or prerefunding and the price at which the redemption will take place.
17. Denominations of the securities if not standard denominations ($1,000 or $5,000 if bearer; multiples of $1,000 up to $100,000 if registered).
18. Whether securities were issued as original issue discount securities.

19. Any special instructions or qualifications affecting payment of principal and interest (securities in default or which pay interest other than on a semiannual basis) or other special conditions of the transaction.

20. If the securities are callable, a statement that the exercise of call features may affect the yield stated and that information about the call features is available upon request.

21. If the securities are zero-coupon securities, a statement that the investor will not receive periodic interest payments and, if the securities are callable and in bearer form, a statement that unless the securities are registered it may be difficult for the customer to determine whether the securities have been called.

Except for items 20 and 21, most of this information also must be included on interdealer confirmations.

Rules G-12 and G-15 also contain standards for delivery of physical securities to dealers and to customers, respectively.

6

The Investors

Of approximately $784 billion of municipal debt outstanding at the end of 1989, households held 38 percent, or $298.1 billion. Commercial banks held 16.5 percent, or $129.7 billion. Property and casualty insurance companies held 19.1 percent, or $149.5 billion, and open-end bond funds held 20.8 percent, or $163.5 billion. (Household investor statistics, as measured by the Federal Reserve, include unit investment trusts and other closed-end bond funds. Investment by open-end bond funds is measured under the mutual funds category.)

Households, commercial banks, and property and casualty insurance companies have dominated the municipal securities market since the mid-1950s. Nonfinancial corporations, as well as state and local governments, have been occasional buyers of the bonds. Life insurance companies, once substantial buyers, no longer invest significantly. Pension funds rarely buy because they are tax-exempt.

The relative importance of each of the major investor categories has shifted over the years. Throughout much of the 1960s, commercial banks absorbed two-thirds of all new municipal issues; in the 1970s, they absorbed less than one-third. Casualty insurance companies became more active purchasers of securities, along with individual investors.

During the 1980s, commercial banks considerably reduced their municipal purchases. This, together with an influx of individual buyers and significant growth in the bond fund sector, resulted in a major shift in the composition of the investors in the municipal bond market. Principally, as a result of tax law changes, as later discussed, banks have substantially reduced their purchases of municipal bonds and have been dis-investing from their municipal bond portfolios since the third quarter of 1986. (See Figure 6-1.)

FIGURE 6-1. Major Investors in State and Local Government Bonds

Percentage Share of Bonds Outstanding for Selected Years, 1955-1989

Year	% of Total Held by Households	% of Total Held by Commercial Banks	% of Total Held by Property and Casualty Insurance Companies	% of Total Held By Mutual Funds and Money Market Funds
1955	42.2%	28.2%	9.1%	—
1960	43.5	25.0	11.4	—
1965	36.3	38.7	11.3	—
1970	31.9	48.6	11.8	—
1975	30.4	46.0	14.9	—
1980	25.2	42.6	23.0	1.8%
1985	33.4	35.3	13.5	10.6
1989	38.0	16.5	19.1	20.8

SOURCE: Federal Reserve Flow of Funds Accounts

The main attraction of municipal bonds to investors is the tax exemption: as outlined in Chapter 1, the bond interest enjoys an exemption from federal income tax. The interest income from state and local issues is usually exempt from income taxes in their states, although it is generally not exempt from taxes in other states. Many municipal securities dealers supply investors with yield-equivalent tables that show yields adjusted for taxes (see Figure 1-2), to help them compute the benefit of tax-exempt yields to them.

The number of investors tends to expand or contract depending upon the spread relationship between municipal bonds and taxable securities. For example, if municipal rates are at 72 percent of rates on comparable corporate securities, individual investors in tax brackets of 28 percent or higher benefit from investing in municipals. If yield spreads narrow, however, and municipals trade at 85 percent of corporates, the group of investors who would benefit from investing in municipals expands to include all those in tax brackets of 15 percent or higher.

The dependence of issuers largely on three major investor groups—individuals, property and casualty insurers, and banks—has been a source of concern in the marketplace for some time. The buying patterns of all three groups are cyclical, dependent on changes in profitability, interest rates, and tax rates. During 1986, because of limitations on tax-exempt debt issuance, municipal issuers began to offer taxable bonds.

Individual Investors

During the 1980s, individual investors dominated the municipal market. In 1989 their holdings represented 38 percent of all outstanding tax-exempt securities. The activity of these investors in the market fluctuates, depending upon the absolute level of interest rates, the relationship of municipal yields to those of taxable securities, and income tax rates.

Individuals generally purchase the greatest volume of municipal securities when municipal rates are near their highest levels. In 1969, to take one example, when interest rates were at a cyclical peak, individuals accounted for the purchase of 94 percent of net new municipal issues. In 1977, with municipal yields at a cyclical low, individuals made no net new purchases of municipal bonds. During that year, property and casualty insurers absorbed the largest portion (49 percent) of the municipal new-issue market.

Beginning in 1980, individuals assumed a position of dominance in the municipal bond market. As interest rates rose and spreads between municipal and taxable bonds narrowed, the market for municipal bonds broadened considerably. In 1980, when the average Bond Buyer Index was 8.58 percent and long-term U.S. Treasury bonds yielded 11.23 percent (a 265 basis-point spread), individuals purchased 22 percent of all net new municipal issues. By 1982, when the average Bond Buyer Index was at its all-time high of 11.79 percent and Treasuries yielded 12.92 percent (a spread of only 113 basis points), individuals had accelerated their purchase activity to account for 54.2 percent of the municipal new-issue market. Between 1983 and 1989, individuals remained the largest municipal bond investor group.

Some observers believe that, based merely on tax rates and their progressive nature, it would make sense for individuals to own more municipal bonds than they actually do. But many who are eligible because of high incomes have not accumulated the wealth to enable them to make substantial purchases, especially if they want to diversify their assets. Generally, bonds now trade in $5,000 denominations. As with most other securities, transaction costs on smaller trades are usually higher than on large trades. The bond funds, both closed-end and open-end, have made municipal bond investments more accessible to the general public.

The interest of individual investors in municipal securities is also affected by various tax law provisions, including the marginal tax rate of an individual under current tax provisions. In addition, under the 1986 Tax Reform Act interest on "private activity bonds" issued after August 7, 1986, is included as a preference item in determining the applicability of and computing the alternative minimum tax imposed upon individual taxpayers. In addition, under current Revenue Code provisions, interest on municipal securities is includable in a taxpayer's "modified adjusted gross income'' for purposes of determining the amount of a taxpayer's Social Security benefits which may be subject to federal income taxation.

Mutual Funds

UNIT INVESTMENT TRUSTS

The first bond fund appeared in 1961 in the form of a unit investment trust. At that time, Congress did not yet allow managed mutual funds specializing in municipal bonds to pass tax-exempt interest income on to investors, though unit investment trusts could do so. The unit trusts issue a set number of shares to investors and invest that finite sum in a portfolio of municipal bonds. The portfolio purchased by a unit trust is usually held to maturity. The life of these funds is usually limited to the life of the bonds originally bought.

Investors can buy units in the funds, usually in multiples of $1,000. Although most investors intend to hold on to their investments until the bonds mature, the fund sponsors ordinarily maintain secondary markets for the units. Investors can also redeem the units through the fund trustees, although the price paid for the units will have declined if interest rates rise. As the bonds in the unit trust mature, or are called, the investors who have held their units are paid back the principal value. Some fund sponsors will reinvest interest income for investors in another fund set up for that purpose. There is normally a sales charge of 2 percent to 5 percent for the unit investment trusts, depending upon the type of fund and size of the purchase.

MANAGED FUNDS

In 1976, Congress allowed managed mutual funds to pass on tax-exempt income to investors, and this category of funds grew rapidly. The managed fund category includes both closed-end and open-end funds. Closed-end managed funds are similar to unit trusts in that a fixed number of shares are offered to investors and that a finite sum is invested in a bond portfolio. Some closed-end funds are traded on a stock exchange. Open-end bond funds conversely may issue shares in relation to the demand for their product and the supply of appropriate investments. New investors may be accepted and the portfolio expanded on an unlimited basis at the manager's discretion. Both types of managed funds investing in municipals can buy and sell bonds in the portfolio as often as they deem necessary. The objective is to produce a higher return by good management than would be available if bonds were simply bought and held. The prices of the bonds in the portfolio will determine the asset value of the funds, and they will shift up and down with general changes in interest rates. Sales charges may amount to 5 percent, although many funds are no-loads, which carry no sales charge. Management fees and expenses typically run to about 1 percent of the assets annually.

The objectives and management styles of the managed funds vary widely. Some funds are devoted to short-term municipal bonds and provide investors with liquidity. Maximum liquidity in a tax-exempt instrument is available through the purchase of units in a tax-exempt money market account. Other funds are dedicated to longer-term sectors of the market and have objectives that range from maximum total return, plus safety of principal, to "high-yield funds," which invest in lower-quality or non-rated bonds and are designed for investors seeking maximum tax-exempt interest income with a higher element of risk.

The philosophies of individual fund managers often differ. Certain bond fund managers try to gauge swings in interest rates and to shift their portfolios among long-term and short-term maturities, as well as cash. Other managers seek out undervalued securities as a method of increasing the return on their portfolios. Managers of municipal bond funds claim that over time they will outperform the unmanaged unit trusts.

Both types of managed bond funds have steadily grown in popularity since their inception. In 1980, managed open-end funds owned 1.3 percent of all outstanding municipal bonds; at the end of 1989, this figure increased to 11.9 percent. The growth of open-end funds is further indicated by 1989 statistics which show that mutual funds' (open-end funds') holdings of tax-exempt securities increased by $60.1 billion over the 1985 level. Closed-end managed funds have recently increased in popularity; however, growth in this sector is not readily measurable as data for these funds are incorporated in totals for the individual investor sector described earlier in this chapter.

MONEY MARKET FUNDS

Tax-exempt money funds began in 1979. They invest in securities so as to produce an average life in the fund portfolio of no more than 270 days and usually much shorter, even though they can invest in securities that go out to 360 days. Such funds are primarily created to provide short-term liquidity and the benefits of tax-exemption to individuals and corporations investing such monies. The advent of tax-exempt money funds led to the growth and the creation of many new tax-exempt products, which are discussed in Chapter 1 under the category variable-rate demand obligations. The rapid growth of tax-free money funds is illustrated in Figure 6-2.

FIGURE 6-2. Tax-Free Money Market Funds' Total Assets, 1983-1989

Using Year-end Totals

($ in millions)

Year	Assets
1983	$16,238.5
1984	$23,066.7
1985	$34,581.1
1986	$60,783.8
1987	$59,257.6
1988	$63,782.2
1989	$69,656.0

SOURCE: IBC/"Donoghue's Money Fund Report®" of Holliston, Massachusetts 01746, 1989.

Commercial Banks

Historically banks' interest in purchasing municipal bonds has been influenced by a combination of factors, including the level of loan demand, overall bank profitability, and the attractiveness of municipal bonds versus alternative investments.

In response to industry conditions, banks have modified their investment behavior over the years. In 1960, municipal bonds represented about 8 percent of all commercial bank assets. During the 1960s, spurred by the institution of certificates of deposit in 1961, banks accelerated their purchases of municipal securities. By allowing the banks to issue these short-term demand deposits to corporations, the Federal Reserve also gave the banks more flexibility to manage their own assets and liabilities. Where banks formerly invested heavily in short-term government issues to stay liquid, they could now raise money when necessary by issuing CDs. With this freedom, the banks started to switch into short- and medium-term municipal bonds for their higher after-tax returns.

By 1971, municipals had reached their peak in terms of total share of commercial bank assets, at approximately 14.5 percent. After that point, municipals declined steadily as a percentage of total bank assets (see Figure 6-3). This decline continued during the 1970s, as banks found other ways to reduce their tax liabilities. Leasing operations, through which banks could make ample use of the investment tax credit, became very popular, and foreign tax credits were significant for many major banks. In addition, early in the 1970s the profits of some banks were drained, due partly to real-estate investment trust losses and partly to a generally weaker economy.

FIGURE 6-3. Share of Commercial Bank Assets Held in State and Local Government Securities, 1960-1989

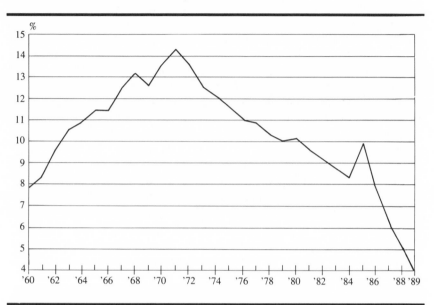

SOURCE: Federal Reserve Flow of Funds Accounts

The amount of municipal bonds as a proportion of commercial bank portfolios increased sharply during the 1960s but declined during the 1970s and 80s.

Beginning in 1982 changes in federal tax legislation further reduced the banks' demand for municipal securities. Formerly, financial institutions were exempt from IRS rules which prohibited the deduction of interest paid on debt incurred to purchase or carry tax-exempt securities. In 1982, the law was changed to allow banks to deduct only 85 percent of such interest expense. In 1984, the law was further tightened to provide only an 80 percent deduction. While overall bank holdings of municipals continued to rise from $82.8 billion in 1971 to $174.2 billion in 1984, municipals' share of total bank assets had fallen to 8.3 percent by 1984. In 1985, banks were temporarily more active in the municipal bond market, due to concern over tax reform, to renewed bank profitability and to the surge in supply of new bond issues which drove up municipals' rates relative to other investments. At the close of 1985, municipals represented approximately 10 percent of total bank assets, and by the close of 1989 had dropped to 4.0 percent, the lowest level recorded since these statistics have been measured. This was a direct result of the Tax Act of 1986, which eliminated the interest expense deduction for all but the smallest local issues.

Property and Casualty Insurance Companies

Investment objectives and high tax rates have encouraged companies in the property and casualty insurance industry to invest in municipal bonds. Considerable volatility in the investment activity of insurance companies is due to the cyclical nature of profits within the industry. During the 1970s, insurers benefited from premium rate increases granted by state regulators. As profitability levels rose, insurers accelerated their purchases of tax-exempt securities. As a percentage of overall insurance company assets, municipal bonds grew from 34 percent in 1970 to a peak of 47 percent in 1979.

Beginning in 1979, the property and casualty insurance industry experienced declining profitability. A period of increased competition among companies drove down premium rates. Insurers attempted to capitalize on historically high interest rates by reducing their premiums in order to attract dollars for investment, but inflation cut sharply into earnings as the cost of claims settlements also rose. Moreover, regulators—generally slow to grant insurance rate increases to compensate for inflation—allowed increases only after significant declines in earnings were reported. As a result of lower profitability, insurers reduced their municipal bond purchases. At the close of 1989, municipal bonds represented 30.4 percent of insurance company assets, a dramatic reduction from the peak of 47 percent. (See Figure 6-4.)

The Tax Reform Act of 1986 altered the investment implications of tax-exempt bonds for property and casualty companies with the imposition of an alternative minimum income tax, as well as changes in the calculation of loss reserves. On the other hand, changes in the way in which income is calculated for insurers may tend to increase their taxable income, thereby generating greater demand for municipal bonds in some cases.

Aside from tax exemption, an important advantage of municipal bonds to casualty insurance companies is that bonds are recorded on their financial statements at cost rather than at market value. According to most state laws, stocks must be recorded at market value for the purpose of computing the surplus of a casualty insurer. The surplus, in turn, determines how much insurance a company is allowed to write. By holding municipal or taxable bonds rather than stocks, the insurer will not be penalized by fluctuations in market prices.

Casualty insurers have typically favored long-term maturities for their municipal bond portfolios. They were principally interested in producing the highest yield possible, given adequate credit quality; and long-term municipal bonds produce the highest returns. Many casualty insurers prefer revenue bonds over general obligation securities to produce higher returns on their investments. However, the changes in the tax implications of municipal bonds discussed above are inducing some to move out of longer maturities into intermediate-term revenue bonds or general obligation bonds.

FIGURE 6-4. Share of Property and Casualty Insurance Company Assets Held in State and Local Government Securities, 1960-1989

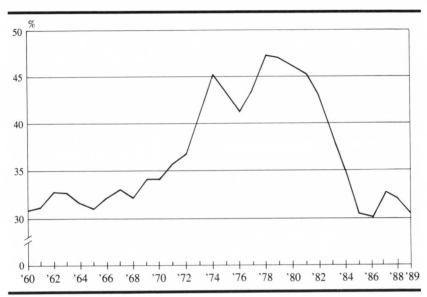

SOURCE: Federal Reserve Flow of Funds Accounts

The proportionate share of property and casualty insurance company assets held in municipal securities has declined considerably since 1979.

The Basic Principles of Investing in Bonds

One fundamental relationship in fixed-income securities is that between interest rates and price: as interest rates rise, prices fall; as interest rates fall, prices rise. However, the degree to which prices shift relative to interest rates is affected by several important factors.

MATURITY

The longer a bond's maturity, the wider will be the swings in price for any change in interest rates. Thus, a bond with a coupon of 5 percent due in one year would sell at $970 to produce an 8 percent yield to maturity, while a 5 percent bond due in 20 years would have to sell at $700 to produce the same 8 percent yield to maturity. In the first example, an extra $30 gain over one year is sufficient to bring the yield up to 8 percent. In the second, a $300 discount is required to generate the same yield because the gain is spread over such a long period of time.

Short-term bonds will trade closer to the $1,000 par value because the investor will receive the full amount of the principal sooner.

COUPON INTEREST RATES

Generally, the higher the coupon interest rate, the smaller will be price movements for a given change in market interest rates. If interest rates fall by two percentage points—say, from 8 percent on ten-year bonds to 6 percent—the price of a par bond will rise by about 15 points to 115. A 6 percent, ten-year bond trading at par would rise more in value if interest rates fell two percentage points from that level. The price would rise to about $116\frac{1}{2}$ if interest rates fell from 6 percent to 4 percent.

DISCOUNTS AND PREMIUMS

Bonds trading at a discount experience wide price swings for a given shift in interest rates, while bonds trading at a premium shift proportionally less. Consider, for example, the case of two noncallable 20-year bonds both yielding 6.5 percent to maturity. One is a discount bond with a 2 percent coupon, and is selling for 50; the other carries an 8 percent coupon and sells for nearly 117. If the market pushes the yield to maturity on both bonds to 7.5 percent, the discount bond will fall in price by about $6\frac{1}{2}$ points to $43\frac{1}{2}$. The premium bond, on the other hand, will fall by $11\frac{1}{2}$ points. But the percentage change in the price of the bonds is the key calculation. The price of the discount bond will have dropped by 13 percent, whereas the price of the premium bond will have dropped by only 10 percent.

The difference in volatility between premium bonds and discount bonds is even more dramatic in the case of so-called cushion bonds—that is, callable bonds selling above the initial call price. In the case of cushion bonds the volatility will be based on the call date rather than the maturity date and the bonds will tend to act like shorter-maturity bonds.

Because gains earned on discount bonds are subject to federal income taxation, the prices of discount bonds will fall even lower than these calculations suggest.

Investor Objectives

A summary of basic investor objectives follows, along with examples of how municipal bonds can meet these objectives.

HIGH CURRENT INCOME

Current yield is the simple coupon rate divided by the price paid for the bond, without regard to maturity date. A wealthy retired couple, for example, might want to live on current investment income. Premium bonds are an investment they might consider as a way to meet their objectives. For instance, if the couple purchased a 7 percent, five-year bond for 108.75, the yield to maturity would be 5 percent. However, the current yield would be 6.44 percent—that is, $70.00 of income for every $1,087.50 invested. (Investors must be mindful that the premium is not deductible as a tax loss.)

For investors more willing to take risks in order to increase their income, lower-rated bonds may be considered. At certain times Baa/BBB rated bonds may yield 250 basis points more than Aaa/AAA rated bonds. Non-rated bonds can produce even greater yield advantages for high-risk investors.

CAPITAL GAINS

Discount bonds are often appropriate for investors less interested in current income than in capital gains. The gains earned when the bond matures are taxable except in the case of original issue discount bonds. But for investors who will be in a lower tax bracket when the bonds come due, municipal discount bonds can meet the capital gains objective and provide some tax-free income in the meantime.

TIMING THE MATURITY

With the broad variety of securities available in the municipal marketplace, it is possible to tailor a bond portfolio to fit special timing needs. For parents who may have children entering college in ten years, for example, discount bonds that mature at the time the cash is needed may be appropriate. One particularly good instrument for meeting such goals is the "zero-coupon" municipal bond. Zeros, which provide no income in the interim but pay out all of the tax-exempt interest in a lump sum at maturity, are an excellent way to accumulate funds for college, retirement, or another such purpose. Investors can stagger maturities if they are uncertain what their future cash needs will be. There is also a variety of suitable instruments for the short-term investor. These include one- to three-year bonds, put bonds, and tax-exempt commercial paper.

IN-STATE TAX EXEMPTION

Investors in high tax states (e.g., New York, California, Minnesota, Massachusetts, Connecticut) that place an income tax on out-of-state bonds will generally wish to invest in bonds issued in their own states and in U.S. territories. The interest on bonds issued in these U.S. territories—American Samoa, the Commonwealth of Puerto Rico, Guam, the Northern Mariana Islands, and the U.S. Virgin Islands—is exempt from all federal, state, and local income taxes.

SWAPS

Swapping is one of the most useful investment techniques among fixed-income investors. The most popular use of municipal bond swaps is to produce a loss for tax purposes that can be used to offset capital gains or, to some extent, ordinary income.

Essentially, a swap is just what its name suggests. An investor sells one security and simultaneously buys another with the proceeds, usually for about the same price. In a tax swap, the investor will have a loss on the bond to be sold, probably because interest rates have risen since the security was bought. The objective is to generate a tax loss to offset gains elsewhere, but without substantially changing the dollar value, risk level, yield, or maturity of the investment.

Investors must realize that they cannot have it all their own way, however. For one thing, the Internal Revenue Service requires that the issues being swapped are not "substantially identical." Otherwise, the trade is ruled a "wash sale" and the tax loss will be disallowed. Tax accountants interpret what is identical or not in different ways, and each tax swap should be carefully reviewed. A trade involving different issuers is considered a good swap for meeting IRS standards. In lieu of this, accountants generally say there must be a significant difference in coupon or maturities to qualify as a tax loss.

There are costs involved in swapping. The dealer will earn a spread, and the perfectly exchangeable issue is not easy to find. Usually, investors will want to maintain quality and keep the total amount of the investment the same. They also usually will want to maintain the same level of current tax-free income. Often, to satisfy all the requirements, an issue with a longer maturity is bought.

An example of a *practical* tax swap follows. An investor owned $50,000 par value of an issue that he bought at par with a 5.50 percent annual coupon rate. Interest rates had risen substantially since the purchase, and the sale of the bond would produce a substantial loss. The investor decided to take the loss by selling the issue and investing the proceeds in a similar issue. His dealer worked out the trade shown in Figure 6-5.

The proceeds from the sale of the issue amounted to $43,000; the original purchase price was $50,000; and the resulting loss was $7,000, which was used to reduce other taxable income. The cost of the purchased issue was $42,875. Through the swap, the investor raised both the current yield and the credit rating slightly, while maintaining the yield to maturity. But something was given up in the process. The maturity on the purchased issue was two years longer than on the former issue. Furthermore, at the issue's maturity, the investor will incur capital gains tax.

Swaps can be used for a variety of other purposes. Investment managers often swap in and out of securities they find more attractive than other securities. Swaps

FIGURE 6-5. Example of a Practical Tax Swap

Rating	Par Amount	Coupon Rate	Date of Maturity	Current Price	Current Yield	Yield to Maturity
SELL						
Aa	$50,000	5.50%	6/1/94	86	6.40%	7.80%
BUY						
Aa1	$50,000	5.75%	4/1/96	85.75	6.70%	7.80%

between bonds in the tax-exempt market and those in the taxable market are not uncommon as a method of capitalizing on changing spread relationships between the two. Generally, swaps are a key investment technique in implementing the more sophisticated investment strategies of institutions and large investors.

Call Provisions

Most municipal securities are issued with call provisions. Call provisions in a bond issue give the issuer flexibility in controlling its borrowing costs through the early retirement of debt, either in whole or in part. Bond call provisions vary widely, and many investors overlook this important element in bond issues when making their investment decisions. Call provisions describe the terms and conditions under which an issuer may redeem bonds.

Bonds can be called at par, at some premium above par or, in the case of zero-coupon bonds, at the compound or straight-line accreted value. Call protection refers to the bond issuer's inability to exercise a call for some specified period of time. Call protection also refers to the protection a specific bond maturity may enjoy over other bonds in the same issue which are called ahead of it. First call refers to the earliest date the issuer can execute a call. Interest accrual or compound value accretion ceases once a bond has been called.

There are three primary types of call features commonly found in municipal bond issues: optional, mandatory sinking fund, and extraordinary (or special redemptions).

The optional call feature describes the manner in which an issuer may voluntarily redeem bonds. A typical optional call provision allows the issuer to retire term bonds at a price above par in five or ten years from the issue date. In such cases, serial bonds due in less than ten years are not subject to optional call. The call price then declines each successive year until it reaches par. In some bond issues, however, no premiums above par are paid if the issuer exercises his optional call rights. Monies available for optional calls come most frequently from the sale of advance refunding or refunding bonds. Refunding bonds are bonds which are sold to provide funds to retire the outstanding debt of an issuer. Sometimes, rather than retiring all the outstanding bonds at the first optional call date, refunding bond proceeds are escrowed to provide sufficient monies to retire bonds at their stated maturities. In some cases, bonds are retired under the optional call feature using surplus funds of the issuer. Investors are provided some protection from optional calls in that the interest savings resulting from retiring the bonds early must exceed the premiums above par that are paid to investors. This normally occurs only when interest rates have dropped substantially. Usually, certain bond maturities such as zero-coupon bonds are protected from the optional call feature.

By ignoring the call features, investors may be missing important opportunities for capital gain or be subjecting themselves to capital losses if the bonds are called at par earlier than expected. For example, many retail investors paid too little attention to the special redemption provisions when they purchased high-coupon single-family mortgage revenue bonds in 1982 and 1983 at substantial premiums above par. Large amounts of these bonds were redeemed a year or two later at par because issuers were unable to spend bond proceeds in the allotted time. Some investors suffered substantial capital losses when their bonds were redeemed at par. Call provisions can limit the capital gains potential on a bond. Additionally, when a call occurs during periods of lower interest rates, the investor is forced to reinvest his principal at lower rates. On the other hand, savvy investors can sometimes purchase market discount bonds subject to par calls from active sinking funds. Purchasing these bonds at prices substantially below par can lead to significant capital gains when the mandatory sinking fund is used to retire debt. Furthermore, fears of bond calls on high-coupon bonds may be overstated and could provide opportunities for astute investors to purchase such bonds at attractive prices.

Sinking funds are monies paid periodically by the bond issuer to redeem term bonds over the life of an issue. This enables the issuer to spread the costs of retiring the term bonds over the issue's life. Sinking funds add some measure of security on the bonds by avoiding one large payment on the term bond at its final maturity. Sinking funds are usually controlled by the bond trustee, and funds can be used either to call bonds or to purchase equal face amounts in the bond market. This latter option is utilized when and if the bonds are trading below par in the market. Open market purchases provide price support for sinking fund bonds during periods when such bonds are selling at a discount because of rising interest rates. On the other hand, sinking fund bonds are called at par when lower interest rate levels would normally make such bonds worth substantially more. When bonds are called they are selected on a random basis within each maturity.

Extraordinary or "special" redemption provisions detail the required uses of specific excess funds of a bond program. Extraordinary redemptions are specifically designed to protect the creditworthiness of the issuer by allowing bonds to be retired in the event extraordinary circumstances impair the issuer's future revenue stream. This call feature is most prevalent in "cash-flow" bonds such as single- and multi-family mortgage revenue bonds and student loan revenue bonds. Extraordinary redemptions occur on such cash-flow bonds from unexpended bond proceeds, prepayment or sale of mortgage loans securing the bonds, loan insurance proceeds, or excess program revenues. Occasionally such call provisions occur in bonds issued for construction of capital projects, allowing special redemptions from unexpended monies if the project is not built, or from insurance proceeds if the project is damaged or destroyed.

Extraordinary redemption provisions vary considerably among bond issues and are often complex. Such redemptions are usually made at par (or accreted value for original issue discount bonds) and can occur at any time after the bonds are issued. For many issues the special redemptions using various funds are mandatory. In other cases they're at the discretion of the issuer. Bond redemptions are most often executed on a pro rata basis across all bond maturities in an issue. This means the redemption funds available are applied to each bond maturity on the basis of what percentage a particular bond maturity bears to the total amount of bonds outstanding. In the case of single-family housing bonds there is one form of bond redemption where monies available for redemption from prepaid mortgage loans are applied to a particular term bond(s) before any other maturity. This type of bond is known as a super sinker and provides call protection for the other term bonds in the issue. The average bond life on a super-sinker is substantially shorter than for other term bonds in the same issue, but the yields tend to be only slightly less. Investors must carefully consider the possibility of such a call when evaluating the purchase of premium bonds.

As noted in Chapter 3, the yield to call shows investors what yield will be earned if the bonds are called. It is the equivalent of the yield to maturity, except that it is calculated to the first call date and price. The yield to call, if lower than the yield to maturity, must be cited in written confirmations of orders. Bonds with little time left to the first call date often trade at lower prices and higher yields to maturity than equivalent bonds with ample call protection, especially when interest rates are high and are expected to fall, a condition that would make a redemption likely.

Investor Strategies

More-aggressive investors, institutional and fund portfolio managers, as well as some individuals, seek other ways to improve their performance. Some basic strategies they may employ are described below:

INTEREST RATE SWINGS

Some investors try to anticipate wide swings in interest rates. If rates are thought to be going up, investors might liquidate, to the extent possible, holdings in all long-term bonds, including municipal bonds. If rates are going down, investors might build up their portfolios. For practical reasons, institutional investors cannot often make radical shifts in the amount of their holdings. One alternative is to move part of a portfolio into short-term maturities in anticipation that interest rates will rise. Short-term securities fall in price less than longer-term issues fall, for a given rise in interest rates. Similarly, investors might choose to accumulate longer-term issues if interest rates are likely to decline.

Bolder investors might invest in deep-discount bonds if interest rates are expected to fall. The faster price movement in these bonds could produce substantial gains. For investors who believe that interest rates will rise, premium bonds serve the purpose of shielding the portfolios somewhat from wide price swings.

Some investors who are particularly uncertain about the course of interest rates adopt a fence-straddling position. They may invest heavily in long-term bonds for the attractive yields; but they may also place a substantial portion of their funds in securities with very short-term maturities. Such a strategy gives them flexibility should interest rates turn sharply in either direction. Because such investors concentrate their holdings at both ends of the maturity spectrum rather than in the middle, this technique has been dubbed a ''barbell'' strategy.

SPREADS

Investors often invest in classes of securities whose yields are historically out of line with those of other securities in the market. Sometimes they do so in anticipation of a shift in these relationships due to changing market conditions. When interest rates are very high and investors are particularly concerned about a weakening in the economy, the gap between the yields of low-rated versus higher-rated securities often widens. Some investors then sell their more risky investments and move into the highest-rated securities. In times of easier credit and greater confidence, some investors begin to buy the lower-rated bonds. Swapping among bonds of different quality is quite common among institutional portfolio managers. (See Figures 6-6a and 6-6b.)

Similarly, the spread between bonds with long maturities and short-term bonds also varies under different market conditions. When these spreads are out of line compared to historical relationships, investors frequently shift into the more attractive segments of the market.

FIGURE 6-6a. Yield Spreads Between Aaa-Rated and A-Rated Municipal Securities

FIGURE 6-6b. Yield Spreads Between Long- and Short-Term Municipal Securities

Aaa-A MUNI SPREAD vs. BBI

30-1 YR. MUNI SPREAD vs. BBI

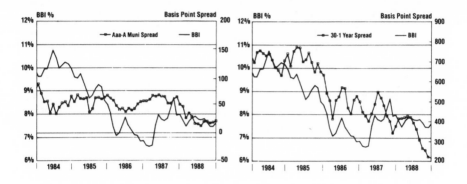

SOURCE: Data Resources

Sophisticated investors try to forecast the spreads between issues of different maturities and different quality ratings. These spreads often follow a cyclical pattern. Figure 6-6a shows how quality spreads have widened nearly coincidentally with the Bond Buyer Index. As shown in Figure 6-6b, maturity spreads are slower to respond to movement in the Bond Buyer Index.

Investors are often concerned with the spread between tax-exempt and taxable securities. At times of very narrow spreads, different classes of investors will purchase municipal securities. Moreover, investors will look to the municipal market outperforming taxable markets during these periods of narrow spreads.

Conversely, when tax-exempt spreads are relatively wide versus taxable securities, investors begin to look at different alternatives for the use of their money. Yield relationships in comparison with taxable investments may also help determine the specific maturities that an investor will wish to purchase.

Other Tax Matters

PREMIUM BONDS

When investors hold tax-exempt bonds to maturity that were bought at a premium, they will not incur a tax loss on the difference between the purchase price and the par value. If the bonds are sold before maturity, the size of the gain or loss will depend on how long the bonds were held, because the federal tax law generally requires that the premium be amortized yearly on a basis reflecting the compounding of interest (at the yield to maturity of the bonds) and deducted from the investor's tax basis in the bonds. If, for example, an investor bought a 20-year bond at 104 and the premium of $40 had been amortized for 10 years in the amount of $28, the investor's basis at the end of 10 years would be $1,012 per bond. A sale at 101 would produce a loss of $2 per bond. The foregoing method of amortizing premium applies to bonds issued after September 27, 1985. The premium on bonds issued on or before that date may be amortized on a straight-line basis at the investor's option.

DISCOUNT BONDS

The gain realized when an investor sells a bond bought at a market discount for a profit or holds it to maturity is considered a capital gain. However, for certain bonds originally issued at a discount—called "original-issue discounts"—the difference between the discount and the par value, under certain circumstances, is not subject to federal income tax. This category includes zero-coupon bonds, which defer the payment of all interest until the final bond maturity. For all original-issue discount bonds, the discount is considered part of the tax-exempt interest being earned on the bond by the investor and, for bonds issued after September 3, 1982 and acquired after March 1, 1984, must be accrued over the life of the bond on a basis reflecting the compounding of interest at the yield to maturity of the bond. Generally, for pre-September 3rd, 1982 bonds the discount is accrued on a straight-line basis. This discount is added to the investor's tax basis as it is accrued. A ten-year bond with an original-issue discount of $20, $13 of which is accrued over the first five years, would generate $7 of capital gain if sold at par at the end of five years. If the same bond were held until maturity, the $20 discount would generate no capital gain subject to federal income tax.

ACCRUED INTEREST

Municipal bonds trade plus accrued interest. The buyer, who will receive the full six months' interest if he or she is the bondholder on the interest payment date, must pay the seller the share of interest earned between the settlement date of the transaction and the last interest payment date. This accrued interest is tax-exempt income for the seller of the bonds.

Evaluations

Because municipal bonds are traded over the counter and because so many issues are traded infrequently, investors often request evaluations of their municipal holdings to determine the market value of their portfolios. Evaluations may also be necessary to satisfy legal or financial requirements for individuals and institutional investors as well as for bond funds.

The types of evaluations vary widely, but essentially they are designed to determine the price for each bond in a portfolio that would be received if the bond were sold that day. Evaluators generally value a portfolio by comparing each bond with the recent trade prices of matching or similar bonds. Many evaluations are mathematical, often computerized, estimates, based on a grid or matrix with three dimensions. Each dimension corresponds to one of the important variables of the bond: coupon, maturity or call date, and quality. The mathematics of the grid allow the evaluator to estimate at what price a bond with a given coupon, maturity, and quality should be currently trading.

By and large, an evaluation is only as good as the information that goes into it. For some evaluations, new market information is fed into the matrix only monthly. Other evaluators' systems are updated far more frequently, in some cases daily. In at least one bond pricing system, a matrix is not used at all; rather, that evaluator attempts to utilize actual quotes as the basis for its prices. The accuracy of the market information is also important. An evaluator needs a good sense of how the market is trading for a full range of bonds. That information must include not only prices, but also shadings in the quality that the market is assigning to different kinds of bonds. Some evaluation systems use a finely differentiated system of quality ratings; others are very simple.

PORTFOLIO INSURANCE

Municipal bond portfolio insurance is a means of buying a "blanket" insurance policy for all the bonds contained in a given portfolio. This option is most frequently used by bond funds. Under certain policies, the bonds remain insured only as long as they are held within the insured portfolio. If a particular bond is sold prior to maturity, the insurance policy on that bond lapses. Other portfolio policies are structured with terms which allow for the continuation of the bond insurance even if the bond is traded out of the insured portfolio. Such a policy offers investors improved liquidity while protecting against credit risk.

7

Credit Analysis

Beginning with the note defaults by New York City, Cleveland, and the New York State Urban Development Corporation in the mid-1970s, interest was rekindled in municipal credit analysis. This interest was heightened by the default of the Washington Public Power Supply System in 1983 on more than $2 billion of debt issued to finance the construction of nuclear power plants. Investors and dealers had been accustomed to comparatively secure payment of principal and interest. There had been few serious municipal credit problems since the Depression: in the 1930s, there were nearly 5,000 recorded defaults, while in the 1960s, there were fewer than 300. One study found that between 1945 and 1965 only $10 million of principal and interest was permanently lost to municipal investors. Even the Depression defaults were almost entirely corrected by 1945, and most investors were paid what they were owed.

During the 1970s, however, the financial and debt environment changed. The Advisory Commission on Intergovernmental Relations, in its March 1985 report, *Bankruptcies, Defaults and Other Local Government Financial Emergencies,* found that the number of municipal bankruptcies grew to 21 between 1972 and 1984, compared with only ten cases filed between 1960 and 1971. Changes in bankruptcy laws and the proliferation of special-district and industrial development bonds were partly responsible for this development. For example, under the revised bankruptcy code, the approval of creditors was no longer required for filing for bankruptcy, so that some entities—for example, the San Jose School District, California—were able to file for bankruptcy in order to avoid the burdens of a labor agreement. The number of general purpose government filings remained small, but—as the financial analyst has come to recognize—defaults and bankruptcies can move independently of each other. For instance, the Washington

Public Power Supply System defaulted on two projects without filing for bankruptcy, while the school district did file, although its debt payments remained intact.

The Bond Investors Association, a trade association which maintains a database of defaulted municipal bonds, reported approximately 500 defaults in the 1980 to 1988 period. Although the number of defaults appeared to increase in the past decade, it is probably due to better data collection efforts. In addition, roughly two thirds of the total number of defaults are primarily concentrated in the industrial revenue bond, retirement center and nursing home sectors of the market, areas in which recent tax law changes will reduce future issuance.

Consequently, the investment community is no longer as calm as it once was, and research departments for dealers as well as for institutional investors have grown markedly. Moreover, where attention once centered almost solely on a handful of debt ratios, research has become much more sophisticated. The economic, financial, administrative, and political environments of the municipalities are now explored in detail. Credit analysts seek more information about population, wealth, and local industry; watch for trends in employment, per-capita income, and the assessed valuation of property; closely analyze the financial statements; and seek fuller disclosure of data where necessary. As more governments move to adopt generally accepted accounting principles, disclosure and comparability will improve.

In addition, the growth in the number of complex revenue bond issues has required a broader and more specialized research effort. Housing, hospital, and resource recovery issues, for example, are financially very intricate. Airport and stadium bonds must be analyzed like those of any new business venture. Traditionally monopolistic enterprises such as public utilities have become larger and more complex. Industrial revenue bonds are monitored closely, as their security is dependent on the continued profitability of the company involved. Hospital revenue bonds also face special challenges in a continually changing regulatory environment.

The two major categories of bonds are analyzed in very different ways. For general obligation bonds, analysts must concentrate on the financial health of the entire entity, noting the extent of its taxing power as well as the potential of its economic base, which will affect the entity's ability to raise the necessary revenues. The analysis of revenue bonds, however, is as varied as the types of revenue bonds issued. An economic analysis of the enterprise being financed is critical, as is an assessment of the economic strength of the area to be served. The legal and financial protective provisions of revenue bonds are also important and should be given close scrutiny.

General Obligation Bonds

THE POLITICAL MOOD

One of the important lessons of the 1970s was that changes in the political mood of taxpayers can prove as important for the value of the bonds as the financial ability to pay. Willingness to pay has always been an issue of municipal bond analysis, but the principle was brought home in a somewhat different way by the referenda in favor of property-tax cutbacks, most notably in California and Massachusetts. The limitation that referenda placed on localities in these states' tax-raising abilities did not affect their outstanding general obligation debt, because any debt already approved was protected. However, lease-rental bonds, which are paid out of general tax revenues, and tax-allocation bonds, which are backed by increases in property tax revenues from added property values due to district redevelopment, were affected.

In short, a community's action can significantly alter the credit of municipal issues that are already outstanding. Although the contractual obligation of issuers to pay off general obligation debt has been strongly reinforced by the courts, an obligation cannot be met if the funds are not available.

Most revenue bonds are not affected by taxpayer limitations on property tax, because they are normally paid from other sources of income. But there is nothing to say that electric utility users, for example, will not stage their own revolt—as they did in the Pacific Northwest during the early 1980s. As a result, assessment of the current political mood of states and localities can prove to be an important part of municipal bond analysis.

Analysts also rely on other information to assess a community's willingness to pay. The details of the state's constitution or of the statutes authorizing bonds and taxes will provide an indication of how difficult it is to raise more debt. Past action to meet budget deficits is another guide. Over the longer term, analysts prefer to see that the final maturity of bonds does not exceed the life of the project for which the proceeds are used. Future taxpayers may not be willing to pay for a public enterprise that is no longer in use or that is in need of substantial repair.

THE DEBT BURDEN

Traditional general obligation bond analysis emphasized the debt burden of the community. The objective was, and still is, to determine whether the debt of the issuer is at a manageable level compared to property values, population, income, and similar data. Measures of debt burden have proved to be inadequate tools in themselves. But coupled with other information, debt burden is still an important gauge of the ability of communities to pay their debt.

The measures most commonly used are a series of debt ratios, which are compared with benchmarks based on averages throughout the country. Trends in these ratios are watched closely for signals of future improvement or of deterioration. The analysis begins with the computation of the municipality's debt. A sample debt statement is shown in Figure 7-1.

The first step in the analysis is to compute the municipality's total bonded debt—that is, the total general obligation debt issued by the municipality, no matter what the purpose. Added to this is any unfunded debt, typically short-term notes. The sum of the two is usually called total direct debt. The next step is to deduct all items that are not actually potential burdens on the municipality's tax resources. The first deduction is for all self-supporting enterprise debt, generally debt issued to support a project and paid for out of the revenues of that project. General obligation debt is often issued to support, for example, water and sewer systems and even airports. Although the debt may ultimately become a claim against the municipality's tax revenues, the issues are often structured to be self-supporting.

Along with deducting the self-supporting debt, the analyst should deduct any sinking funds or reserve funds established to pay off future debt. The buildup in such reserves reduces the burden to the issuer. Tax anticipation notes and revenue anticipation notes—notes that will be paid off automatically out of earmarked revenues—are usually deducted.

Bond anticipation notes, which are ultimately refinanced into long-term debt, are not deducted from total debt in the computation unless they have been issued for a self-supporting enterprise.

When these items are deducted from total direct debt, the figure remaining is called net direct debt. To this must be added the debt of overlapping or underlying units of government. Such units include but are not limited to school districts, parks, and other services in which the municipality shares, such as police or sanitation. Because the local population and economic wealth must also bear this debt, the pro rata or proportional part of the debt of these units is assigned to the municipality. The amount assigned is the proportion of the municipality's full market value to the full market valuation of the whole unit, including the municipality. This overlapping debt is totaled and added to the net direct debt to arrive at the final figure, the overall net debt. The overlapping debt for Dallas is shown in Figure 7-1.

With overall net debt tallied, the analyst is ready to compute a variety of ratios. One popular measure is the ratio of overall debt to full valuation. Analysts prefer to use full market value of property rather than an assessed valuation. Assessed valuation is generally a percentage of the full value of the property as set by the municipality or state. Because these percentages vary widely, a comparison of different municipalities is difficult to make. By using full valuation, the analyst does not have to worry about variations in state formulas. Many municipalities, however, have diversified their tax bases, making debt to valuation a less important measure than it once was. Other debt ratios can be more meaningful since they include annual debt service and other fixed costs such as leases and pensions as a percentage of the operating funds.

FIGURE 7-1. Determining a Municipality's Debt Burden

CITY OF DALLAS DEBT STATEMENT as of April 1, 1985

Estimated Full Valuation of Taxable Property

1984 Taxable Assessed Valuation (100%)		$42,792,236,827
Total General Obligation Debt:		
General Purpose Bonds	$491,023,383	
Airport Land Acquisition Warrants (D/FW Airport)	547,710	
Airport Improvement Bonds (Love Field Airport and Redbird Airport) (Note 1)	233,700	
Assumed Water District Bonds (Note 1)	27,000	
Combination Tax and Revenue Certificates of Obligation (Note 1)	55,460,000	
Certificates of Obligation (Note 1)	2,000,000	
Combination Tax and Revenue Certificates of Obligation	2,185,000	
Combination Tax and Parking Revenue Certificates of Obligation (Note 1)	15,880,000	
Convention Center Improvement Bonds (Note 1)	4,576,200	
Solid Waste Improvement Bonds (Note 1)	886,239	
Municipal Produce Market Improvement Bonds (Note 1)	6,261,428	
The Series 1985 Certificates of Obligation (Note 1)	5,400,000	$584,480,660
Less Self-Supporting Debt (Note 1)		90,724,567
Total Funded Debt Payable from Ad Valorem Taxes		493,756,093
Cash Balance in Interest and Sinking Fund (as of 4-1-85)		56,812,663
Net Funded Debt		$436,943,430

(continued onto next page)

Net Overlapping Debt

Dallas Independent School District	$192,882,400	93.99%	$181,290,168
Dallas County	244,285,000(2)	61.85%	151,090,273
Dallas County Community College District	50,500,000	61.85%	31,234,250
Dallas County Hospital District	77,600,000	61.85%	47,995,600
Dallas County Road District No. 1	770,000	61.85%	476,245
Denton County	9,835,000	.09%	8,852
Carrollton-Farmers Branch Independent School District	46,575,000	10.49%	4,885,718
Collin County	35,949,000	.05%	17,975
Duncanville Independent School District	19,299,000	30.98%	5,978,830
Garland Independent School District	82,480,000(3)	5.25%	4,330,200
Grand Prairie Independent School District	31,387,000	8.23%	2,583,150
Highland Park Independent School District	10,060,000	9.72%	977,832
Irving Independent School District	22,895,000	10.25%	2,346,738
Lancaster Independent School District	19,217,000(4)	1.78%	342,063
Mesquite Independent School District	79,049,660	.06%	47,430
Plano Independent School District	84,470,000	.09%	76,023
Richardson Independent School District	69,625,000	34.98%	24,354,825
Wilmer-Hutchins Independent School District	11,290,000	49.39%	5,576,131
Net Overall Funded Debt			$900,555,733

Population, January 1, 1985 Est. 987,350

Per Capita Overall Net Debt $912

Ratio of Overall Net Debt to Est. Market Valuation   2.10%

Notes:
(1) Transfers are and will be made from the respective revenue funds to the General Fund and the General Obligation Debt Service Fund in amounts sufficient to pay both principal and interest.
(2) Includes $41,000,000 to be sold June 10, 1985.
(3) Includes $20,000,000 sold April 2, 1985.
(4) Includes $9,500,000 sold April 5, 1985.

SOURCE: Dallas Official Statement dated May 20, 1985

A debt worksheet, such as the one illustrated, shows how the debt burden of a local community is computed.

One commonly used ratio is that of overall debt to population. The per-capita debt of a highly rated municipality would almost certainly be less than $1,000 and would normally be less than $500. Comparison of debt to personal income is another useful measure.

Comparing annual debt service to tax and other revenues provides a measure of an issuer's ability to pay. It is a common tool for analyzing state credits, where there usually is no property tax.

The moral obligation bonds issued by states present a special situation for analysis. Although the full backing of the state is implied for these bonds, there is always some doubt as to how readily states will rescue issues in trouble. Analysts concentrate, therefore, on the degree to which these bonds are self-supporting and will not need the state's help. Standard & Poor's usually assigns a lower rating to a moral obligation bond than it would assign to a full faith and credit bond of the same guarantor, unless the project can be rated better on its own. Moody's simply ignores the moral obligation and rates the issue on its own pledged revenue support. The record in New York and New Jersey is well established in that the states will aid housing and port authority debt service payments through the legislative appropriation process.

The best sources of financial information are the municipality's or unit's official statement and annual report as well as other financial statements it makes available on request. Moody's and Standard & Poor's provide services that summarize much of the most important data for thousands of issues.

ECONOMIC ANALYSIS

To many analysts, the state of the local economy is the most important single factor in determining a state's or municipality's creditworthiness. Communities at different stages of growth may require more or less debt. A young, booming city often needs to issue more bonds than a mature or deteriorating city. However, an older community that has elected to keep up with capital improvements will probably need to embark on major borrowing to keep its economy healthy—or risk economic decline. A high per-capita total debt or rising trends in total debt might be acceptable to investors in the first case and present a danger in the second.

Key indications of a community's economic strength include income levels, population trends and prospects, employment statistics, and industry or employer composition. Per-capita income and its rate of growth are among the first measures analysts examine. Some analysts also look at income per household because per-capita data can often be misleading. It can be distorted by large student or prison populations, for example.

Analysts caution against relying too heavily on unemployment numbers to measure the strength of employment. Patterns of unemployment can be disguised by a number of factors, including population shifts and changes in the composition of the labor force. Labor force growth is a more accurate measure.

A comparison of a municipal population's income levels and of its labor force growth with national averages can provide analysts with a measure of the community's economic standing in the country. Moreover, comparing a municipality with its neighbors along similar lines can help identify problems that might otherwise go unnoticed.

Other readily available data are also good indicators of economic health. The valuation of property per capita is often cited. The age and condition of housing and rent levels are also good indicators of local wealth.

Population, too, can be a key indicator. A growing population is usually a sign of strength, although unusually rapid growth could lead to problems. A falling population is generally associated with deteriorating cities and regions. Occasionally, however, a city may lose population to its suburbs, but retain its economic strength as a place of employment if it has maintained its infrastructure in reasonably good shape.

Once an overall direction of the local economy is established, scrutiny of the specific industries and companies that dominate the community's employment is important. The two principal questions are whether the main industries are healthy and growing, and whether the region is diversified economically so that it does not depend too heavily on any one industry or on one sector, such as manufacturing. Expansion plans for major companies can be important, and the amount of construction under way in a municipality provides one means of assessing these expansion plans. Overbuilding, of course, can be as dangerous as no building at all. A mix of new, sprouting companies and mature, steady companies is usually most desirable. Often, the credit analyst will consult his or her corporate research department for specific information on companies in a particular region.

Diversity not only protects a community from deterioration should the major employer leave town or suffer a business setback; it can also shield the municipality, to some extent, from a severe downturn during economic recessions. A good yardstick for a municipality's strength is how well it did in the last recession. Did employment recover in line with the rest of the economy? Did personal income hold up? Did the municipality run an operating deficit?

Analysts must also examine the changes taking place in the nation's economic base. Generally, the country has, to a large degree, moved away from manufacturing toward services and trade. The object of this examination is to determine the derivation of personal income in a given community, as well as its employment categories. For example, although job dependency on the automobile industry is far less important in Michigan today than in the past, it is likely that personal income levels still remain very largely dependent on the health of that industry.

TAX REVENUES

Analysis of a locality's economic structure must be translated into how this affects its tax base. A strong economic structure will normally mean plenty of taxing potential, but there are several factors that should be analyzed further. Again, diversity is key. A corporation in the region may be even more dominant in terms of the proportion of taxes paid than in the employment it provides.

Major sources of revenues besides property tax are also welcome. How significant are revenues from sales taxes, income tax, fees, and concessions? Because most states do not levy property taxes, a careful analysis of their various sources of income is important.

A superior tax system is one that captures a wide range of economic activity. For example, if a state's tax structure depends heavily upon declining oil and gas activity, budget constraints are not likely to be far behind.

For many municipalities, federal and state aid can comprise as much as 30 percent or more of revenues. Most analysts regard too much reliance on aid as a danger. For one thing, it is usually out of the control of the municipality (except in the case of school bonds, where the state may supplement local property taxes). For another, the amount of aid can be changed not only by legislative actions on the state and national levels, but sometimes by administrative decisions, all of which are subject to political vagaries.

Finally, once the sources of revenue are reviewed, analysts can determine what potential there is for raising tax rates. Generally, if taxes are already high, the potential for increases is less likely. The percentage of taxes collected in some state and local governments can run dangerously low, even when other factors look good. A poor collection rate, especially compared to rates in adjoining regions, could reflect either economic shifts or simply an inefficient government. A temporary drop in property taxes may sometimes occur as a result of property revaluation. This trend should be watched for any evidence of a tax resistance movement.

FINANCIAL FACTORS

The emphasis on long-term factors in determining municipal financial health has certainly increased in the last ten years. But what has received even more emphasis has been the current financial status of the municipalities and their methods of reporting.

Deficits in any of the various funds municipalities use to account for their finances are red flags that require more investigation. In the 1970s, the size of the deficits of several major cities was far larger than what was reported. The cause of any deficit, and whether the factors are temporary and easily remedied or chronic and longer term, must be understood. An occasional deficit is not necessarily a problem. A dip in the economy, a change in state aid, or a local corporate bankruptcy could tilt a municipality's main operating fund into temporary deficit. A deep or ongoing deficit, however, must be investigated further.

In relation to this, analysts look carefully at short-term financing. Many state and local governments have adopted active short-term financing programs to provide funds when the timing of revenues and expenditures does not match. The volume of the short-term notes can reach dangerously high levels, however— which is precisely what happened in the case of New York City in the 1970s.

An operating deficit or surplus must be analyzed in light of a municipality's past operations. The surplus or deficit in the fund balance is the sum of past surpluses and deficits, and a surplus there may more than compensate for an operating deficit in any given year. Balance sheets must also be examined. A healthy level of working capital and highly liquid current assets are beneficial. Reserves for items such as uncollected taxes and payables should be adequate.

Close analysis of the budget is another valuable tool. Has the municipality stayed within the budget in the past? What specific items account for the cost overruns or excesses? Is the next year's budget reliable? Some localities have adopted procedures for carefully allotting funds which must be examined.

OFF-THE-FINANCIAL-STATEMENT CONSIDERATIONS

Pension liabilities and other deferred obligations. The extent of pension fund liabilities for municipalities has drawn widespread concern. For one thing, it has often been difficult to obtain reliable information on the amount of such liabilities, although reporting has improved in recent years. Second, a great proportion of pension liabilities is unfunded. Analysts generally want to know how pension obligations will affect expenditures over the years. If there are heavy unfunded liabilities, will the state or local government be obliged to increase outlays substantially? If pension liabilities are funded, are actuarial assumptions about inflation and investment returns on the funds realistic or is funding set too low?

OTHER FACTORS

The opinion of bond counsel should not be taken lightly. For this reason, the reliability of counsel is critical. The role of bond counsel is discussed in greater detail in Chapter 2.

The independent audit is becoming more common among larger issuers of municipal debt. The Governmental Accounting Standards Board (GASB), the Government Finance Officers Association (GFOA), and rating agencies recommend that an independent audit of financial statements be undertaken annually. To the analyst, the independent audit helps ensure that the financial data being presented are accurate and consistent with prior financial statements. Because the audit is undertaken in accordance with the GASB's generally accepted accounting standards, the uniformity and consistency of accounting methods can be relied on. Audits supervised by state officials (most states require some kind of audit) or made to ensure compliance with a government program will not necessarily address the same areas as those covered in an audit conducted by an independent accountant using GASB principles.

Finally, many analysts try to assess the general capability and responsibility of a state or local government's fiscal officers. More and more, analysts have come to emphasize how well a city or state is managed, how carefully programs are documented, and how diligently and imaginatively the future programs of the municipality are planned. Political structure can be particularly important. For example, a strong mayoral system or a council-manager form will often be able to control finances better than a weak system. When rating an issuer's credit, analysts are placing increasing weight on such factors, however subjective. Additionally, better-managed governments are developing performance objectives that are both measurable and reported to their constituencies. It may be beneficial to examine any such reports.

Revenue Bonds

The analysis of revenue bonds is conducted in quite a different manner from that of general obligation bonds. Virtually every revenue bond is unique, so an economic analysis of the demand for services, cost and operating efficiency, and competition is imperative to every analysis. Moreover, the economic health of the service area is an important and complicated factor.

Most revenue bonds are traditionally protected by a number of legal and financial agreements that can often be more important to bondholders than is the project itself. The first step in any analysis is close examination of the provisions of the bond resolution. The provisions are summarized in the issuer's official statement, but attention is paid to the full text of all legal documents. Final documents may differ in material respects from preliminary information in connection with the offering of new debt.

THE RESOLUTION

Flow of Funds

The bond resolution is a document that sets forth the order in which funds generated by the enterprise will be allocated to various purposes. The funds are used to pay for operations and debt service and to establish reserves. Different kinds of bonds require different flows of funds. But generally, all funds are first recorded in the revenue fund. The flow of funds described below is typical of many revenue bonds.

Operations and maintenance. The money necessary to meet the ongoing budgeted expenses of the enterprise is placed, monthly, in the enterprise's operations and maintenance fund. Normally, one-twelfth of an enterprise's annual budget is shifted from the revenue fund to the operations and maintenance fund each month. From there, expenditures are made to meet expenses. Occasionally, enough money is placed in the fund both to cover budgeted expenses and to provide a reserve.

Debt service. Funds are set aside monthly that will equal, over the course of a year, the amount necessary to meet annual debt service. This fund frequently maintains separate accounts for principal and interest. Sometimes, separate bond-redemption funds or accounts are set up. There may also be a note-repayment fund or account and a sinking fund account.

Debt service reserve fund. Funds are apportioned to the debt service reserve fund after annual debt service is ensured. These funds are tapped only if the debt service fund itself is insufficient to meet annual payments. The reserve fund is usually set at an amount equal to one year's debt service, although it may equal only average annual payments rather than the maximum annual payments. This fund can be set up initially out of bond proceeds or built up over time. The Tax Reform Act of 1986 has made the creation of reserve funds financially unattractive for municipal issuers and many high-quality issues are now forgoing them.

Reserve maintenance fund. Allocations are made to this fund to meet unanticipated maintenance expenses, usually at the recommendation of the consultants in charge.

Renewal and replacement fund. The fund is established to replace equipment and make repairs over the life of an enterprise. A set payment is made into this fund according to the enterprise's budget for such replacements. When more construction is planned, a construction fund is normally set up for expansion or new projects.

Surplus monies. Most bond resolutions carefully itemize where the balance of revenues will be directed should they exceed what is required for all funds. The monies are sometimes used to redeem bonds or reduce tax payments. Many municipalities take surplus funds from revenue enterprises for use in their own general fund. The resolution also specifies what kinds of securities can be bought with the excess funds.

Analysts assess all these funds to be sure they are sufficient to meet the enterprise's requirements. Figure 7-2 describes the flow of funds for a typical revenue bond issue.

FIGURE 7-2. Flow of Funds Account for a Typical Revenue Bond Issue

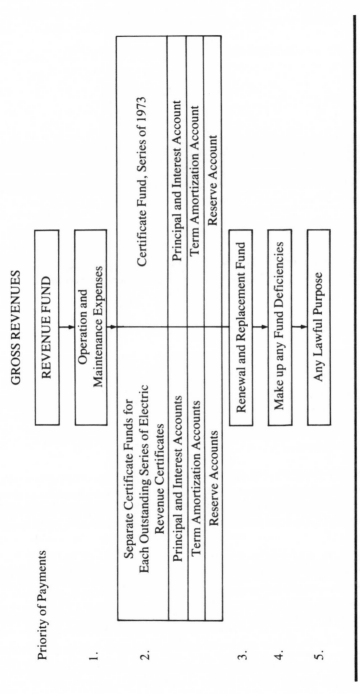

GROSS REVENUES

Priority of Payments

REVENUE FUND

1.   Operation and Maintenance Expenses

2.   Separate Certificate Funds for Each Outstanding Series of Electric Revenue Certificates   Certificate Fund, Series of 1973

    Principal and Interest Accounts   Principal and Interest Account

    Term Amortization Accounts   Term Amortization Account

    Reserve Accounts   Reserve Account

3.   Renewal and Replacement Fund

4.   Make up any Fund Deficiencies

5.   Any Lawful Purpose

The flow of funds is the order in which the revenues generated by the project financed from the proceeds of the revenue bond issue will be allocated to various purposes.

Covenants

A sensible flow of funds and ample reserves are not the only assurances investors seek. For user-charge bonds, a rate covenant is important. By such a covenant, the issuer pledges that rates will be set sufficiently high to meet operation and maintenance expenses, renewal and replacement expenses, and debt service. Another form of the rate covenant requires that rates be set to provide a safety margin of revenues above debt service, after operation and maintenance expenses are met.

Additional covenants might include a provision for insuring the project, requirements for a periodic review by a consulting engineer, or guarantees that no free services shall be offered to municipalities or customers and that separate books will be kept to record the accounts of the project. Other covenants contain provisions for independent audits and prohibitions against the sale of the project or of its facilities before the bonds are paid off. In some cases, a covenant stipulates the retention of an outside expert for periodic review of the enterprise's operations or maintenance.

Claims on Revenues

Most bonds are backed by a first lien on net revenues. Bonds with second or third liens usually are rated significantly lower than those with first liens. Some contract obligations, though, have priority even over first-lien bonds; for example, a power supply contract is usually treated as an operating expense.

Additional Bonds

Once the claim on revenues has been established, a very important covenant written into most revenue bond resolutions involves provisions for additional bonds. If the issuer retains the right to offer bonds at a later time that have an equal or prior claim on revenues, the bondholder may be placed in a riskier position. Most issuers will provide one of two types of protective bond clauses. The less common one stipulates that any additional bonds will be junior and subordinate to the current bonds, except those that may be necessary for the completion of the enterprise. This is called a closed-end provision, the drawback being that subordinated bonds will be more difficult to market.

An open-end provision allows for bonds of equivalent lien on earnings to be issued, subject to certain requirements. Generally, the limitation is that the earnings coverage of debt service, including that for the new bonds, not fall below a set minimum—for example, 125 percent. Earnings of the enterprise can be defined in several ways to meet this test, however. Some define the earnings to be covered as the most recent fiscal year's earnings or the average of earnings over the preceding 24 months. The latter is the most conservative of the methods commonly used. Another method is to base the test on future estimates of earnings. This usually requires reports by reliable consultants. The past several years have seen a steady trend towards weaker covenants, with resulting lower ratings.

ECONOMIC ANALYSIS

Most revenue bonds are supported by enterprises that must be analyzed like any other business venture. The factors affecting various kinds of revenue enterprises differ markedly from enterprise to enterprise. However, the issuer generally provides a great deal of the data to investors through preliminary official statements, feasibility and other engineering studies, capital improvement programs, bond resolutions, and various reports.

Some types of projects require more scrutiny than others. By and large, water, sewer, and electric utility bonds are backed by monopolistic enterprises and are quite secure. In contrast, housing and hospital bonds usually require much more research. See Figure 7-3 for the major uses of revenue bonds in 1989.

Financial and legal considerations are often paramount in the analysis of this kind of debt. However, the effective demand for the service—which includes the ability of customers to pay for it—is a key consideration. Some of the most important factors affecting the credit of different kinds of revenue bonds are outlined below.

Electric utility bonds. The strength of an area's economy and the cost of the service are key factors in determining that area's effective demand for electricity. Analysts prefer to see that sources of power generation are diversified among different types of fuels. The power supply itself must be adequate to support the area's growth, and any future capital outlays should be considered. On the other hand, underutilization of generation facilities can become a burden.

Water and sewer system bonds. Water bonds usually relate to the water supply for a community, an issue of importance to established cities, where often the water supply system has to be either enlarged or renovated, and to new cities or communities where water supply may have to be created. Sewer system bonds relate largely to the disposal of the water we use in our personal, daily, or business lives, and at the end of nearly all sewer systems is a wastewater treatment plant that "treats" the sewage prior to disposal into a river, lake, or ocean. Treatment plants have to meet federal environmental standards, and this may require special and expensive technologies. The economic mix of the area being serviced and the potential for growth are factors important in determining demand for either water supply or disposal. Reduced federal financial support, especially in wastewater treatment, will probably contribute to enlarged local financing requirements.

Toll road bonds. Once potential traffic is estimated, the major question for the success of this kind of enterprise concerns the elasticity of the demand for it. In other words, if toll rates increase, will the amount of traffic decrease substantially? A mix of different types of users helps ensure stable demand levels, but competition from other roadways needs to be assessed. Often, bond resolutions contain provisions calling for limitations on the construction of potentially competitive projects. Economic trends in the area being serviced are also analyzed, as are the price and availability of fuel. Bridge and tunnel authority bonds are often examined using the same criteria.

FIGURE 7-3. Major Uses of Revenue Bonds in 1989

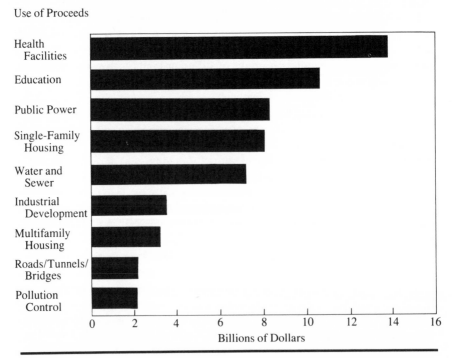

SOURCE: IDD Information Services/PSA Municipal Securities Database

Transit revenue bonds. In recent years, both new and older public transportation systems have developed revenue bond programs to build, expand, or renovate their systems. As no public transit system has been able to support itself entirely from fares, other financial resources have had to be provided. These include ongoing federal and state capital and operating subsidies, taxes such as a sales or gasoline tax, or a combination of several such resources. Debt financing may take the form of a gross revenue pledge from fares, as in the case of the New York Metropolitan Transportation Authority, or of a special sales tax pledge, as in the cases of the Bay Area Rapid Transportation District and the Metropolitan Atlanta Regional Transportation Authority. Key factors in such cases are the need and demand for the service, the importance of the service to the local economy, the outlook for non-fare revenues, and management factors, particularly labor relations.

Industrial revenue and pollution control bonds. These credits are as sound as the corporations behind them. They are backed by leases to those corporations and are usually analyzed as unsecured corporate debt. Often, however, the bonds are guaranteed by a corporate subsidiary and not by the parent company. In the more secure issues, the investor has a first mortgage on the property involved.

Airport bonds. Generally, a feasibility study is a must in analyzing the prospects for an airport. The potential traffic through the airport is the main consideration. Is it an airport for a single, major city? Are there competing airports? Could it become a hub airport? Some airport bonds are secured directly by leases with participating airlines and are analyzed much like industrial revenue bonds. More often revenues are derived from contracts with airlines based upon airport usage. The economy of the service area and pricing policies of the airlines are also factors.

Hospital bonds. Among the most complex of issues, hospital bonds usually require feasibility studies. The location, level, and quality of services offered are important. A teaching hospital will normally have a good flow of well-trained physicians. Third-party payments by insurance companies, Medicare, and Medicaid make up the bulk of a hospital's revenues, and analysts prefer commercial insurance company payments to government payments. Care should be taken that a "certificate of need" is secured on the financing involved where required and, where it is not required, that the need for the enterprise be amply demonstrated.

Housing bonds. There are essentially two types of housing revenue bonds: multifamily and single-family. Multifamily housing revenue bonds finance rental housing developments for low- and moderate-income families and the elderly. Multifamily bonds are usually secured by the principal and interest payments on a mortgage. These payments consist of the aggregation of monthly rental payments. Earlier multifamily issues were typically subsidized and/or insured under federal housing programs. As the federal government reduced its involvement in housing programs, multifamily issues have come to use market-based rental units to subsidize a dedicated portion of units at below-market rents for defined beneficiaries. Credit enhancements such as bond insurance, surety bonds, collateralized mortgage pass-through certificates, and letters of credit are employed. The key analytical variables related to multifamily bonds include the occupancy rate and the ability of the occupants to pay. Proper construction of the enterprise as well as the quality of ongoing management are also important; maintenance of reserves, for example, should be adequate. Legal documents relating to redemption provisions and credit enhancement must be studied.

Single-family housing revenue bonds provide below-market-rate mortgages to qualified individual borrowers financing one- to four-family owner-occupied dwellings. Security for a bond issue is derived from individual monthly mortgage payments contained in a portfolio of mortgages. The level of delinquencies, foreclosures, and prepayments are key considerations in analyzing these bonds. The level of reserves, type of insurance coverage, and investment policies of an issuer help to define credit quality. The demand for mortgages in the area served is also an important point to be assessed, since a lack of demand can mean that a portion of the bond issue will have to be called, resulting in a lower coverage of program costs.

College and university bonds. Private and public colleges have issued a significant amount of debt either directly or through state-established finance authorities. The bonds are usually direct obligations of the institution and may be a general obligation of the institution or a special revenue bond for housing or a stadium. To a large degree, the state-supported institutions have an advantage over private institutions, due to the public nature of their financial resources. However, the top-tier private institutions have continued to do well with their substantial endowments, wide scope of programs, and enhanced management and financial techniques; they are highly regarded in the bond market. Enrollment trends, diversity of curriculum, demand for an institution as evinced by its application pool, selectivity, and the strength of an institution's asset base provide the major clues to its financial health and prospects.

Student loan bonds. They are typically issued through a separately organized entity to meet students' needs for aid in covering tuition costs. Most of these student loan bonds are "structured" in that they are based upon assumptions regarding prepayments, delinquencies, investment income, insurance coverage, and guarantees.

FINANCIAL FACTORS

Financial ratio analysis is a useful way to assess the strength of a revenue project. The most frequently used measure of an enterprise's well-being is the coverage ratio—the ratio of revenues (less operation and maintenance expenses, but before provision for depreciation) to debt service. The pertinent information is found in the issuer's operating statement.

Analysts also emphasize that projecting future debt service coverage is important. Debt service coverage may be adequate when bonds are issued, but if additional bonds are planned or if revenues fall off, that coverage could drop sharply. Analysis of the efficiency of current facilities and the potential need for new facilities play roles here.

Other Factors Affecting Credit

In assessing how secure certain securities in fact are, analysts must also take into account two final factors. These are the existence of letters of credit backing an issue or of bond insurance policies that perform much the same function.

LETTERS OF CREDIT

Letters of credit (LOCs) are used to increase market access for an issuer that may have difficulty in selling its bonds due to a perceived weakness in its ability to meet its obligations. An LOC, issued by a suitable bank or lending institution, will enhance the quality and appeal of the bond issue by substituting the paying ability of the bank for that of the bond issuer.

A letter of credit is generally issued by a commercial bank and represents a contract between the issuing bank and the bond trustee. Under the letter, the bank irrevocably agrees to pay to the trustee upon demand monies in an amount necessary to cover all payments due on the bonds. As with all contracts, the specific terms are negotiated and can vary with each bond sale. Within the context of the municipal market, however, terms and conditions tend to be standardized, especially as far as the investor is concerned.

Letters of credit are used for two purposes: to facilitate credit and to enhance liquidity. The LOC was first used in the municipal market to enhance the credit of a bond issue. For this purpose, the bank issuing the LOC irrevocably pledges to provide funds to meet debt service payments in the event that the bond issuer cannot do so. The terms of the LOC empower the bond trustee to draw on the letter of credit directly if the bond issuer fails to make deposits sufficient to provide for timely payment of interest or principal or both. Thus, the letter of credit is used to protect investors from a default.

The expanded use of tender or put option bonds spawned the second use of the LOC: to increase liquidity. Under the terms of this kind of contract, the bank issuing the LOC agrees to advance any funds necessary to purchase bonds tendered by investors. The bank, in effect, provides for extraordinary demands for cash if a substantial number of bonds are tendered.

A well-capitalized and financially strong bank substituting its own paying ability for that of a bond issuer may, at first glance, seem to be an ideal situation for the risk-averse investor; and, in most cases, bonds carrying this kind of assurance of timely payment of principal and interest are rated double- or triple-A. An LOC, however, is normally issued for only three to seven years for bonds which may have a maturity of 20 to 30 years. It is necessary, therefore, that the letter be renewed or a substitute obtained periodically. The bond indenture typically provides that if the letter of credit is not renewed or if a suitable substitute cannot be found, the bonds must be redeemed prior to the expiration of the letter of credit.

Hence, the question of timely payment, while reduced, continues to exist. At the time of issuance of the bonds, a substitution of credit took place—the bank's for the issuer's. Attention must be paid to the creditworthiness of the bank itself since a rating change for the bank's obligations will affect all financings supported by the bank. However, in very basic terms, banks generate revenues by investing money (loans, mortgages, and other securities). Money for investing is obtained by borrowing, deposits (savings and checking), and earnings on investments. Should a bank lose money on its investments or lose its sources of funds, it will encounter financial difficulties. It is important, therefore, that the bank issuing the LOC have a sound financial history and a diverse loan portfolio, and that it have adequate assets.

BOND INSURANCE POLICIES

Basically, a municipal bond insurance policy is a noncancellable guarantee designed to protect the bondholder from nonpayment on the part of the issuer. In the event that an issuer fails to meet a scheduled principal or interest payment, the insurer, acting as a third-party guarantor, will make the debt service payment directly to the paying agent or trustee. The insurer has received an up-front premium for the guarantee, the amount of which is determined primarily by the perceived risk associated with the financing.

It is important to remember that the issuer invariably remains the first source of payment of principal and interest. Hence, the underlying credit characteristics of the issuer remain very important and can vary considerably. Refer to Chapter 3 for more detailed coverage of the bond insurance companies.

8

Understanding Municipal Bond Interest Rates

To the underwriter or trader in municipal bonds, fluctuations in the price of securities seem a constant, everyday affair. However, underlying the short-term shifts in securities prices and interest rates are longer-run factors that have a profound effect on long-term trends in interest rate movements. The basic factors that determine interest rates in general also determine the level of municipal rates; municipal bond yields tend to rise and fall in accordance with rates on other fixed-income securities, at least over time. A nearly 20-year comparison of the Bond Buyer Index with rates on federal securities demonstrates clearly the close relationship between markets for the two kinds of securities (see Figure 8-1).

Over shorter periods of time, however, municipal bond yields can move independently of general market rates. Municipal rates are particularly affected by the supply of new issues and the cyclical buying habits of the principal investors. The tax exemption, as discussed in Chapter 6, limits the market to those who can best take advantage of it: insurance companies, bond funds, individuals, and, in the past, commercial banks.

Municipal rates are also usually lower than rates on other securities of equivalent maturity and risk because of the tax exemption. During most of 1989, for example, long-term municipal rates averaged approximately 75 percent of rates on equivalent corporate securities. In 1986, however, some municipal yields moved above those on taxable issues due to uncertainties raised by proposed tax legislation. However, municipal rates fluctuate more widely over time than taxable rates. Before the Sixteenth Amendment established the income tax,

FIGURE 8-1. Interest Rate Trends in the Municipal and U.S. Government Securities Markets, 1969-1988

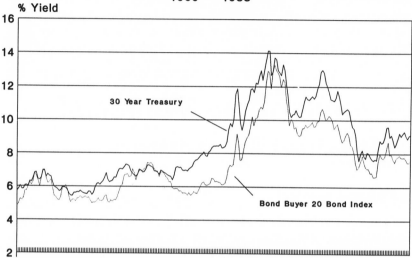

Yield Comparison
Bond Buyer 20 Bond Index and 30 Year Treasury Bond
1969 - 1988

SOURCE: Merrill Lynch Capital Markets

Rates on municipal securities generally rise and fall with changes in other interest rates, although the extent and timing of those shifts can vary.

municipal securities traded at about the same rate as corporate securities. Within a few years of the passage of the Sixteenth Amendment, the gap between the two widened. At the end of World War II, rates on municipal bonds were as low as 41 percent of corporate rates. The gap slowly began to narrow.

Prior to the 1980s short-term municipal notes, typically bought by large institutions taxed at corporate rates, traded at approximately 50 percent of comparable yields on corporate securities. Since then such notes have traded closer to 70 percent of comparable yields on corporate securities as the importance of large institutions declined and that of individuals represented by money funds increased.

Determinants of the Overall Level of Interest Rates

THE BUSINESS CYCLE

One well-established observation of most economists is that, as economic activity picks up, borrowing demand increases across the board, and interest rates rise. Financial institutions and capital markets compete with each other for a limited supply of funds. Consequently, banks raise both the rates they are willing to pay to lenders and the interest rates they demand from borrowers. To attract more capital to the money and bond markets, rates then have to rise further.

This process has been borne out in business cycle after business cycle. Interest rates peak at about the same time that the rate of real (inflation-adjusted) economic growth begins to decline. In inflationary periods, interest rates have generally peaked a little later in the cycle. Therefore, efforts to forecast the business cycle play an important part in interest rate forecasting.

THE FEDERAL RESERVE

The nation's central bank—the Federal Reserve—is one of the most powerful forces in the economy. It has considerable influence over key interest rates, both directly and indirectly (via its control over the amount of reserves in the banking system that support the creation of money through bank deposits). To many economists, the growth of the money supply is the most important variable in determining the growth of aggregate spending. Others claim that fiscal policy—the primary tools being tax expenditure policies of the federal government—is also influential.

The Federal Reserve has several methods by which it can influence interest rates and the money supply. It sets the discount rate, the rate at which banks that are members of the Federal Reserve system can borrow directly from the Fed. It also establishes reserve requirements for its members: banks must keep a set portion of every deposit or loan on hand as a reserve. The Fed's most flexible means of control, and one it most frequently uses, works via the policy directions of its Open Market Committee. Through guidelines established by this committee, the Fed buys and sells U.S. government securities in order either to add or withdraw reserves from the banking system. This not only alters the total amount of reserves outstanding, but also has a direct effect on the interest rates of those kinds of securities the Federal Reserve is buying or selling.

In recent years, the Fed has tried to maintain control over both the money supply and interest rates. The economists known as monetarists claim that the Fed should, by and large, not attempt to control interest rates but rather concentrate on controlling the money supply. Other economists hold that the level of interest rates is more important than the money supply.

Whatever the theory behind its moves, the Fed has a great influence on interest rates in the short run. When the money supply is growing too quickly or the Fed wants rates to move higher, it will direct its open-market operation to sell government securities. The added supply of securities should drive prices down and yields up. In the meantime, the Fed is draining bank reserves from the system in payment for the securities it is selling. That can reduce the money supply. Conversely, if the Fed wants to drive down rates or to boost the money supply, it will usually buy government securities.

An entire industry of Fed watchers has grown up in recent years. These economists try to anticipate the Fed's activities and to explain the reasoning behind what the Fed does. In the late 1970s and early 1980s, the securities markets became so sensitive to Federal Reserve policy that most interest rates would rise or fall whenever the Fed took any action whatsoever. Often, the market would rise or fall on the announcement of the weekly change in the money supply. If the money supply rose unexpectedly, interest rates rose in anticipation that the Fed would withdraw funds from the market and push rates up. An unanticipated drop in the money supply would send rates lower in anticipation that the Fed would buy securities. In the mid-1980s almost the opposite has been true; little attention has been paid to money growth and the focus has returned to movements in the discount rate.

INFLATION

Many economists believe that inflation expectations are built into interest rates. The basic theory is that there is a stable, ''real'' (inflation-adjusted) rate of interest that would prevail if prices were stable, and that ''nominal'' interest rates (the rates actually paid by borrowers and received by lenders) will be equal to the sum of this real rate and the expected rate of inflation.

For example, even if there were no inflation, lenders would demand compensation for giving up current purchasing power, while borrowers would be willing to pay for the credit in the expectation that they could use the money productively. The interest rate paid under these conditions—of zero inflation—is called the real rate of interest. History suggests that the real rate of interest for long-term corporate borrowing in the United States has been approximately 3 percent. For short-term securities, the real rate has been much lower.

On the other hand, when consumer prices are rising, lenders demand a higher rate to compensate for their lost purchasing power, while borrowers are willing to pay higher rates because they will be paying back the loan in the future with money that has lost value. If investors expected inflation to stay at 4 percent for the life of a bond, for example, they would demand an additional 4 percent in interest on top of the real rate. According to this view, the 4 percent "inflation premium" plus the real rate of interest would approximate the long-term nominal interest rate, under these conditions.

Because future inflation cannot be known with certainty, the degree to which inflation is built into nominal interest rates reflects investors' and borrowers' long-run expectations of inflation. Even short-term interest rates respond to these expectations. Most economists do agree that, for whatever reasons, as the inflation rate rises, so will interest rates. A clear indication of the direction of inflation is one of the most important factors in forecasting the level of interest rates.

THE NATION'S FLOW OF FUNDS

Interest rates are essentially the prices of different kinds of credit—prices that tend to equalize the supply and demand for credit throughout the economy. If there is a high demand for credit, interest rates will rise. This simultaneously makes it more costly to borrow (thereby reducing credit demand) and attracts prospective lenders (increasing credit supply). If demand for credit falls, the opposite results occur.

Changes in the supply of credit will affect interest rates in the opposite way. More funds available to buy securities will push rates down. Many economists at brokerage firms and banks closely analyze the nation's capital flows to forecast interest rates. The object is to project the major demands for borrowing, on one hand, and to project the major sources of the supply of lending, on the other. The projections, of course, are closely related to forecasts of the business cycle in general.

The Federal Reserve publishes an invaluable series of accounts to facilitate such an analysis. It is called the "Flow of Funds," and traces just how money flows through the entire economy. With this tool, economists attempt to forecast the various components of the supply and demand for credit. Unusually heavy needs on the part of municipalities or the federal government, for example, can be assessed in this light. Heavy demand from these borrowers may be offset by diminished borrowing needs on the part of corporations. Regarding credit supply, economists can get a better notion of just how much strain will be placed on different kinds of financial institutions, as well as on the direct money and capital markets themselves. Any great increase in the demand for money by major institutions would lead to a tightening in the availability of credit and to higher interest rates.

In 1988, total credit supplied came to $839.8 billion, a level only exceeded in 1985 and 1986, years in which the credit markets were affected by the impending implementation of the Tax Reform Act of 1986 (see Figure 8-2). The Act had far reaching implications for the credit markets and as such caused distortions in the supply and demand for funds. The demand for credit increased sharply in 1985, and to a lesser extent in 1986, as borrowers rushed to fund their capital needs before the effective date of the Act. The supply of credit declined after these aberrations and totalled $757.1 billion in 1987, a decrease of 17% and 15% from the levels in 1985 and 1986, respectively. Of particular note is the amount of credit supplied by foreign investors. Their investment has increased substantially since 1983, rising almost five fold from $17.0 to $83.5 billion. This increase can be attributed to the United States' continuing trade deficits which have increased the wealth of its trading partners and the relatively high returns available on de-nominated assets, both of which make U.S. investments attractive to foreigners.

Term Structure of Interest Rates

Why do fixed-income securities of about the same risk but with different maturities trade at different yields? The relationship between yield and maturity among bonds of different maturities is known as the term structure of interest rates. This relationship can be represented graphically by what is known as a "yield curve."

A yield curve for government securities is given in Figure 8-3. The vertical axis shows the yield and the horizontal axis marks the years to maturity. Following the curve across to the vertical axis, one can see that a security maturing within one year would yield 6.03 percent, whereas a 20-year bond would yield 7.74 percent. The points that make up the curve are the actual yields for securities with the stated number of years left to maturity.

The yield curve in Figure 8-3 is typical because it is positively, or upwardly, sloped. The yield curve is usually more positively sloped when the economy is near its cyclical low in a recession. Short-term rates are particularly low at that point. When the economy is at its peak growth rate and starting to strain its resources, the yield curve is usually inverted. A sample curve taken in 1981 (see Figure 8-4) shows how short-term rates were higher than long-term rates as money tightened at the height of economic growth. Short-term rates tend to fluctuate much more widely over an interest rate cycle than do long-term rates.

FIGURE 8-2. The Supply and Demand for Credit

($ in billions)

	Annual Net Increases in Amounts Outstanding, Dollars in Billions					
	1983	1984	1985	1986	1987	1988
Net Demand						
Privately Held Mortgages	$100.2	$145.0	$133.3	$142.3	$157.8	$178.9
Corporate & Foreign Bonds	43.7	83.9	124.6	163.6	140.5	133.2
Total Long-Term Private	143.9	228.9	258.0	305.9	296.3	312.1
Short-Term Business Borrowing	52.6	141.3	116.5	114.3	74.5	161.1
Short-Term Other Borrowing	58.0	88.4	96.2	61.3	39.0	62.9
Total Short-Term Private	110.6	229.6	212.7	175.5	113.4	224.0
Privately Held Federal Debt	240.0	260.5	286.9	363.1	307.7	243.8
Tax-Exempt Notes and Bonds	51.6	87.5	159.2	47.0	37.7	59.8
Total Government Debt	291.6	348.0	446.2	410.1	345.4	303.6
Total Net Demand for Credit	$546.2	$806.6	$916.9	$891.5	$757.1	$839.8
Net Supply						
Thrift Institutions	$135.6	$150.2	$83.0	$105.5	$140.4	$107.0
Insurance and Pensions	100.6	123.0	151.1	182.8	215.4	226.6
Investment Companies	−6.3	69.2	86.5	161.7	23.5	23.5
Other Nonbank Finance	24.0	65.1	63.5	74.0	16.1	45.2
Total Nonbank Finance	253.8	407.6	384.0	524.1	395.4	402.3
Commercial Banks	139.9	170.8	206.9	194.5	124.5	158.5
Nonfinancial Corporations	21.3	23.9	15.7	31.6	10.8	−1.4
State and Local Governments	27.0	26.8	66.7	41.8	41.2	22.5
Foreign Investors	17.0	30.2	24.6	49.1	48.0	83.5
Subtotal	459.1	659.3	697.9	841.1	619.9	665.3
Residual: Households Direct	87.1	147.3	219.0	50.4	137.2	174.5
Total Net Supply of Credit	$546.2	$806.6	$916.9	$891.5	$757.1	$839.8
Memo						
Net Issuance Corporate Stock	$25.8	−$81.7	−$61.9	−$64.1	−$138.4	−$153.6
Total Credit and Stock	572.0	724.9	855.0	827.3	618.7	686.2
Percentage of Total Absorbed by						
Households	45.5%	46.0%	42.5%	46.1%	57.8%	50.9%
Nonfinancial Business	13.9	9.6	6.5	8.0	−3.0	4.5
Financial Institutions	5.3	10.3	12.5	14.1	15.9	13.0
Government	35.6	34.2	38.2	30.6	27.6	27.3
Foreigners	−0.3	−0.2	0.3	1.3	1.7	4.4

SOURCE: Salomon Brothers Inc

Interest rates are essentially the prices that will equalize the supply and demand for credit, and a detailed look at credit flow is an important tool for forecasting rates.

FIGURE 8-3. The Yield Curve

The Term Structure of Interest Rates for U.S. Government Securities, December 1986

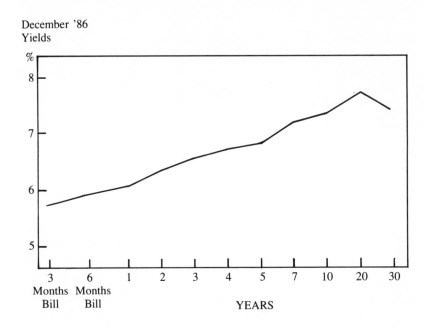

The yield curve, which plots the interest rates of securities with equivalent risk but different maturities, typically slopes upward; the longer the maturity, the higher the rate.

Several theories attempt to explain the shape of the yield curve. A summary of the most important ones follows.

EXPECTATIONS

A theory to which most economists adhere in one form or another is that investors' and borrowers' expectations of future changes in interest rates are the primary determinants of the term structure of rates. The theory in its pure form assumes that investors seek to maximize their returns, regardless of the maturity

FIGURE 8-4. Inverted Yield Curve

The Term Structure of Interest Rates for U.S. Treasury Securities, February 1981

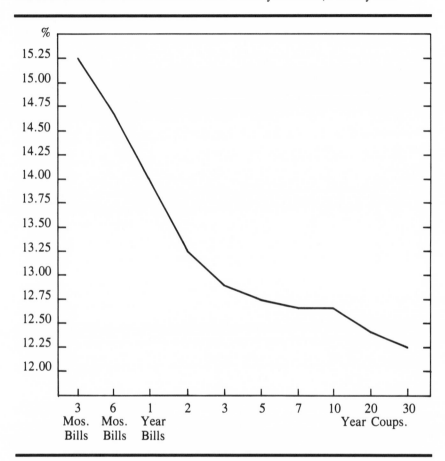

SOURCE: Merrill Lynch Securities Research Division

Occasionally, the yield curve is inverted with short-term rates higher than longer-term rates. This occurs when the economy is near the peak rate of growth and the availability of credit tightens significantly.

of the fixed-income securities they buy. Borrowers too are considered indifferent to the maturity of their debt. As a result, the long-term interest rate becomes the average of the current short-term rate and the expected level of future short-term rates. As expectations of short-term rate levels change, so do current levels of both short-term and long-term rates.

For example, when investors expect short-term rates to rise more than the general market does, some will buy short-term securities and sell longer-term securities, reasoning that they will earn a better return by rolling over their short-term investments than by keeping their funds in long-term securities. Their action forces current short-term yields down as they buy, and longer-term yields up as they sell. As a result, borrowers seek out longer-term loans in anticipation that short-term rates will be higher in the future. This move on the part of borrowers, together with the decrease in investors' demand for long-term debt (and increase in its supply), drives long-term rates up, while the accompanying rise in investors' demand for short-term debt (and drop in its supply) forces short-term rates down. The result is that the yield curve slopes upward more steeply, reflecting expectations that interest rates will indeed be higher in the future.

When investors and borrowers expect short-term rates to decline more than the general market does, the opposite result occurs. Investors sell their short-term securities and buy longer-term securities because they believe the return will be greater. Borrowers defer their longer-term debt issues and instead borrow short term. Their combined actions cause short-term rates to rise and longer-term rates to fall, so that the yield curve flattens or turns downward.

LIQUIDITY PREFERENCE

One major problem with this theory, say many economists, is that longer-term securities fluctuate more in price than short-term securities when interest rates shift. If yields rise, the price of a long-term security falls much more than that of a short-term security. The investor who wants to sell may have to take a significant loss.

These economists claim that, to make up for the risk of interest rate fluctuations, yields for longer-term securities must be higher than the expectations theory described above implies. The longer the maturity, the greater this premium. If investors and lenders all believe that future short-term rates will equal current short-term rates, the expectations theory predicts that the yield curve will be flat. Those who believe there must be a risk premium argue that the curve will still be sloped upward.

SEGMENTED MARKETS

At the other end of the theoretical spectrum are those economists who believe that interest rates are primarily a function of the supply and demand for bonds at different maturities. These economists argue that most investors and borrowers will not be willing to shift into different maturities simply because yields change.

They will tend to buy and sell within a range of maturities for a variety of reasons. Banks, for example, tend to lend in shorter-term ranges. The supply and demand for funds at those maturities would then be the principal determinant of rates.

At one point, for example, there may be a very light investment demand for securities with maturities between five and ten years. Or it may happen that very few borrowers come to market with issues that mature in more than 20 years. In each of these so-called segmented markets, rates will be set independently of what is going on in other maturities, claim proponents of this theory. The greater the supply of bonds compared to demand in a maturity, the higher the rate will be, regardless of rates for other maturities. Conversely, the smaller the supply, the lower the rate. In this view, then, the shape of the yield curve will depend mostly on the supply and demand for securities at different maturities.

Municipal Bond Rates

Economists generally take all the above factors into consideration when making forecasts of the overall level and term structure of interest rates. The municipal bond market, however, has several special features that must be emphasized. By far the most important of these is the unusual nature of the demand for municipal securities. As discussed in Chapter 6, the advantages of the tax exemption historically limited the universe of investors to commercial banks, property and casualty insurance companies, and higher-income individuals.

SUPPLY AND DEMAND

Because of the specialized market for tax-exempt securities, highly cyclical demand factors are probably more important in determining municipal rates than in determining the rates of most other types of fixed-income securities. The particular characteristics of the major buyers of municipal bonds make for a cyclical pattern of demand.

Commercial banks typically were heavy buyers of municipal bonds when most interest rates were falling and in the earlier stages of an economic upturn. At that time, loan demand was not yet strong, credit was readily available, and banks had plenty of funds to invest. As rates on other securities rose faster, and as credit tightened and loan demand picked up, funds became tighter for the banks. They began to divert funds into their highly profitable loans and started liquidating some municipal bond holdings. Moreover, they preferred short- and medium-term bonds because such bonds were more liquid and better matched the maturities of the banks' liabilities.

Casualty insurance companies have also purchased municipal securities in a cyclical pattern. The level of their purchases depends mostly on their taxable profits. Profits are strongest when inflation is stable or after regulatory commissions grant rate increases. As inflation rises, the value of claims against insurance companies also rises, which squeezes profits. Inflation often peaks at the top of, or for several months after, a downturn in the business cycle. Insurance companies then typically start to reduce their purchases. Such companies, which owned about 19.1 percent of all municipal securities outstanding in 1989, usually made their heaviest purchases later in the business cycle than did commercial banks. They tended to buy long-term bonds and lower-quality bonds than banks did. Insurance companies have tended to be major purchasers of revenue bonds.

Individual investors generally are the last in the business cycle to start buying heavily. Their major inducement is high interest rates. As rates move up, individuals jump aboard and can be purchasing the majority of municipal bonds when rates are at their very highest.

The emergence of open-end municipal bond funds has altered this pattern somewhat. Sold in much the same way that equity mutual funds are sold, they tend to attract a lot of money when the net asset value of the fund is rising—that is, when interest rates are falling and bond prices are rising. The purchasing power of such bond funds may be greatest when bond prices are near their peaks and yields are at cyclical lows. Consequently, as economic expansion proceeds and rates increase, bond funds will sell some of their holdings.

Figure 8-5 shows the flow of funds during the period 1984 to 1989.

CAPITAL GAINS TAX EFFECTS

One other factor that has a different effect on municipal rates than on the rates of other securities is the treatment of capital gains. Although municipal bond interest payments are tax-exempt, capital gains earned upon selling bonds are taxed. [The one exception is original-issue discounts (see Chapter 6).] The buyer of a discount municipal bond, for example, will receive his or her interest payments tax-free. But when the bond is cashed in at maturity, the difference between the par value and the original purchase price of the bonds will be subject to federal income tax.

The Differences in Municipal Rates

The special characteristics of the municipal bond market result in two distinct differences between municipal and other rates.

FIGURE 8-5. Net Changes in the Holdings of State and Local Government Securities by Major Investing Groups, 1984-1989

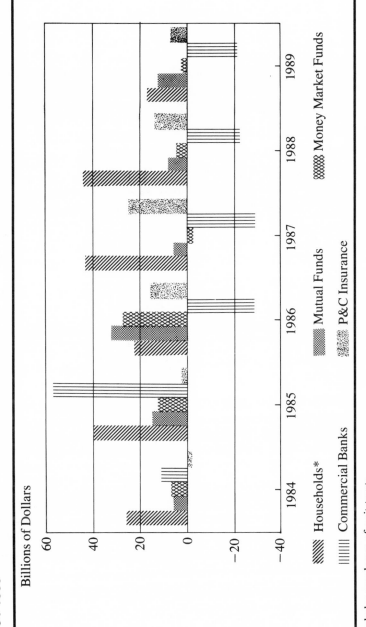

Billions of Dollars

Households*   Mutual Funds   Money Market Funds

Commercial Banks   P&C Insurance

*Includes purchases of unit trusts.

SOURCE: Federal Reserve Board

VOLATILITY

In percentage terms, municipal rates are generally more volatile than other rates. A casual observation of Figure 8-1 reveals how much wider the yield fluctuations are for the Bond Buyer Index than for U.S government securities. Several more sophisticated studies have corroborated this.

The causes of the volatility have already been discussed. The cyclical pattern of demand for municipal securities adds volatility to the market. Corporate and government bonds fluctuate less, because the base of demand for taxable instruments is greater and because changes in tax rates have no effect on many of the large institutional buyers who dominate the taxable market.

FIGURE 8-6. Yield Curve for Municipal Securities*

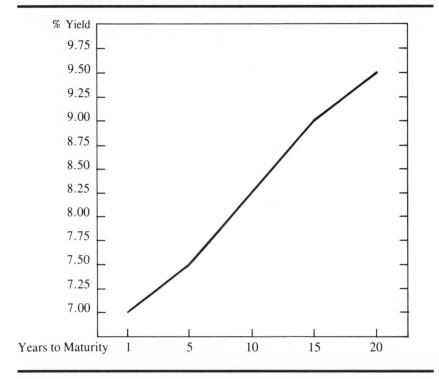

SOURCE: Merrill Lynch Securities Research Division

* Moody's Aaa-rated general obligation securities, average new-issue reoffering yields, February 1981

UPWARD-SLOPING YIELD CURVES

The yield curve for municipal bonds is almost always upward-sloping, even when interest rates are near cyclical peaks. A sample yield curve from 1981 is shown in Figure 8-6. By contrast, the 1981 yield curve for Treasury securities, shown in Figure 8-4, slopes downward, reflecting the market's expectation that future rates would fall.

The composition of demand is the main reason for this upward-sloping curve. Short-term instruments trade very close to the after-tax return for corporations and individuals in the highest tax brackets, except during brief periods of abnormally heavy supply of short-term instruments or seasonal withdrawal of assets from money funds.

Long-term municipal securities will trade at somewhat higher relative rates. Even if the market expects rates in general to fall (when the corporate yield curve would be downward-sloping), the municipal yield curve would generally slope upward. The primary reasons are: (1) the greater volatility of longer-term municipal bonds, (2) the heavy supply of intermediate- and long-term bonds as a percentage of the total market, and (3) the relatively limited demand for longer-term securities by purchasers of tax-exempt bonds.

9

Regulatory and Disclosure Requirements

Federal Regulation of Municipal Securities Transactions

Until the late 1960s the municipal securities market was relatively free of federal legislative restrictions, and the issuance of municipal securities was not subject to extensive regulation by any federal agency. Since the enactment of the Sixteenth Amendment to the U.S. Constitution in 1913 authorizing the modern federal income tax system, each version of the Internal Revenue Code enacted by Congress had expressly exempted interest on municipal securities from federal income taxation. Similarly, when Congress enacted the Securities Act of 1933, the Securities Exchange Act of 1934, and related laws governing securities transactions, it expressly exempted municipal securities and the issuers of municipal securities from the registration, reporting and regulatory requirements imposed by those federal securities laws.

Beginning in the late 1960s and early 1970s, federal involvement in the municipal securities markets significantly increased, and it has continued to grow. This involvement has occurred in two distinct areas: the enactment of federal tax laws and the promulgation of Treasury regulations restricting the types of municipal securities which qualify for the municipal securities tax exemption and imposing other requirements, and the enactment of federal securities laws providing for the development of a comprehensive regulatory scheme, under the jurisdiction of the Municipal Securities Rulemaking Board (MSRB), covering the activities of brokers and dealers in municipal securities transactions. More recently, the Securities and Exchange Commission has adopted a rule (Rule 15c2-12) imposing disclosure document review and distribution requirements on municipal securities underwriters. In connection with the publication of the Rule, the SEC also published a release setting forth its views concerning underwriter responsibilities in municipal securities offerings.

The development of federal regulatory involvement in municipal securities market activity is best understood in the broader context of federal-state relationships.

The Basis of Federal Tax Exemption

The tax-exempt status of municipal securities is closely intertwined with the development of the federal income tax system. The historical basis for the exemption initially rested upon an application of the constitutional doctrine of "intergovernmental tax immunity" and the 1895 case applying that doctrine to municipal securities, *Pollock v. Farmers' Loan and Trust Company,* also produced the need for the Sixteenth Amendment to the Constitution authorizing a modern income tax system.

At issue in *Pollock* was whether the Wilson-Gorman Tariff Act of 1894, which levied a federal tax on certain types of income, including interest on municipal securities, was constitutionally valid. Article I, Section 2 of the U.S. Constitution required that direct taxes among the states be apportioned according to population; and Article I, Section 8 of the Constitution required that indirect taxes, such as duties and imports, be uniform throughout the United States.

In *Pollock*, the Supreme Court decided that the 1894 Tariff Act was unconstitutional because taxes levied were not apportioned according to population. The court also ruled that interest on municipal securities was not subject to federal income taxation because a tax on interest would impermissibly burden state government and interfere with its power to borrow money. In so ruling, the Court reasoned that the states were "immune" from federal interference with their borrowing power, applying the doctrine of intergovernmental tax immunity. That doctrine, established in the landmark case of *McCulloch v. Maryland* (containing Justice Marshall's famous dictum, "The power to tax involves the power to destroy"), limits the ability of federal and state governments to levy taxes on each other which impermissibly intrude upon governmental sovereignty.

The *Pollock* decision produced the necessity for the Sixteenth Amendment to the U.S. Constitution in order to permit an effective federal tax structure which was not constrained by appointment and population requirements. The amendment, which was enacted by Congress and submitted to the states for ratification in 1913, reads as follows:

> The Congress shall have the power to lay and collect taxes on incomes, from whatever source derived, without apportionment among the several states, and without regard to any census or enumeration.

During the ratification process, an issue arose over the wording of the Sixteenth Amendment and its potential effect on the municipal securities tax exemption established by the *Pollock* decision. The concern was that the words authorizing a tax on incomes ''from whatever source derived'' expanded the areas of potential federal taxation to include the income on municipal securities. Several U.S. Congressmen, including sponsors of the Sixteenth Amendment, disputed that interpretation and disavowed any congressional intent to achieve that result. Thus, for example, Senator William E. Borah of Idaho stated in the Congressional Record that:

> To construe the proposed amendment so as to enable us to tax the instrumentalities of the state would do violence to the rules laid down by the Supreme Court for a hundred years, wrench the whole Constitution from its harmonious proportions and destroy the object and purpose for which the whole instrument was framed.

The Sixteenth Amendment, in the form proposed, was eventually ratified by the states. The question of whether the term ''from whatever source derived'' expanded the substantive areas of federal taxation was addressed by the Supreme Court in *Evans v. Gore*, decided in 1920, where the Court concluded:

> . . . the genesis and words of the amendment unite in showing that it does not extend the taxing power to new or excepted subjects, but merely removes all occasion otherwise existing for an apportionment among the states of taxes laid on income, whether derived from one source or another. And we have so held in other cases.

Although *Pollock* established the constitutional basis of tax exemption and later cases made clear that the Sixteenth Amendment did not expressly eliminate it, federal efforts to restrict or significantly limit the exemption have been made through the years, as discussed in the next section. Moreover, subsequent to *Pollock*, several Supreme Court decisions in other areas of federal-state relationships significantly limited the scope of the intergovernmental immunity doctrine, producing strong debate concerning the continuing vitality of *Pollock*, particularly as federal tax restrictions on municipal securities increased.

That debate led, eventually, to a challenge of federal restrictions and a reexamination of the *Pollock* holding in *South Carolina v. Baker*, decided by the

Supreme Court in 1988. In that case, South Carolina contested the provisions of the Tax Equity and Fiscal Responsibility Act of 1982 requiring most municipal securities to be issued in registered form and conditioning tax exemption upon compliance with the registration requirement. The Supreme Court upheld the validity of the provision and, in doing so, expressly overruled the *Pollock* holding that municipal bond interest is immune from a nondiscriminatory federal tax.

The *South Carolina* decision removes the claim to historical constitutional protection for the municipal securities exemption and makes the continuation of that exemption and the nature of tax restrictions generally subject to the political dynamics of the federal legislative processes. The Court's ruling in *South Carolina* has produced concern among some state and local governments about the need for a constitutional amendment expressly protecting the municipal securities tax exemption from federal intrusion.

Federal Tax Legislation Affecting Municipal Securities

Although the first Internal Revenue Code enacted after the adoption of the Sixteenth Amendment contained a specific stated exemption for interest on municipal securities, federal efforts to constrict or eliminate that exemption began and continued after that enactment. Thus, the House of Representatives passed a proposed constitutional amendment in 1923 to authorize the taxation of income derived from future issues of municipal securities, but the proposal failed to pass the Senate. Other federal attempts to tax municipal bonds were made in the 1930s and 1940s without success. For example, during consideration of the Revenue Revision of 1942, the Treasury Department strongly urged the imposition of a tax upon the interest on all state and municipal bond issues, including both present and future issues. This proposal was rejected by the U.S. House of Representatives Committee on Ways and Means but was accepted by the Senate Finance Committee with respect to future issues. After extensive debate on the floor of the Senate, this proposal was defeated and stricken from the bill. In 1969, the House passed a bill that included interest earned on all municipal securities within its minimum-tax provisions. The Senate did not accept the measure. Finally, in the late 1970s, a number of proposals were made in Congress to give municipal issuers the option of issuing taxable securities and receiving an interest subsidy from the federal government. Proposals of this nature (called the Taxable Bond Option) were opposed by municipal issuers who feared that federal intervention would accompany the subsidies.

Although there have not been, since the Taxable Bond Option proposals of the late 1970s, any general federal legislative attempts to eliminate completely, or to provide a substitution for, the municipal securities tax exemption, the federal statutory authorization for such exemption has been the subject of significant restrictions. This process began in 1968 with enactment by Congress of the industrial development bond statute restricting the uses for which industrial development bonds could be issued and still retain the federal tax exemption. The list of eligible uses included in that statute, as amended, included residential real property for family units; sports facilities; convention or trade show facilities; airports, docks, wharves, mass commuting facilities, parking facilities, or storage or training facilities directly related to any of the foregoing; sewage or solid waste disposal facilities or facilities for the local furnishing of electric energy or gas; air or water pollution control facilities; facilities for the furnishing of water under certain conditions; development of industrial parks; and "small issue" industrial development bonds that are subject to dollar-amount limitations.

In 1969, Congress eliminated the statutory exemption for "arbitrage bonds"— that is, municipal securities whose proceeds were used to acquire other securities with a yield greater than the yield on the municipal securities. Congress was concerned that some state and local governments were misusing the tax exemption by investing the proceeds from bond issues in higher-yielding federal or other obligations, the interest on which was not taxable in their hands. Both the industrial development bond and the arbitrage bond statutes have spawned extensive and intricate Treasury regulations governing the statutory concepts and their application to particular instances.

Further and increasingly extensive federal tax regulation of municipal securities occurred in 1980, with the enactment of the Mortgage Subsidy Board Tax Act which imposed substantial limits and requirements on tax-exempt residential mortgage bonds; in 1982, with the enactment of the Tax Equity and Fiscal Responsibility Act, which imposed additional industrial development and arbitrage bond restrictions and required all municipal securities to be issued in registered form; and in 1984, with the enactment of the Deficit Reduction Act which, among other things, imposed volume limitations on private activity bonds and other restrictions. Finally, as summarized in the next section, with the enactment of the Tax Reform Act of 1986, Congress restructured and further added substantially to the provisions governing the issuance of municipal securities.

The Current Statutory Exemption

The Tax Reform Act of 1986 continues the basic exemption for interest on municipal securities set forth in Section 103 of the Internal Revenue Code of 1954.

However, the 1986 Act significantly added to and changed prior law by imposing new restrictions on all types of municipal securities, further expanding the definition of "private activity" bonds, further restricting the aggregate volume of private activity bonds, and imposing new arbitrage-related restrictions and procedures.

Although any discussion of the full detail of the provision of the 1986 Internal Revenue Code applicable to municipal securities is beyond the scope of this book, certain basic concepts are important and can be broadly, if imprecisely, summarized. In general, Section 103 of the 1986 Internal Revenue Code exempts interest on any municipal security except for certain specified "private activity bonds" and "arbitrage bonds."

Private activity bonds under the 1986 Code include all municipal securities, irrespective of the purpose for which they are issued or the source of payment, if 10 percent or more of the proceeds will be used to finance property which will be used by any private entity and if more than 10 percent of the proceeds of the issue will be secured by property or payments used in a private entity's trade or business. These two tests—the "private business use test" and the "security interest test"—must be examined in connection with the issuance of any municipal security. For example, care must be taken that municipal securities issued to finance a government office building do not violate the tests by virtue of underlying leasing and operating arrangements. Any municipal security which is a private activity bond will not be tax-exempt unless it falls within the category of a "qualified bond" under the 1986 Code and meets other requirements. Qualified bonds include those issued for "exempt facilities" such as publicly owned airports, docks, wharves and mass commuting facilities; water-furnishing facilities; sewage facilities; certain solid waste disposal facilities; qualified hazardous waste facilities; qualified residential rental projects; facilities for the local furnishing of electric energy or gas; and local district heating or cooling facilities. Qualified bonds also include municipal securities meeting specific tax law requirements and issued to finance qualified residential mortgages, qualified veterans' residential mortgages, qualified small issue industrial development projects for manufacturing and farming purposes, qualified student loans, qualified redevelopment projects, and qualified expenditures of 501(c)(3) organizations, such as hospitals and educational institutions.

Among the additional restrictions which apply to qualified private activity bonds are specified state volume limitations imposed on an annual basis, public hearing requirements, informational reporting requirements, and restrictions on the amount of proceeds which can be used other than for qualifying expenditures. In addition, certain restrictions applicable to all municipal securities, such as the arbitrage requirements discussed below, also apply to private activity bonds.

The second major area of restriction—applicable to all municipal securities—is that of the arbitrage restrictions. The arbitrage restrictions essentially preclude investment of the proceeds of municipal securities in higher-yielding securities. There are limited exceptions to this general rule for temporary periods, for reasonably required reserve funds not exceeding 10 percent of proceeds, and for a minor portion of bond proceeds. In addition, and importantly, the 1986 Code requires, with limited exceptions, that *all* earnings on bond proceeds derived from investments with a yield higher than the bond rate be paid to the federal government at specified intervals. The exceptions from this rebate requirement include an exception for municipal securities issues where all the proceeds are expended for the applicable governmental purpose within six months after the date of the issue and an exception for certain small-volume issues.

The 1986 Code also imposes restrictions on the advance refunding of municipal securities—that is, securities issued to retire an outstanding issue of securities prior to its maturity date. Among other things, the 1986 Code prohibits the advance refunding of private activity bonds [except for obligations issued for 501(c)(3) organizations] and restricts the number of times and conditions under which all other municipal securities issues can be advance refunded.

In addition to the restrictions summarized above on the types of municipal securities eligible for the federal tax exemption and the use of the proceeds of those securities, the 1986 Code imposed a number of related restrictions affecting the municipal securities market. Thus, under the 1986 Code, interest on private activity bonds [other than 501(c)(3) obligations] issued after August 7, 1986, is treated as a preference item for purposes of computing the corporate and individual alternative minimum tax imposed by the 1986 Code. Similarly, interest on all municipal securities (whenever issued) is required to be entered into the minimum tax computation for corporations through the "book income" provisions of the 1986 Code. With limited exceptions, the 1986 Code also eliminated the prior law provision which permitted financial institutions to deduct 80 percent of the amount of interest attributable to purchasing or carrying tax-exempt obligations. The effect of these, and other provisions of the 1986 Code, has been to alter significantly investor participation in the municipal securities markets. Other discussions related to specific provisons of the Tax Reform Act of 1986 are included in Chapters 1 and 6.

Application to Municipal Securities of Federal Securities Laws

The Securities Act of 1933 established the Securities and Exchange Commission as the federal regulatory authority over the issuance and trading of securities in the national capital markets and imposed registration requirements governing the issuance of such securities. However, Congress specifically exempted municipal securities from the registration and reporting requirements of the 1933 Act. Similarly, Congress exempted persons issuing or engaging in municipal securities transactions from the reporting, registration, and related requirements of the Securities Exchange Act of 1934. The legislative history of the 1933 and 1934 Acts indicates that the basis for the municipal securities exemption stemmed from potential constitutional questions over the ability of Congress to regulate state and local governments in the issuance of securities, and from a sense that the municipal securities markets did not require the same type of regulation and oversight as the corporate capital markets.

In the early and middle 1970's, however, Congress refocused its attention on the municipal securities market as a result of the "boiler room" sales and trading practices of a few municipal securities dealers. This renewed federal oversight resulted in the enactment of the Securities Acts Amendments of 1975. Those amendments imposed registration requirements upon municipal securities dealers and established the Municipal Securities Rulemaking Board as the regulatory authority with rulemaking authority over municipal securities transactions affected by dealers.

An important issue raised during congressional consideration of the Securities Acts Amendments of 1975 was whether the legislation should also extend regulation to issuers of municipal securities. This raised the possibility of the promulgation by the SEC of disclosure requirements for municipal bond issues.

In response to those concerns, provisions were added to the 1975 Act prohibiting the SEC and the MSRB from requiring an issuer to make any filing with the SEC or MSRB prior to the sale of its securities. In addition, the "Tower Amendment" was added prohibiting the MSRB from requiring an issuer, through a broker, dealer or municipal securities dealer, to furnish information to a purchaser of its securities.

Even though the imposition of federal disclosure requirements for issuers was thus restricted by the Securities Acts Amendments of 1975, those amendments did provide for an expanded definition of the term "person" to include issuers of municipal securities for certain purposes. This change clarified any uncertainty over the applicability of the antifraud provisions under Section 10(b) of the 1934 Act to all municipal market participants, including issuers.

Proceeding under its rulemaking authority under the antifraud provisions, the SEC adopted Rule 15c2-12 effective January 1, 1990, imposing disclosure document review and distribution responsibilities upon municipal securities underwriters. In practical effect, those requirements, discussed later in this Chapter, indirectly require issuers to prepare and distribute official statements for offerings covered by the Rule to permit underwriters to comply with the requirements of the Rule.

The Municipal Securities Rulemaking Board

As noted above, in 1975, the MSRB was created as an independent, self-regulatory organization charged with primary rulemaking authority for the municipal securities industry. The MSRB's regulatory authority covers dealers, dealer banks, and brokers in municipal securities, but, as discussed earlier, its jurisdiction does not extend to the issuers of municipal securities. All market participants subject to MSRB jurisdiction are required to register with the SEC. In 1986, more than 2,400 dealers, dealer banks, and brokers were so registered. As a self-regulatory organization, the MSRB is financed not by the federal government but solely by the municipal securities industry. Its operations are supported by fees and assessments paid by firms and bank dealers engaged in the municipal securities business. These include an initial fee paid by a firm or bank dealer prior to commencing municipal securities actions, an annual fee, and an assessment fee based on the volume of new-issue underwriting in which a firm or bank dealer participates.

THE REGULATORY STRUCTURE

The MSRB was designed by Congress as the rulemaking body for the municipal market with a view to the unique nature of the municipal market and its participants—banks, securities firms engaged in a general securities business, and sole municipal firms. The MSRB is composed of 15 members. Five members represent broker-dealers, another five represent bank dealers, and the remaining five, the "public representatives," cannot be associated with or controlled by a municipal securities broker or dealer. One of the five public representatives must represent investors and another must represent issuers of municipal securities.

The initial 15 members of the Board were appointed by the SEC in September 1975. Subsequently, new Board members have been nominated and elected by the MSRB under a procedure that allows for recommendations of individuals for nomination by the industry and by interested members of the public. While not involved directly in the election procedures, the SEC must, pursuant to statute, approve the selection of public members of the Board.

The Securities Acts Amendments of 1975 grant the MSRB general rulemaking authority over municipal market participants, and specify several areas of mandatory rulemaking in which the Board is required "as a minimum" to propose and adopt rules. These enumerated areas include standards of professional qualification, rules of fair practice, record keeping, the minimum scope and frequency of periodic compliance examinations, the form and content of quotations relating to municipal securities, sales of new-issue municipal securities to related portfolios during the underwriting period, the definition of a "separately identifiable department or division of a bank" for purposes of SEC registration and enforcement of Board rules, the internal operation and administration of the board, and assessments.

The MSRB's rulemaking procedures involve several steps. Typically, the Board drafts proposals for rule changes, and asks for public comments, to be offered within 60 days. Upon adoption by the MSRB in final form, rule proposals are filed with the SEC and the federal bank regulatory agencies. Each proposed rule is published in the *Federal Register* and is subject to a public comment period of up to 35 days from the date of publication. The Board's rules are ordinarily subject to approval by the SEC prior to becoming effective. Exceptions are rules relating solely to the administration of the MSRB and to assessments that are effective upon filing but which may be rescinded by the SEC within 60 days thereafter.

Even though the MSRB is charged with primary rulemaking responsibility over municipal market professionals, the SEC retains ultimate regulatory authority and may add to or delete from the Board's rules if it finds such action necessary or appropriate.

In recognition of the existing regulatory structure for banks and securities firms, the MSRB does not have inspection or enforcement authority. Instead, the National Association of Securities Dealers, Inc., for its members, and the three federal bank regulatory agencies, as appropriate, are charged with the responsibility for inspection and enforcement of the Board's rules, which have the force of federal law under the legislation.

The Rules

The Board completed writing most of its rules within the first two years of its existence. Since the adoption of those basic rules, it has been concerned with amendments to and interpretation of the existing rules. These rules are separated into three major categories. The first two are administrative and definitional. The third group, the general rules, are the substantive rules of the Board. The details of the most important of these rules have already been discussed. A brief summary of the major rules is given below, but the descriptions are at best simplifications, meant only as a guide. According to the Board's rule G-29, all dealers must keep a copy of the rules on the premises.

Administrative Rules

The administrative rules, A-1 through A-15, cover such areas as membership, powers, and meetings of the board. The rules outline the rulemaking procedures and set fees for registered dealers, as well as rates for underwriters' assessments.

Each dealer pays an annual fee of $100. Assessments are based on the volume of underwriting a dealer had undertaken. The assessment rate at the end of 1989 was 2 cents for every $1,000 par value of bonds underwritten.

Definitional Rules

These are a short set of rules (D-1 through D-11) that provide formal definitions of certain key but legally ambiguous terms. A bank dealer, a customer, and a discretionary account, for example, are carefully defined.

General Rules

As of May 31, 1990, there were 36 general rules. (The key rules are discussed in previous chapters of this volume.) Rule G-1 defines exactly what operations qualify, under the rules, as independent dealer departments in banks. Professional qualifications are generally covered in rules G-2 through G-7. G-3 is the most far-reaching rule, classifying employees and establishing qualifying examinations. Chapter 3 discusses this rule at some length.

The principal record-keeping rule is G-8, the details of which are summarized in Chapters 4 and 5. Rule G-9 specifies how long records must be preserved, and rule G-27 designates people to be responsible for record keeping.

Syndicate practices have been among the more controversial areas of coverage. Rule G-11 lists the MSRB's requirements. They are summarized in Chapter 4. The MSRB has set uniform practices for clearing, processing, and settling transactions under rule G-12, the key points of which are summarized in Chapters 4 and 5. Rule G-15 contains requirements for written confirmations to customers, the most important of which are outlined in Chapter 5.

Rule G-13 requires that all quotations by dealers must represent actual bids and offers—that is, the dealer must be prepared to make the trade at the yield or price quoted, at the time the quotation is made. Dealers can, however, give mere indications of yields or prices when requested, as long as they make it clear that these indications are not actual quotations. Rule G-16 states that every municipal securities dealer will be examined for compliance with the rules by the assigned enforcement agency at least once every two years.

Most of the remaining rules—G-17 through G-36—are known as the fair practice rules. In the words of the Securities and Exchange Act of 1934, these are designed:

> . . . to prevent fraudulent and manipulative acts and practices, to promote just and equitable principles of trade, to foster cooperation with persons engaged in regulating, clearing, settling, processing information with respect to, and facilitating transactions in municipal securities, to remove impediments to and perfect the mechanism of a free and open market in municipal securities, and, in general, to protect investors and the public interest.

The first of these rules (G-17) states simply:

> . . . In the conduct of its municipal securities business, each broker, dealer, and municipal securities dealer shall deal fairly with all persons and shall not engage in any deceptive, dishonest, or unfair practice.

An equally important rule is rule G-19, on suitability, which requires that a dealer make "suitable" recommendations to customers. Some of the other fair practice rules involve gifts, relationships between underwriters and issuers, dissemination of official statements or similar disclosure documents, advertising, the fairness of prices and commissions, quotations, and the improper use of assets.

Rule G-35 establishes arbitration procedures for dealers and customers who have disputes or claims involving municipal securities transactions. The MSRB has written an arbitration code that provides a forum for the resolution of municipal securities disputes. The code covers the initiation for proceeedings by a dealer or customer, the conduct of hearings, and awards. A simplified procedure has been established for claims of $5,000 and less. Under rule G-35, a customer or dealer may compel another dealer to arbitrate a dispute.

On May 31, 1990 the SEC approved MSRB Rule G-36 which requires underwriters to forward to the MSRB copies of official statements and refunding documents for bond issues subject to SEC Rule 15c2-12. This rule will insure that the MSRB has the necessary disclosure documentation for its proposed repository.

Disclosure and the Antifraud Provisions of the Federal Securities Laws

Although the federal securities laws do not impose direct registration or disclosure document content requirements upon the issuers of municipal securities, a number of factors have resulted in increased efforts by municipal issuers and other municipal market participants to assure that disclosure information provided for municipal securities is as accurate, cogent, and comprehensive as possible. First, the difficulties of New York City and other major municipal issuers in the mid-1970s have resulted increasingly in investor requirements that full disclosure information about municipal securities transactions be provided. These investor requirements, together with industry concerns about potential federal imposition of regulation and disclosure requirements, have prompted municipal securities market participants to develop and follow fairly standard disclosure practices. In this connection, the Government Finance Officers Association led the development, in 1976, of "Disclosure Guidelines for State and Local Government Securities." The GFOA Guidelines, which were revised in January, 1988, have evolved into voluntary industry standards followed by many market participants in preparing municipal securities disclosure documents. Other industry initiatives, including improvements in government financial accounting and reporting under the auspices of the Government Accounting Standards Board (GASB) have also contributed to more standardized disclosure practices.

A second major factor influencing the nature and extent of disclosure in connection with municipal securities is the applicability of the antifraud provisions of both the Securities Act of 1933 (Section 17) and the Securities Exchange Act of 1934 [Section 10(b)]. It is commonly acknowledged that these provisions — which impose liability for failure to disclose material information in connection with securities offerings — do apply to municipal securities market participants, including issuers, in particular circumstances.

The SEC Staff Report concerning the Washington Public Power Supply System, released in September of 1988, refocused industry and federal agency efforts on improving municipal securities disclosure practices and developing more effective means for assuring the availability and distribution of disclosure information. Although not recommending enforcement actions against market participants, the SEC Staff Report was critical of the adequacy of disclosure practices followed in connection with Supply System financings. The conclusions reflected in the Staff Report prompted the SEC to publish and finally adopt Rule 15c2-12 imposing specific disclosure document review and distribution requirements upon municipal securities underwriters.

In general, Rule 15c2-12 requires all underwriters participating in a primary offering of municipal securities with an aggregate amount of $1 million or more to obtain and review a nearly final official statement before bidding on or purchasing the offering unless the offering qualifies for the ''limited placement'' exemption prescribed by the Rule or comprises securities having maturities or variable-rate demand features of less than nine months. The Rule also requires each participating underwriter in negotiated offerings to mail preliminary official statements to potential customers by the business day following a customer request, and to contract with an issuer for the receipt by the underwriter of final official statements in sufficient time to permit the underwriter to include a copy of that document with customer payment confirmations. Under the terms of the Rule, a participating underwriter of a municipal securities offering retains an obligation to deliver a copy of the final official statement to each potential customer upon request until specified periods following the underwriting period.

The SEC accompanied Rule 15c2-12 with an interpretative statement setting forth its views concerning the investigatory responsibilities of underwriters in reviewing official statements. In that interpretative statement, the SEC emphasized that municipal securities underwriters had a responsibility, under the antifraud provisions, to satisfy themselves concerning the accuracy of key issuer representations contained in disclosure documents. In articulating that position, the SEC declined to set forth explicit investigatory procedures for underwriters to follow. It did, however, list factors which would be relevant in determining the extent of underwriter investigatory activity in particular cases and acknowledged that competitively-bid offerings presented fewer opportunities to complete an investigatory review than negotiated municipal offerings.

It seems clear that municipal disclosure practices will continue to be the subject of industry and federal regulatory focus. An area of increasing and particular interest is the development of methods to centralize or standardize information gathering, storage and retrieval. To that end in publishing Rule 15c2-12 for comment, the SEC also solicited industry comments concerning the creation of a repository of municipal securities disclosure documents. The development of a repository, the nature of information to be submitted to it and the degree of industry participation in providing that information on a regular basis are issues that are actively under discussion by the MSRB and all municipal securities market participants. The resolution of them will significantly influence future disclosure practices in both the new-issue and secondary markets for municipal securities. As noted earlier, the MSRB under its Rule G-36 requires underwriters to send to the MSRB copies of official statements and refunding documents for bond issues subject to SEC Rule 15c2-12. This rule will insure that the MSRB has the necessary disclosure documentation for its proposed repository.

Appendix:
Mathematical Calculations

The proliferation of desk calculators, as well as the growing use of the computer, has made most hand calculations concerning municipal bonds obsolete. Desk calculators will compute bond yields and prices in a matter of seconds. They can handle virtually any combination of yield or price and time to maturity. Traditionally municipal bond calculations are made on the basis of 12 months of 30 days each and 360-day years.

Most major dealers either have their own computer programs or access to outside computer companies to make calculations on bids for new bond issues. Once a laborious process, the calculation of the bid is now almost instantaneous. The growth of more complicated types of issues, such as housing issues and advance refundings, has required still more complex calculations. The flow of funds in these issues, and the rates at which they are invested, are very important in pricing the bonds. Again, sophisticated computer programs have been developed to deal with the intricacies of these issues.

The concepts behind these calculations, however, are very important. The market value of a bond simply cannot be understood without a thorough grounding in how yields and prices are calculated. The value of a bid, similarly, cannot be understood without such fundamental principles.

Present Value Theory

The most important concept underlying most bond calculations is discounted present value. It is a way to take into account the time value of money. One dollar received today is worth more than one dollar tomorrow and a lot more than one dollar received ten years from now. The compound interest formula follows.

$$\text{Future value} = (1 + k)^n$$

The annual interest rate is k. The number of years the investment is being held is n. The investor would earn $1 + k$ in the first year. That would be reinvested and earn interest in the second year at the same rate. The total at the end of the second year is arrived at by multiplying $(1 + k)$ times $(1 + k)$. In the third year, the investor has a total of $(1 + k)^3$, and so on. With k equal to 6 percent and the investment held for ten years, the formula looks as follows.

$$\text{Future value} = (1 + .06)^{10} = 1.79$$

Finding the present value is the reverse of finding the future value. What would an investor pay today for the promise of one dollar to be paid in ten years? That depends at what rate money could be invested. Assuming it could be invested at a 6 percent rate of interest, the value today of one dollar received ten years from now is 56¢. This is known as the present value. The 6 percent rate is known as the discount rate. In other words, if an investor put 56¢ in a bank account that pays 6 percent compounded annually (which means that interest is paid and reinvested once a year), he or she will have one dollar at the end of ten years.

The equation to solve for present value is the inverse of the compound interest equation.

$$\text{Present value} \quad = \frac{1}{(1 + k)^n}$$

To find the present value of one dollar received ten years from now, we must assume a discount rate. For the above example, it is 6 percent.

$$\text{PV} = \frac{1}{(1 + .06)^{10}} = \frac{1}{1.79} = .56 = 56¢$$

THE INTERNAL RATE OF RETURN

Present value theory is used in another important way. A borrower might offer a lender one dollar seven years from now in return for a loan of 75¢ today. Alternatively, another borrower might offer one dollar in six years for 85¢ today. How does the lender compare the offers? The so-called internal rate of return must be calculated for each offer. What annual return will the investor earn if he or she puts 75¢ in the equivalent of a savings account today and withdraws one dollar in seven years? The answer is about 4 percent. It is the internal rate of return, interest compounded annually, of the first offer. What annual rate of return will be earned on 85¢ with a payoff of one dollar in six years? The answer is about 3 percent.

Clearly, the first offer is better, provided the investor does not mind keeping his money tied up for another year.

The internal rate of return cannot be computed as cleanly as the present value can. There is no algebraic formula for it. Instead, it is found by a trial-and-error search through the present value tables, a process now made instantaneous by computers and calculators. These readily available tables are compilations of the present values for a range of discount rates and maturities. An excerpt is shown in Figure A-1.

When the present value and maturity are known, the tables can be scanned for the appropriate rate of return. Although the computer will do the work, it is important to understand the process. In the lending example above, the 75¢ the lender would have to give up today is the present value. The maturity or duration of the loan is seven years. The question is what discount rate—internal rate of return—would make one dollar received in seven years equal to 75¢. The answer is found in the seven-year row of the present value table. Run across the seven-year row to .75, or, for the sake of simplicity, the closest value to .75, which in this case is .7599. Look up the column to see what the internal rate of return is. It is 4 percent. To put it another way, 75¢ (75.99¢, more precisely) invested in a savings account paying 4 percent a year, compounded annually, would be worth one dollar at the end of seven years. A very precise answer can be found by interpolating, as explained in a later section.

Yield to Maturity

Given the coupon, current price, and time to maturity, the yield to maturity is the internal rate of return an investor earns from payments of bond interest and principal, with interest compounded semiannually. The price of the bond is precisely the present value of all the cash flows—interest and principal—discounted by the yield to maturity.

As with the concept of the internal rate of return, the yield to maturity takes into account the time value of money. The current yield does not. It is simply the annual coupon payment divided by the current price of the bond. A bond with a 6 percent coupon selling for 90 has a current yield of 6.67 percent.

$$\frac{\$60}{\$900} \text{ or } \frac{.06}{.90} = .0667$$

The current yield does not take into account the gain or loss to the investor when the bonds are redeemed, either. In the case of the discount bond above, the investor will receive $100 above the purchase price at maturity. One way to

FIGURE A-1. Excerpt from Present Value Table

SCAN TABLES

PRESENT WORTH OF 1

ANNUAL COMPOUNDING

Description: This table shows what $1 to be paid in the future is worth today. Present Worth is the value today of a single payment tomorrow. Interest is computed and compounded annually.

Example: A note promising to pay $10 000 in 5 years is discounted. The discounted value of the note is $8 219.27 at a 4% rate of interest, computed and compounded annually.

YEAR	4.00 %	4.25 %	4.50 %	4.75 %	5.00 %	5.25 %	5.50 %	5.75 %
1	0.961538	0.959233	0.956938	0.954654	0.952381	0.950119	0.947867	0.945626
2	0.924556	0.920127	0.915730	0.911364	0.907029	0.902726	0.898452	0.894209
3	0.888996	0.882616	0.876297	0.870037	0.863838	0.857697	0.851614	0.845588
4	0.854804	0.846634	0.838561	0.830585	0.822702	0.814914	0.807217	0.799611
5	0.821927	0.812119	0.802451	0.792921	0.783526	0.774265	0.765134	0.756133
6	0.790315	0.779011	0.767896	0.756965	0.746215	0.735643	0.725246	0.715019
7	0.759918	0.747253	0.734828	0.722640	0.710681	0.698949	0.687437	0.676141
8	0.730690	0.716789	0.703185	0.689871	0.676839	0.664084	0.651599	0.639377
9	0.702587	0.687568	0.672904	0.658588	0.644609	0.630959	0.617629	0.604612
10	0.675564	0.659537	0.643928	0.628723	0.613913	0.599486	0.585431	0.571737
11	0.649581	0.632650	0.616199	0.600213	0.584679	0.569583	0.554911	0.540650
12	0.624597	0.606858	0.589664	0.572996	0.556837	0.541171	0.525982	0.511253
13	0.600574	0.582118	0.564272	0.547013	0.530321	0.514177	0.498561	0.483454
14	0.577475	0.558387	0.539973	0.522208	0.505068	0.488529	0.472569	0.457167
15	0.555265	0.535623	0.516720	0.498528	0.481017	0.464161	0.447933	0.432309
16	0.533908	0.513787	0.494469	0.475922	0.458112	0.441008	0.424581	0.408803
17	0.513373	0.492841	0.473176	0.454341	0.436297	0.419010	0.402447	0.386575
18	0.493628	0.472749	0.452800	0.433738	0.415521	0.398109	0.381466	0.365555
19	0.474642	0.453477	0.433302	0.414070	0.395734	0.378251	0.361579	0.345679
20	0.456387	0.434989	0.414643	0.395293	0.376889	0.359383	0.342729	0.326883
21	0.438834	0.417256	0.396787	0.377368	0.358942	0.341457	0.324862	0.309109
22	0.421955	0.400246	0.379701	0.360256	0.341850	0.324425	0.307926	0.292302
23	0.405726	0.383929	0.363350	0.343920	0.325571	0.308242	0.291873	0.276408
24	0.390121	0.368277	0.347703	0.328324	0.310068	0.292866	0.276657	0.261379
25	0.375117	0.353263	0.332731	0.313436	0.295303	0.278258	0.262234	0.247167
26	0.360689	0.338862	0.318402	0.299223	0.281241	0.264378	0.248563	0.233728
27	0.346817	0.325047	0.304691	0.285655	0.267848	0.251190	0.235605	0.221019
28	0.333477	0.311796	0.291571	0.272701	0.255094	0.238661	0.223322	0.209002
29	0.320651	0.299085	0.279015	0.260335	0.242946	0.226756	0.211679	0.197637
30	0.308319	0.286892	0.267000	0.248530	0.231377	0.215445	0.200644	0.186891

SOURCE: *The Thorndike Encyclopedia of Banking and Financial Tables*

include this in the calculation would be to amortize the discount of $100 over the ten-year life of the bond on a straight-line basis. This would come to $10 a year. But it is a misleading calculation because the investor does not have use of the $100 over ten years. The yield to maturity does account for both the timing and amount of interest and principal payments. To use the savings account analogy again, it is the annual rate of return the investor would earn if he or she put the $900 paid for the bond into a savings account, received a check every six months that represented semiannual interest payments of $30, and withdrew $1,000 at the end of ten years. The answer is easily found with a bond calculator and almost as easily in the basis books published by the Financial Publishing Company, in Boston. As with any internal rate of return, there is no direct algebraic formula to compute yield to maturity. The answer is approximately 7.50 percent, as can be seen in Figure A-2.

The yield to maturity on a premium bond is handled similarly. A 6 percent ten-year bond bought at 110 has a lower yield to maturity than current yield. The investor paid $1,100 for the bond and will receive only $1,000 back if it is held to maturity. The current yield is 5.45 percent. Again, the premium could be amortized on a straight-line basis, reducing each interest payment for the sake of computation by $10 a year. But that distorts the true picture. The yield to maturity is the internal rate of return that an investment of $1,100 is earning from semiannual interest payments of $30 and a return of principal in ten years of $1,000—it is about 4.75 percent.

To repeat, yield to maturity calculations for most bonds assume that interest is being compounded semiannually. Also, interest paid is assumed to be reinvested at the same rate for all present-value-type calculations. If an investor knows that this will not be the case, adjustments can and should be made to the calculations to get a truer internal rate of return.

Calculating the Yield to Maturity

To understand fully just how the yield to maturity is calculated, it is necessary to demonstrate how the price of a bond is found when the yield to maturity is known. Municipal bonds are generally quoted in terms of yield to maturity. The investor or dealer can then determine the price of the bond. The price of a bond is precisely the sum of the present values of the cash flows—interest and principal—discounted by the yield to maturity. For example, if a bond quoted at a 7 percent yield to maturity has a coupon of 6 percent and is due in three years, the price will be the sum of the present values of each semiannual interest payment of $30, plus the present value of $1,000 received in three years, all discounted by 7 percent. In other words, what would an investor have to put up now to earn a 7 percent annual return, compounded semiannually, from interest of $30 received every six months

FIGURE A-2. Excerpt from a Basis Book

YEARS and MONTHS   6% ↓

Yield	8-3	8-6	8-9	9-0	9-3	9-6	9-9	10-0
4.00	113.93	114.29	114.64	114.99	115.33	115.68	116.01	116.35
4.20	112.43	112.76	113.06	113.37	113.67	113.98	114.27	114.58
4.40	110.96	111.24	111.51	111.79	112.04	112.31	112.57	112.83
4.60	109.51	109.76	109.98	110.22	110.44	110.68	110.89	111.12
4.80	108.09	108.30	108.48	108.69	108.87	109.07	109.25	109.44
5.00	106.68	106.86	107.01	107.18	107.32	107.49	107.63	107.79
5.20	105.30	105.44	105.56	105.69	105.81	105.94	106.05	106.18
5.40	103.94	104.05	104.13	104.23	104.31	104.41	104.49	104.59
5.60	102.60	102.68	102.73	102.80	102.85	102.92	102.96	103.03
5.80	101.29	101.33	101.35	101.39	101.41	101.45	101.46	101.50
6.00	99.99	100.00	99.99	100.00	99.99	100.00	99.99	100.00
6.10	99.35	99.34	99.32	99.32	99.29	99.29	99.26	99.26
6.20	98.71	98.69	98.65	98.64	98.60	98.58	98.54	98.53
6.30	98.08	98.05	97.99	97.96	97.91	97.88	97.83	97.80
6.40	97.45	97.41	97.34	97.30	97.23	97.19	97.12	97.08
6.50	96.83	96.77	96.69	96.63	96.55	96.50	96.42	96.37
6.60	96.22	96.14	96.05	95.98	95.88	95.81	95.72	95.66
6.70	95.61	95.52	95.41	95.33	95.22	95.14	95.03	94.96
6.80	95.00	94.90	94.78	94.68	94.56	94.47	94.35	94.26
6.90	94.40	94.28	94.15	94.04	93.91	93.80	93.68	93.58
7.00	93.80	93.67	93.53	93.41	93.26	93.15	93.01	92.89
7.10	93.21	93.07	92.91	92.78	92.62	92.49	92.34	92.22
7.20	92.62	92.47	92.30	92.15	91.98	91.84	91.68	91.55
7.30	92.03	91.87	91.69	91.53	91.35	91.20	91.03	90.89
7.40	91.46	91.28	91.09	90.92	90.73	90.57	90.38	90.23 ←
7.50	90.88	90.70	90.49	90.31	90.11	89.94	89.74	89.58
7.60	90.31	90.11	89.89	89.71	89.49	89.31	89.11	88.93
7.70	89.75	89.54	89.31	89.11	88.88	88.69	88.48	88.29
7.80	89.18	88.97	88.72	88.51	88.28	88.08	87.85	87.66
7.90	88.63	88.40	88.14	87.92	87.68	87.47	87.23	87.03
8.00	88.07	87.83	87.57	87.34	87.09	86.87	86.62	86.41
8.10	87.53	87.28	87.00	86.76	86.50	86.27	86.01	85.79
8.20	86.98	86.72	86.44	86.19	85.91	85.67	85.41	85.18
8.30	86.44	86.17	85.88	85.62	85.33	85.09	84.81	84.58
8.40	85.90	85.63	85.32	85.05	84.76	84.50	84.22	83.98
8.50	85.37	85.08	84.77	84.49	84.19	83.93	83.64	83.38
8.60	84.84	84.55	84.22	83.94	83.63	83.35	83.05	82.79
8.70	84.32	84.01	83.68	83.39	83.07	82.78	82.48	82.21
8.80	83.80	83.48	83.14	82.84	82.51	82.22	81.91	81.63
8.90	83.29	82.96	82.61	82.30	81.96	81.66	81.34	81.06
9.00	82.77	82.44	82.08	81.76	81.41	81.11	80.78	80.49
9.10	82.27	81.92	81.55	81.23	80.87	80.56	80.22	79.92
9.20	81.76	81.41	81.03	80.70	80.34	80.02	79.67	79.37
9.30	81.26	80.90	80.52	80.17	79.80	79.48	79.12	78.81
9.40	80.76	80.40	80.00	79.65	79.28	78.94	78.58	78.26
9.50	80.27	79.90	79.50	79.14	78.75	78.41	78.05	77.72
9.60	79.78	79.40	78.99	78.63	78.23	77.89	77.51	77.18
9.70	79.30	78.91	78.49	78.12	77.72	77.37	76.99	76.65
9.80	78.82	78.42	77.99	77.62	77.21	76.85	76.46	76.12
9.90	78.34	77.93	77.50	77.12	76.70	76.34	75.94	75.60
10.00	77.86	77.45	77.01	76.62	76.20	75.83	75.43	75.08
10.20	76.93	76.50	76.05	75.64	75.21	74.83	74.41	74.05
10.40	76.00	75.56	75.10	74.68	74.24	73.84	73.42	73.04
10.60	75.09	74.64	74.16	73.73	73.28	72.87	72.44	72.05
10.80	74.20	73.73	73.24	72.80	72.33	71.92	71.47	71.08
11.00	73.31	72.84	72.34	71.88	71.41	70.98	70.53	70.12
11.20	72.45	71.96	71.44	70.98	70.49	70.06	69.60	69.19
11.40	71.59	71.09	70.57	70.10	59.60	69.15	68.68	68.26
11.60	70.75	70.24	69.70	69.22	68.71	68.26	67.78	67.36
11.80	69.91	69.40	68.85	68.36	67.85	67.39	66.90	66.47
12.00	69.10	68.57	68.01	67.52	66.99	66.53	66.03	65.59

SOURCE: Reproduced from Publication No. 83, *Expanded Bond Values Tables,* Copyright 1970, Page 589, Financial Publishing Company, Boston, Massachusetts.

and return of principal of $1,000 in three years? The problem can be formulated as follows.

Time from the Purchase	Cash Received	Present Value at a Discount Rate of 7%
6 months	$ 30.00	$ 28.99
12 months	30.00	28.01
18 months	30.00	27.06
24 months	30.00	26.14
30 months	30.00	25.26
36 months	$1,030.00	837.91
Total	$1,180.00	$973.36*

The total cash payments come to $1,180. But the sum of the present values—which is the price of the bond—is only $973.36.

Bond calculators will compute prices. Knowing the yield to maturity, coupon, and time to maturity, one can also merely look for the right price in a basis book. *As shown in the short excerpted page from the basis book in Figure A-3, the price, $973.40, is the same as the sum of the present values found above, except for errors due to rounding.

To find the yield to maturity when the price is known is simply the reverse of this process. The price of the bond is the present value of all future payments. In the above example, had the price of 97.34 been known, the yield to maturity would be found by hunting for the discount rate that would produce a sum of present values equal to 973.40. As pointed out in the section on internal rate of return, a trial-and-error search is unavoidable if computed by hand. For a 6 percent ten-year bond bought at 90, the present value of all future cash flows must come to 900. To find the yield to maturity, a discount rate would have to be applied to each semiannual payment to derive the present value. If the sum of these present values did not equal 900, another rate would be tried, and so on.

Interpolation

Before the sophisticated desk calculator, the basis book was an essential tool for all professionals in the municipal bond industry. In practice, however, no matter how detailed the basis book, all permutations are not recorded. Basis books typically record the values for bonds with increments in yields of .05 percent. Occasionally, municipal bonds are quoted in increments of $1/8$ of 1 percent, or other odd rates. Maturities are usually broken down on a monthly basis. But most frequently, a bond will have an odd number of days to maturity.

FIGURE A-3. Excerpt from a Basis Book

6%			**YEARS** and MONTHS				
Yield	2-9	2-10	2-11	3-0	3-1	3-2	3-3	3-4
4.00	105.15	105.30	105.45	105.60	105.74	105.89	106.03	106.18
4.20	104.62	104.75	104.89	105.02	105.15	105.28	105.41	105.54
4.40	104.09	104.21	104.33	104.45	104.56	104.67	104.79	104.90
4.60	103.57	103.67	103.78	103.89	103.98	104.07	104.17	104.27
4.80	103.05	103.14	103.23	103.32	103.40	103.48	103.56	103.65
5.00	102.53	102.60	102.68	102.75	102.82	102.89	102.96	103.03
5.20	102.02	102.07	102.13	102.20	102.25	102.30	102.35	102.41
5.40	101.50	101.55	101.59	101.64	101.68	101.72	101.76	101.80
5.60	101.00	101.03	101.06	101.09	101.11	101.14	101.16	101.19
5.80	100.49	100.51	100.52	100.54	100.55	100.56	100.57	100.59
6.00	99.99	99.99	99.99	100.00	99.99	99.99	99.99	99.99
6.10	99.74	99.73	99.73	99.73	99.72	99.71	99.70	99.69
6.20	99.49	99.48	99.47	99.46	99.44	99.42	99.41	99.40
6.30	99.24	99.22	99.21	99.19	99.16	99.14	99.12	99.10
6.40	98.99	98.97	98.94	98.92	98.89	98.86	98.83	98.81
6.50	98.75	98.71	98.68	98.66	98.62	98.58	98.54	98.51
6.60	98.50	98.46	98.42	98.39	98.34	98.30	98.26	98.22
6.70	98.26	98.21	98.17	98.13	98.07	98.02	97.97	97.93
6.80	98.01	97.96	97.91	97.86	97.80	97.74	97.69	97.64
6.90	97.77	97.71	97.65	97.60	97.53	97.47	97.41	97.35
7.00	97.52	97.46	97.40	97.34	97.26	97.19	97.12	97.06
7.10	97.28	97.21	97.14	97.07	96.99	96.92	96.84	96.77
7.20	97.04	96.96	96.89	96.81	96.73	96.64	96.56	96.49
7.30	96.80	96.71	96.63	96.55	96.46	96.37	96.28	96.20
7.40	96.56	96.47	96.38	96.29	96.19	96.10	96.01	95.92
7.50	96.32	96.22	96.13	96.04	95.93	95.83	95.73	95.64
7.60	96.08	95.98	95.88	95.78	95.67	95.56	95.45	95.35
7.70	95.84	95.73	95.63	95.52	95.40	95.29	95.18	95.07
7.80	95.61	95.49	95.38	95.27	95.14	95.02	94.90	94.79
7.90	95.37	95.25	95.13	95.01	94.88	94.75	94.63	94.51
8.00	95.13	95.00	94.88	94.76	94.62	94.49	94.36	94.23
8.10	94.90	94.76	94.63	94.50	94.36	94.22	94.09	93.96
8.20	94.67	94.52	94.39	94.25	94.10	93.96	93.82	93.68
8.30	94.43	94.28	94.14	94.00	93.85	93.69	93.55	93.41
8.40	94.20	94.04	93.90	93.75	93.59	93.43	93.28	93.13
8.50	93.97	93.81	93.65	93.50	93.33	93.17	93.01	92.86
8.60	93.74	93.57	93.41	93.25	93.08	92.91	92.75	92.59
8.70	93.50	93.33	93.17	93.00	92.82	92.65	92.48	92.32
8.80	93.27	93.10	92.92	92.76	92.57	92.39	92.22	92.05
8.90	93.04	92.86	92.68	92.51	92.32	92.13	91.95	91.78
9.00	92.82	92.63	92.44	92.26	92.07	91.88	91.69	91.51
9.10	92.59	92.39	92.20	92.02	91.82	91.62	91.43	91.24
9.20	92.36	92.16	91.96	91.77	91.57	91.36	91.17	90.97
9.30	92.13	91.93	91.73	91.53	91.32	91.11	90.91	90.71
9.40	91.91	91.70	91.49	91.29	91.07	90.86	90.65	90.44
9.50	91.68	91.47	91.25	91.05	90.82	90.60	90.39	90.18
9.60	91.46	91.24	91.02	90.81	90.57	90.35	90.13	89.92
9.70	91.23	91.01	90.78	90.56	90.33	90.10	89.88	89.66
9.80	91.01	90.78	90.55	90.33	90.08	89.85	89.62	89.40
9.90	90.79	90.55	90.31	90.09	89.84	89.60	89.36	89.14
10.00	90.57	90.32	90.08	89.85	89.60	89.35	89.11	88.88
10.20	90.13	89.87	89.62	89.38	89.11	88.86	88.61	88.36
10.40	89.69	89.42	89.16	98.90	88.63	88.36	88.10	87.85
10.60	89.25	88.97	88.70	88.44	88.15	87.88	87.61	87.34
10.80	88.82	88.53	88.25	87.97	87.68	87.39	87.11	86.84
11.00	88.39	88.09	87.90	87.51	87.21	86.91	86.62	86.34
11.20	87.96	87.65	87.35	87.05	86.74	86.43	86.13	85.84
11.40	87.53	87.21	86.90	86.60	86.27	85.96	85.65	85.35
11.60	87.11	86.78	86.46	86.14	85.81	85.48	85.17	84.86
11.80	86.69	86.35	86.02	85.69	85.35	85.02	84.69	84.37
12.00	86.27	85.92	85.58	85.25	84.90	84.55	84.21	83.89

SOURCE: Reproduced from Publication No. 83, *Expanded Bond Values Tables*, Copyright 1970, Page 584, Financial Publishing Company, Boston, Massachusetts.

Interpolation is used to compute prices and yields for bonds that fall between the published increments of the basis book. (Calculators can generally compute values of bonds with odd terms.) For small increments, there is very close to a constant linear relationship between yields to maturity and prices. By taking an average or proportion between two values in a bond table, the yield or price can be very closely approximated.

For example, a 5 percent bond yielding 4 percent to maturity is due in ten years and three months. The bond table shows that the price for a bond due in exactly ten years is 108.18. The price of a bond due in ten years and six months is 108.51. The price of a bond due in ten years and three months would fall precisely between those two prices. Simply take the sum of the two, which equals 216.69. Then divide by two. The price of the bond in question is 108.35.

Calculations can be made for maturities with an odd number of days by taking the proportion of those days to the period for where there are values in the bond table. If the bonds were due in ten years and 20 days, price or yield would lie between the ten-year and ten-year-six-month values in a proportion of 20 to 180. Remember, in most municipal bond calculations, all months have 30 days. Similarly, the prices of bonds with odd yields can be found by interpolating between the given values.

Yield to Call

Most municipal bonds are issued with call provisions. This feature gives the issuer the right to redeem the bonds after a specified period of time at a specified price. The yield to call measures the yield (internal rate of return) that would be earned if the bonds were called at the call price. Typically, dealers will quote both the yield to maturity and the yield to call to investors if the yield to call is lower. In written confirmations of orders, the Municipal Securities Rulemaking Board requires that the yield to call be stated if it is lower than the yield to maturity.

A typical call provision allows the issuer to redeem the bonds ten years after they are issued at a price of 103. The yield is calculated in the same way as the yield to maturity except that the redemption price is $1,030 and the time to maturity is ten years. With such a call provision, a 6 percent 20-year bond would have a yield to call of 6.22 percent. If the above bond had been bought at the end of the fifth year at 105, its yield to call would be only 5.35 percent. Its yield to maturity at the same time would be 5.50 percent.

Capital Gains Taxes

An adjustment to yield to maturity must be made for bonds bought below par because the discount is subject to capital gains taxes. The taxes must be deducted from the principal in computing the after-tax yield to maturity. It is generally difficult for an investor to know what the capital gains tax will be when the bonds are due. This preference was eliminated for 1987 through 1990. Beginning in 1991, long-term capital gains will be taxed at a maximum rate of 28 percent, three percent lower than the maximum 31 percent statutory rate on ordinary income.

A 6 percent bond (face amount of $1,000) bought at $900 and due in 20 years would be subject to capital gains tax at maturity on the $100 difference between face amount and purchase price. Assuming a capital gains rate of 28 percent, the $100 gain at maturity would be reduced by 28 percent, or $28. The yield to maturity, then, would be computed by assuming the investor would get back $972 rather than the full $1,000. The yield to maturity, after a 28 percent tax on the accreted return, is 6.86 percent. Without capital gains tax, the yield to maturity would be 6.93 percent. The tax consequences of premium bonds are discussed in Chapter 6.

Discount Notes

Treasury bills and other short-term government securities, as well as commercial paper, are usually issued on a discounted basis. The certificate does not bear interest—that is, traditional interest payments are not made. Rather, the security is issued at a discount and then paid in full at maturity. The difference between the purchase price and the value at maturity is the interest earned.

Occasionally, short-term tax-exempt notes are issued on a discounted basis, although the practice has become rare. Computation of the interest earned is straightforward. It is the amount of the discount divided by the amount paid for the security. A $1,000 one-year note issued at $950 has a discount of $50. The investor will receive the full $1,000 in one year. The actual interest income earned equals $50/$950, or 5.26 percent. Note that the interest is always slightly more than the percentage amount of the discount because the investor is putting up less than the full amount that will be paid back.

Calculating the Bid

Computing the interest cost on a new issue generally is not a simple matter. The issuer must be able to determine which bid by competing syndicates produces a lower interest cost. This would obviously be quite straightforward for an issue with all bonds maturing at one date. The lower the coupon rate on such an issue, the lower the interest cost to the issuer, provided the bonds are not issued at a premium or discount.

But because municipal bonds are generally issued in serial maturities, the determination of the total interest cost can be quite complex. To deal with this problem, the industry developed a simplifying formula that ignores the time value of money in measuring interest costs. The computation, known as the net interest cost (NIC), can be calculated relatively quickly by hand. The NIC has continued as the primary method of submitting bids, although computers have made more complex methods just as easy to compute. NIC is a way to measure the total amount of interest, without regard for the time value of money, that will be paid over the life of an issue.

With the growing use of the computer, a method of determining the interest cost that does account for the time value of interest payments has been growing in use. The measure is called true interest cost, or TIC (occasionally referred to as Canadian Interest Cost, or CIC). Returning to present value theory, TIC is the internal rate of return that will be paid by the issuer to investors. It is that discount rate that will equalize the sum of the present values of the issuer's cash payments to the bond proceeds collected by the issuer when the bonds are issued. This will be explained more fully below, but it is important to note that TIC and NIC can be significantly different for the same offering.

NET INTEREST COST

NIC is derived by adding the total volume of interest payments for the entire offering and dividing by the amount of bonds outstanding multiplied by the years they are outstanding. If the bonds were issued at a discount, the amount of the discount would be added to the interest payments as if it were an outlay by the issuer. If the bonds were issued at a premium, the amount would be subtracted from interest payments. The formula is as follows:

$$ \text{NIC} = \frac{\text{total interest payments* + discount (or } - \text{ premium)*}}{\text{bond year dollars}} $$

*Accrued interest *may* be treated as an issuance premium to the issuer and is treated accordingly in the computation of the NIC (i.e., as a deduction from total interest payments).

Bond year dollars measure the amount of bonds outstanding over the time they are outstanding—in other words, how much is outstanding for how long. Bond years alone are simply the number of bonds outstanding (in $1,000 denominations) multiplied by the number of years they are outstanding. One bond year is one $1,000 bond outstanding for one year. Bond year dollars are the cumulative number of bond years multiplied by $1,000 for each bond.

The former Center for Capital Market Research at the University of Oregon, which did a great deal of research into these methods, provided the following example of the NIC calculation. The Center was founded and directed by Dr. George Kaufman, who is now at the School of Business Administration, Loyola

University, Chicago. The NIC is computed for a $3,000 offering with three serial maturities and a constant coupon of 5 percent for each maturity.

EXAMPLE 1

Years to Maturity	Par Value	Coupon Rate	Coupon Payments per Maturity	Bond Year Dollars
1	$1,000	5%	$ 50	$1,000
2	1,000	5	100	2,000
3	1,000	5	150	3,000
Total	$3,000		$300	$6,000

The total interest payments come to $300. Fifty dollars is paid out for the first maturity, which is due in a year. Fifty dollars a year is paid out for two years on the second maturity, and for three years on the third maturity. The bonds were issued at par so there is no addition or deduction from the total interest payments for a discount or premium. Bond year dollars equal $6,000. The NIC equals 5 percent.

$$\text{NIC} = \frac{\text{total coupon payments}}{\text{bond year dollars}} = \frac{\$300}{\$6,000} = .05 = 5\%$$

Because the coupon rate was the same for all three issuers, the NIC was precisely equal to the coupon rate. A somewhat more complicated example will help make the calculation clearer. An issuer chooses to sell $10,000 of bonds in five separate maturities. The serial maturities and the coupon rates follow. There are no discounts or premiums.

EXAMPLE 2

Years to Maturity	Par Value	Coupon Rate
1	$1,000	5.00%
2	2,000	5.10
3	2,000	5.20
4	2,000	5.25
5	3,000	5.30

The total interest payments and bond year dollars follow, in order of maturity.

	Coupon Payments per Maturity	Bond Year Dollars
	$ 50	$ 1,000
	204	4,000
	312	6,000
	420	8,000
	795	15,000
Total	$1,781	$34,000

$$\text{NIC} = \frac{\text{total interest}}{\text{bond year dollars}} = \frac{\$1,781}{\$34,000} = .05238 = 5.24\%$$

Had the issue been sold at a discount, the NIC would have been higher. If the issue had sold at an average price of, say, 97, the issuer would have had $300 less in proceeds. To compute the NIC, the $300 would be added to total interest payments. The NIC rises to 6.12 percent.

$$\text{NIC} = \frac{\$ 1,781 + 300}{\$34,000} = \frac{\$ 2,081}{\$34,000} = .06121 = 6.12\%$$

TRUE INTEREST COST

There are a growing number of critics of NIC. They argue that because the method entirely ignores the timing of interest payments, it can often mislead an issuer into choosing a bid with a higher cost to the issuer. In the previous example, the NIC was a function only of the total amount of interest, and did not take into account the consideration of when the interest payments were made. In other words, all $1,781 of interest could have been paid in the first year and the NIC would have still equaled 5.24 percent.

TIC does account for the time value of money. The underlying theory is the same as that which supports the yield to maturity. TIC is the yearly interest rate an issuer would be paying if it were a bank whose savers deposited the bond proceeds and withdrew the interest and principal according to the maturity schedule.

The TIC for Example 2 is not significantly different from the NIC, but a look at how it is computed is valuable. The TIC is 5.236 percent. The NIC is 5.238 percent.

Time to Maturity (Months)	Total Interest Paid	+	Principal Paid	Present Value of Cash Flow Discounted by 5.236%
6	$ 260.00			$ 253.37
12	260.00		$ 1,000.00	1,196.53
18	235.00			217.47
24	235.00		2,000.00	2,015.50
30	184.00			161.70
36	184.00		2,000.00	1,870.30
42	132.00			110.15
48	132.00		2,000.00	1,733.80
54	79.50			63.00
60	79.50		3,000.00	2,378.18
Total	$1,781.00		$10,000.00	$10,000.00

The TIC is the rate that will discount all future cash payments so that the sum of their present value will equal the bond proceeds. Note that the sum of the present value of all the cash flows will equal $10,000 when discounted at 5.236 percent. Interest is assumed to be compounded semiannually. If the offering has been issued at 97, the TIC would have differed more sharply from the NIC. The bond proceeds would have equaled $9,700. The TIC that would discount the present values to equal $9,700 is 6.24 percent. The NIC for the issue at discount would have been 6.12 percent.

Because there is no algebraic formula, the TIC can be found only with a search through the present value tables. The best way to start out is by computing the NIC. Then a yield slightly above or below the NIC can be tried out to discount the cash flows to their present value. If the sum of the present values is too high, a higher discount rate must be tried. If the sum is less than the proceeds, a lower rate must be tried. After many attempts, you can zero in on the final yield.

Computers can calculate such bids almost instantaneously. The information is fed into a computer program, which, in effect, searches for the right answer in much the same way it would be done by hand. The spreading use of the computer has enabled issuers to demand TIC as a basis for assessing bids more frequently.

Differences Between NIC and TIC

The Center for Capital Market Research of the University of Oregon prepared several examples to show how NIC and TIC can be significantly different. The problem with NIC is that it does not account for the time value of interest payments. As we discussed earlier, the NIC would not change, whether all the interest payments were made in the first year or the last year. Before TIC a few issues were structured with high coupons for early maturities, offset by low coupons on later ones. The net effect is to lower NIC, although such a structure would usually result in higher TIC.

Again, the reason this works is that NIC ignores the time value of interest payments. Higher coupons on early maturities result in higher bond prices. But to get the same price premium on a short-term bond as a long-term bond requires a lower total interest payment. Likewise, for every dollar of interest paid over the life of a bond, one would get a higher price on short-term securities than on longer-term securities. The yield to maturity calculations do take the time value of money into account.

An example will help clarify this principle. A one-year bond with an 8 percent coupon would be priced at 100.95 to yield 7 percent to maturity. A ten-year bond with an 8 percent coupon would be priced at 107.11 to yield 7 percent to maturity. The $10 of extra interest paid on the one-year bond results in a price premium of $9.50, or 95¢ for every dollar of interest paid in excess of what would have been paid if the bond were priced at par. On the ten-year bond, a total of $100 in extra interest is paid over the life of the bond. The premium paid is $71.11, or only 71¢ per dollar of interest paid in excess of what would have been paid if the bond were priced to sell at par.

Because NIC will be minimized if the dollar amount of interest paid is minimized while the price of the securities is maximized, some underwriters use the "high-low" technique to price offerings. When taking the time value of money into account, however, the higher coupons on early maturities do penalize the issuer that must pay out the money sooner than would otherwise be necessary. TIC reflects this. It rises if the bulk of interest is paid early and falls if interest payments are pushed back.

The Center for Capital Market Research provided a couple of simple examples based on Example 1 that illustrate this important point. For both the following issues, interest payments equal $300 and total debt service equals $3,300. The NIC for both issues is 5 percent. But the TIC for Issue A is 5.04 percent because coupon payments are made earlier. The TIC for Issue B is only 4.98 percent because interest payments are made later.

		Issue A NIC = 5% TIC = 5.04%			Issue B NIC = 5% TIC = 4.98%	
Years to Maturity	Par Value	Coupon Rate	Annual Debt Service	Coupon Rate	Annual Debt Service	
1	$1,000	12%	$1,190	2%	$1,130	
2	1,000	3	1,070	5	1,110	
3	1,000	4	1,040	6	1,060	
Total	$3,000		$3,300		$3,300	

In addition, economists at the University of Oregon argued that high- and low-coupon bonds that are otherwise equivalent will often trade at higher yields to maturity than bonds priced closer to par. This penalty yield arises for several reasons. With premium bonds, there is more coupon to be reinvested, which increases the risk and transaction cost of reinvestment. Similarly, discount bonds will also sell at comparatively higher yields, largely because the discount is subject to ordinary income tax. Bids with high and low coupons are often inefficient, said the Center, and result in a somewhat higher total interest cost to the issuer.

The Center for Capital Market Research constructed a set of restrictions that bring the NIC more closely in line with the TIC. Among the most common of these is for the issuer to place a maximum limit on the coupon rate to avoid bonds with large premiums in the early years. A maximum limit can also be placed on the size of any discount for which the issue is sold. A discount is just like a coupon payment at the beginning of the issue. One other popular restriction is to require that coupon rates on succeeding maturities are equal to or higher than the rate on the preceding maturity. This keeps underwriters from frontloading the issue with heavy coupon payments. See the Center's publication *Improving Bidding Rules to Reduce Interest Costs in the Competitive Sale of Municipal Bonds* for a complete discussion of bidding rules.

Average Life of Serial Bonds

The average life of a municipal bond offering is the number of bond years divided by the total number of bonds in the issue. In Example 2, the total number of bond years is 34. There are ten bonds in the $10,000 issue. The average life = $34/10 = 3.4$ years.

Glossary of Municipal Terminology

accrued interest—(1) The dollar amount of interest accrued on a municipal security, based on the stated interest rate on that security, from its date to the date of delivery to the original purchaser. This is usually paid by the original purchaser to the issuer as part of the purchase price of the security. (2) The dollar amount of unpaid interest that has accrued to a certain date, such as to a call date.

ad valorem tax—[Latin: to the value added] A tax based on the value (or assessed value) of property.

advance refunding—The refunding of an outstanding issue of bonds by the issuance and delivery of a new issue of bonds prior to the date on which the outstanding issue of bonds can be redeemed or paid in accordance with its terms. Thus, for a period of time both the issue being refunded and the refunding issue are outstanding, although the trust agreement or indenture securing the issue being refunded may be defeased by the deposit of the proceeds of the new issue into an escrow fund for the issue being refunded.

agency transaction—A sale and purchase of bonds when the dealer places bonds with the buyer on a commission basis rather than selling bonds that he owns.

arbitrage—Investment earnings representing the difference between interest paid on bonds and the interest earned on purpose and nonpurpose securities in which bond proceeds are invested. The Internal Revenue Code regulates the amount and conditions under which arbitrage on the investment of bond proceeds is permissible and the 1986 Tax Reform Act requires, with limited exceptions, that arbitrage from nonpurpose investments must be rebated to the federal government.

arbitrage certificate—Transcript certificate evincing compliance with the limitations on arbitrage imposed by the Internal Revenue Code and the applicable regulations.

ascending or positive yield curve—The interest rate structure which exists when long-term interest rates exceed short-term interest rates.

asked price—The price at which securities are offered by sellers (other than issuers) to potential buyers.

assessed valuation—The value of property against which an *ad valorem* tax is levied, usually a percentage of "true" or "market" value.

basis point—Shorthand reference to $1/100$ of 1 percent (.01 percent).

basis price—The price of a security expressed in yield or percentage of return on the investment. Price differentials in municipal bonds are usually expressed in multiples of $5/100$ of 1 percent, or "05."

bearer security—A security that has no identification as to owner. It is presumed to be owned by the bearer or the person who holds it. Bearer securities are freely and easily negotiable since ownership can be quickly transferred from seller to buyer.

blue sky memorandum—A memorandum specifying the way a specific issue will be treated under state securities laws, frequently of all 50 states, Puerto Rico, Guam, and the District of Columbia. This memorandum is prepared first in preliminary form, which may note that certain steps need to be taken in various jurisdictions in order to qualify the issue for sale within these jurisdictions. The memorandum is then issued in supplemental form, and generally the supplemental form reports that the required actions in the various jurisdictions have been taken.

bond—(1) The written evidence of debt, bearing a stated rate or stated rates of interest or stating a formula for determining that rate, and maturing on a date certain, on which date and upon presentation a fixed sum of money plus interest is payable to the holder or owner. An issue is usually composed of many bonds that mature over more than just a few years. (2) For purposes of computations tied in to "per bond," a $1,000 increment of an issue (no matter what the actual denominations are).

bond anticipation note (BAN)—A note issued in anticipation of later issuance of bonds, usually payable from the proceeds of the sale of the bonds anticipated or of renewal notes.

bond bank—Agencies created by some states to buy entire issues of bonds of municipalities. The purchases are financed by the issuance of bonds by the bond bank. The purpose is to provide better market access for small, lesser-known issuers.

bond counsel—A lawyer or law firm, with expertise in bond law, deliver an opinion, upon the closing of an issue of bonds, as to legality of issuance and other matters that may include the description of security pledge and, in the case of a tax-exempt bond, an opinion as to the tax-exempt nature of the bond.

bond funds—Registered investment companies whose assets are invested in diversified portfolios of bonds.

bond insurance—Insurance as to timely payment of interest and principal of a bond issue. The cost of insurance is usually paid by the issuer in case of a new issue of bonds, and the insurance is not purchased unless the cost is more than offset by the lower interest rate that can be incurred by the use of the insurance.

bond purchase agreement—The agreement between the issuer of bonds and the underwriter or underwriters which have agreed to purchase the bonds setting forth the terms of the sale, the price of the bonds, including any premium or discount, the interest rate or rates which the bonds are to bear, the conditions to closing, including the contents (or a description of the contents) of the opinions to be rendered on the date of closing and of certain certificates which are to be delivered on the date of closing, any restrictions on the liability of the issuer, and, occasionally, indemnity provisions if there is not a separate indemnity letter or agreement. Generally, if a matter is to be considered a prerequisite to closing, it must be stated as such in this agreement. (Also called "contract of purchase" or "underwriting agreement.")

bond year—An element in calculating average life of an issue and in calculating net interest cost and net interest rate on an issue. A bond year is the number of 12-month intervals between the date of the bond and its maturity date, measured in $1,000 increments. For example, the "bond years" allocable to a $5,000 bond dated April 1, 1980, and maturing June 1, 1981, is 5.830 [1.166

(14 months divided by 12 months) x 5 (number of $1,000 increments in $5,000 bond)]. Usual computations include "bond years" per maturity or per an interest rate, and total "bond years" for the issue.

brokers—In the municipal securities market, "brokers" play an important role in the secondary market by buying from and selling to dealers on an agency basis.

call—Actions taken to pay the principal amount of the bonds prior to the stated maturity date, in accordance with the provisions for "call" stated in the proceedings and the bonds.

callable—Subject to payment of the principal amount (and accrued interest) prior to the stated maturity date, with or without payment of a call premium.

call premium—A dollar amount, usually stated as a percentage of the principal amount called, paid as a "penalty" or a "premium" for the exercise of a call provision.

closing date—The date on which a new issuance of bonds is delivered to the purchaser upon payment of the purchase price and the satisfaction of all conditions specified in the bond purchase agreement.

commission—The fee paid to a dealer when the dealer acts as agent in a transaction, as opposed to when the dealer acts as a principal in a transaction (see "net price").

competitive underwriting or sale—A sale of municipal securities by an issuer in which underwriters or syndicates of underwriters submit sealed bids (or oral auction bids) to purchase the securities. This is contrasted with a negotiated underwriting.

concession—The allowance (or profit) that an underwriter allows a non-member of the underwriting syndicate; sometimes referred to as the dealer's allowance.

confirmation—A written document confirming an oral transaction in municipal securities that provides pertinent information to the buyer and seller concerning the securities and the terms of the transaction.

coupon—(1) The part of a bearer bond that denotes the amount of interest due and on what date and where the payment is to be made. Coupons are presented to the issuer's designated paying agent or deposited in a commercial bank for collection. Coupons are generally payable semiannually. (2) Coupon is also often used to refer to the interest rate of a bond.

coverage—This is a term usually connected with revenue bonds. The margin of safety for payment of debt service, reflecting the number of times (e.g., "120 percent coverage") by which annual revenues either on a gross or net basis exceed annual debt service.

current yield—This is sometimes called "stock yield." The rate of return on a bond based on the ratio of the coupon income to the purchase or market price. For example, a $1,000 par value bond with a coupon of 8 percent pays $80 in coupon income. If the bond is bought at a price of 90 ($900), the current yield is 80 divided by 900, or 8.9 percent. If the bond is bought at 110 ($1,100), the current yield is 80 divided by 1,100, or 7.3 percent.

CUSIP—The Committee on Uniform Security Identification Procedures, which was established under the auspices of the American Bankers Association to develop a uniform method of identifying municipal, U.S. government, and corporate securities.

dated date (or issue date)—The date of a bond issue from which the bondholder is entitled to receive interest, even though the bonds may actually be delivered at some other date.

dealer—A securities firm or department of a commercial bank that engages in the underwriting, trading, and sales of municipal (or other) securities.

debt limit—Statutory or constitutional limit on the principal amount of debt that an issuer may incur (or that it may have outstanding at any one time).

debt service—Principal and interest.

debt service requirements—Amounts required to pay debt service, often expressed in the context of a time frame (such as "annual debt service requirements").

debt service reserve fund—The fund into which are paid monies which are required by the trust agreement or indenture as a reserve against a temporary interruption in the receipt of the revenues or other amounts which are pledged for the payment of the bonds. A common deposit requirement for a "debt service reserve fund" is one year's debt service on the bonds. The "debt service reserve fund'' may be initially funded out of bond proceeds, over a period of time from revenues, or by a combination of the above. Many of the old trust agreements provided for a maximum amount to be retained in the ''debt service reserve fund'' with no provision for adjusting that amount as the outstanding indebtedness decreases. For a number of reasons, it has recently become the practice to provide for a reduction in the balance in the ''debt service reserve fund'' to an amount equal to the maximum annual debt service required in any of the remaining years during which the bonds are outstanding.

deep discount—A discount greater than traditional market discounts of 1 percent to 3 percent.

default—Failure to pay debt service when due, or failure to comply with other covenants in financing documents.

defeasance—Termination of the rights and interests of the trustee and bondholders under a trust agreement or indenture upon final payment or provision for payment of all debt service and premiums, and other costs, as specifically provided for in the trust instrument.

denomination—The face amount or par value of a bond or note that the issuer promises to pay on the maturity date. Most municipal bonds are issued in a minimum denomination of $5,000, although a few older issues are available in $1,000 denominations. Notes are generally available in a $25,000 minimum denomination.

discount—(1) Amount (stated in dollars or a percent) by which the selling or purchase price of a security is less than its face amount. (2) Amount by which the amount bid for an issue is less than the aggregate principal amount of that issue.

dollar bond—A bond that is quoted and traded in dollar prices rather than in terms of yield.

double-barreled bond—A bond is said to be ''double-barreled'' when it is secured by the pledge of two (or more) sources of payment. In some states a bond secured in the first instance by a user charge, e.g., water or sewer, may be additionally secured by *ad valorem* taxes.

double exemption—Securities that are exempt from state as well as federal income taxes are said to have ''double exemption.'' In states where this exemption occurs, the exemption is usually only for bonds issued by the state or its local governments. An exception to this rule is the bond debt of U.S. territories such as Guam. Debt of Puerto Rico is also double exempt.

exempt facilities bond—Refers to those types of privately owned or privately used facilities which are authorized to be issued on a tax-exempt basis under the Internal Revenue Code. The Tax Reform Act of 1986 amended prior law to exclude the following types of facilities from those which can be financed on a tax-exempt basis: sports facilities; convention and trade show facilities; air and water pollution control facilities; privately owned airports, docks, wharves, and mass-commuting facilities; and most parking facilities, among others.

extraordinary redemption—This is different from optional redemption or mandatory redemption in that it occurs under an unusual circumstance such as destruction of the facility financed.

face amount—The par value (i.e., principal or maturity value) of a security appearing on the face of the instrument.

financial advisor—A consultant to an issuer of municipal securities who provides the issuer with advice with respect to the structure, timing, terms, or other similar matters concerning a new issue of securities.

financial and operations principal—A municipal securities employee who is required to meet qualifications standards established by the MSRB. The individual is the person designated to be in charge of the preparation and filing of financial reports to the SEC and other regulatory bodies.

flow of funds—Refers to the structure which is established in the trust instruments or bond legislation for the handling of the revenues or other funds or monies pledged for the payment of the bonds as and when received.

fully registered—A security that is registered as to principal and interest, payment of which is made only to or on the order of the registered owner.

general obligation bond (GO)—A bond secured by the pledge of the issuer's full faith, credit, and, usually, taxing power. The taxing power may be an unlimited *ad valorem* tax or a limited tax, usually on real estate and personal property. Most states don't tax real estate, but leave that power to local units of government.

initial delivery—The delivery of a new issue by the issuer to the original purchaser, upon payment of the purchase price. Also called "original delivery."

initial offering price—The price (based upon yield to maturity) stated as a percentage of par at which the underwriting account determines to market the issue during a set period of time, called the initial offering period. Members of the account may not offer any part of the issue at any other price during that period.

interest—Compensation paid or to be paid for the use of money. Interest is generally expressed as an annual percentage rate.

inverted or negative yield curve—The interest rate structure which exists when short-term interest rates exceed long-term interest rates (see "ascending or positive yield curve").

issuer—The public entity that issues securities and is named as the issuer-obligor on those securities. The public entity is the "issuer" even in those cases where the actual source of the money to pay debt service is to be an entity other than the issuer.

joint managers—Underwriting accounts are headed by a manager. When an account is made up of several groups of underwriting firms that normally function as separate accounts, the larger account is often managed by several underwriters, usually one from each of the several groups, and these managers are referred to as "joint managers."

legal opinion—An opinion of bond counsel concerning the validity of a securities issue with respect to statutory authority, constitutionality, procedural conformity, and usually the exemption of interest from federal income taxes.

letter of credit (LOC)—A security document usually issued by a bank that backstops, or enhances, the basic security behind a bond. In the case of a direct pay "LOC," the bondholder can request the bank to make payment directly rather than through the issuer.

level debt service—The result of a maturity schedule that has increasing principal amounts maturing each year so that the debt service in all years is essentially "level." "Level debt service" is often used with revenue bond issues (and, in a familiar area, in the traditional approach to monthly payments on home mortgages).

limited tax bond—A bond secured by a pledge of a tax or category of taxes limited as to rate or amount.

manager (or senior manager)—The underwriter that serves as the lead underwriter for an account. The "manager" generally negotiates the interest rate and purchase price in a negotiated transaction or serves as the generator of the consensus for the interest rate and purchase price to be bid in a competitive bidding situation. The "manager" signs the contracts on behalf of the account and generally receives either a fee or slightly larger spread for its services in this capacity (see "joint managers").

mandatory sinking fund redemption—A requirement to redeem a fixed portion of term bonds, which may comprise the entire issue, in accordance with a fixed schedule. Although the principal amount of the bonds to be redeemed is fixed, the specific bonds which will be called to satisfy the requirement as to amount are selected by the trustee on a lot basis.

marketability—A measure of the ease with which a security can be sold in the secondary market without an undue price concession.

maturity date—The stated date on which all or a stated portion of the principal amount of a security is due and payable.

maturity schedule—The schedule (by dates and amounts) of principal maturities of an issue.

monetary default—Failure to pay principal or interest promptly when due.

moral obligation bond—A type of municipal security, issued by a state agency, that is not backed by the full faith and credit of a state, but state law may provide that the agency request an appropriation from the legislature to replenish the issuer's debt service reserve fund if necessary. The legislature is not required to make the appropriation.

mortgage revenue bond—A security issued by a state, certain agencies or authorities, or a local government to make or purchase loans (including mortgages or other owner-financing) with respect to single-family or multifamily residences.

municipal securities principal—A municipal securities employee under MSRB rules who has supervisory responsibility for the municipal securities operations of the firm.

municipal securities representatives—The broadest class of municipal securities professionals who are required to pass a qualifications examination under the rules of the MSRB. This group includes individuals who underwrite, trade, or sell municipal securities, do research or offer investment advice, provide financial advisory services, or communicate with investors in municipal securities.

Municipal Securities Rulemaking Board (MSRB)—An independent self-regulatory organization established by the Securities Acts Amendments of 1975, which is charged with primary rulemaking authority over dealers, dealer banks, and brokers in municipal securities. Its 15 members are divided into three categories—securities firms representatives, bank dealer representatives, and public members, each category having equal representation on the Board.

negotiated underwriting—In a negotiated underwriting the sale of bonds is by negotiation with an underwriter rather than by competitive bidding. In many states general obligation bonds must be sold at a competitive sale.

net direct debt—Total direct debt of a municipality less all self-supporting debt, any sinking funds, and short-term debt such as tax anticipation notes and revenue anticipation notes.

net interest cost—The traditional method of calculating bids for new issues of municipal securities. The total dollar amount of interest over the life of the bonds is adjusted by the amount of premium or discount bid, and then reduced to an average annual rate. The other method is known as the true interest cost (see ''true interest cost'').

net price—This is the price paid to a dealer for bonds when the dealer acts as principal in a transaction, i.e., the dealer sells bonds that he owns, as opposed to an agency transaction (see ''agency transaction'').

noncallable bond—A bond that cannot be called for redemption at the option of the issuer before its specified maturity date.

notes—Short-term promises to pay specified amounts of money, secured usually by specific sources of future revenues, such as taxes, federal and state aid payments, and bond proceeds.

notice of sale—An official document disseminated by an issuer of municipal securities that gives pertinent information regarding an upcoming bond issue and invites bids from prospective underwriters.

offering price—The price at which members of an underwriting syndicate for a new issue will offer securities to investors.

official statement—The document prepared by or for the issuer that gives in detail security and financial information about the issue.

optional redemption—A right to retire an issue or a portion thereof prior to the stated maturity thereof during a specified period of years. The right can be exercised at the option of the issuer or, in pass-through issues, of the primary obligor. ''Optional redemption'' usually requires the payment of a premium for its exercise with the amount of the premium decreasing the nearer the option exercise date is to the final maturity date of the issue.

original delivery—See ''initial delivery.''

Over-the-Counter Market (OTC)—A securities market that is conducted by dealers throughout the country through negotiation of price rather than through the use of an auction system as represented by a stock exchange.

overlapping debt—On a municipal issuer's financial statement ''overlapping debt'' is the debt of other issuers which is payable in whole or in part by taxpayers of the subject issuer. As an example, a county usually includes several smaller governmental units and its debt is apportioned to them for payment based on the ratio of the assessed value of each smaller unit to the assessed value of the county. Another example is when a school district includes two or more municipalities within its bounds. In each example ''overlapping debt'' is the proportionate share of the county and/or of the school district borne by included subject issuer.

par value—The principal amount of a bond or note due at maturity.

parity debt—Securities issued or to be issued with equal and ratable claim on the same underlying security and source of payment for debt service.

paying agent—Place where principal and interest are payable. Usually a designated bank or the office of the treasurer of the issuer.

point—Shorthand reference to 1 percent. In the context of a "bond," a "point" means $10 since a "bond" with this reference means $1,000 (no matter what the actual denominations of the bonds of the issue). An issue or a security that is "discounted two points" is quoted at 98 percent of its par value.

pollution control bond—A debt security issued by a state, certain agencies or authorities, a local government, or a development corporation to finance the construction of air or water pollution control facilities or sewage or solid waste disposal facilities pursuant to federal law. The bonds are backed by the credit of the beneficiary of the financing rather than the credit of the issuer. New issues of these bonds are prohibited under the 1986 Tax Reform Act.

premium—The amount by which the price of or offered for an issue or a security exceeds its par value. Stated in terms of "priced at 102" (i.e., 102 percent of the face amount) or, in the case of the original purchase price from an issuer, of a premium of specified dollars (a "premium of $X").

prepayment provision—Provision specifying that, and at what time and on what terms, repayment of the principal amount may be made by the issuer prior to the stated maturity. Includes "call," but "prepayment" usually connotes less formal procedures than a call.

price—Security price, generally quoted either in terms of percent of par value (e.g., premium price = 102, discount price = 99) or in terms of annual yield to maturity (e.g., "yielding 7³/₈ percent").

primary market (new-issue market)—Market for new issues of municipal bonds and notes.

principal—The face amount of a bond, which the issuer promises to pay at maturity.

put bond—A put is an option given to the holder of a bond to "put," or tender, the bond to an issuer (or trustee or tender agent) and demand purchase of the bond at a stated time before maturity, or upon the occurrence of particular circumstances.

rate covenant—A covenant in the financing proceedings requiring the charging of rates or fees for the use of specified facilities or operations at least sufficient to achieve a stated minimum coverage (see "coverage").

ratings—Designations used by rating services to give indications of relative credit quality.

refunding—Sale of a new issue, the proceeds of which are to be used, immediately or in the future, to retire an outstanding issue by, essentially, replacing the outstanding issue with the new issue. The purpose of ''refunding'' may be to save interest cost, extend the maturity of the debt, or to eliminate existing restrictive covenants.

remarketing—A formal re-underwriting of a bond for which the form or structure is being changed. Most commonly used in connection with changing variable rate to fixed rate financings, typically because ''the construction phase is over''; or rates are at a level the issuer feels comfortable with for the long-term; or because of indenture requirements (probably relating to arbitrage).

registered securities—Securities registered ''on the books'' of the issuer or trustee as to ownership, the transfer of ownership (and of the right to payment) of which must be registered with the issuer or trustee.

revenue anticipation note (RAN)—RANs are issued in anticipation of other sources of future revenue other than taxes, typically federal or state aid.

revenue bond—A bond on which the debt service is payable solely from the revenue generated from the operation of the project being financed or a category of facilities, or from other non-tax sources.

secondary market—Market for issues previously offered or sold.

selling group—A selling group includes dealers or brokers that have been asked to join in the offering of a new issue of securities, but are neither liable for any unsold syndicate balance nor share in the profits of the overall syndicate. They obtain securities for sale less the takedown.

serial bonds—All or a portion of an issue with stated maturities (as opposed to mandatory sinking fund redemption amounts) in consecutive years.

settlement date—The date, usually five business days after the trade date, on which payment is made and securities are delivered for payment (see ''trade date'').

sinking fund—Separate accumulation of cash or investments (including earnings on investments) in a fund in accordance with the terms of a trust agreement or indenture, funded by periodic deposits by the issuer (or other entity responsible for debt service), for the purpose of assuring timely availability of monies for payment of debt service. Usually used in connection with term bonds.

special tax bond—A bond secured by a special tax, such as a gasoline tax or a sales tax.

spread—The difference between the price at which an issue is purchased from an issuer and that at which it is reoffered by the underwriters to the first holders.

swap—A transaction in which an investor sells one security and simultaneously buys another with the proceeds, usually for about the same price and frequently for tax purposes.

syndicate—A group of underwriters formed for the purpose of participating jointly in the initial public offering of a new issue of municipal securities. The terms under which a "syndicate" is formed and operates are typically set forth in an "agreement among underwriters." Those terms will establish the pro rata participation of each syndicate member, the methods by which offering prices and other terms of sale will be established, in what priority orders for securities will be taken and confirmed and the joint or several nature of the liability assumed by each member for the purchase of unsold securities. The purpose of a "syndicate" formation is to share the risk of the offering among participating underwriters and to establish a distribution network in which to market the offered securities. One or more underwriters will act as manager of the "syndicate" and one of the managers will act as lead manager and "run the books." A "syndicate" is also often referred to as an "account" or "underwriting account."

takedown—The discount from the list price allowed to a member of an underwriting account on any bonds purchased from the account.

tax anticipation note (TAN)—TANs are issued by states or municipalities to finance current operations in anticipation of future tax receipts.

tax base—The total property and resources subject to taxation (see "assessed valuation").

tax-exempt commercial paper—This is a short-term promissory note issued for periods up to 270 days, and is often used in lieu of BANs, TANs, and RANs because of the greater flexibility offered in setting both maturities and determining rates.

technical default—A default under the bond indenture terms, other than nonpayment of interest or principal. Examples of technical default are failure to maintain required reserves or to maintain adequate fees and charges for service.

term bonds—Bonds of an issue that have a single stated maturity date. Typically, an issuer is required to call or purchase a certain amount of the term bonds at regular intervals before the stated maturity date using money set aside in a sinking fund.

total bonded debt—Total general obligation bond debt outstanding of a municipality, regardless of the purpose.

total direct debt—The sum of the total bond debt and any unfunded debt (typically short-term notes) of a municipality.

trade date—The date that a trade, or sale and purchase, is consummated, with settlement to be made later (see ''settlement date'').

transcript of proceedings—Documents relating to a municipal bond issue.

true interest cost—A method of calculating bids for new issues of municipal securities that takes into consideration the time value of money (see ''net interest cost'').

true yield—The rate of return to the investor taking into account the payment of capital gains at maturity on a bond bought at a discount.

trust agreement—Agreement between an issuer and a trustee acting on behalf of bondholders (1) authorizing and securing the bonds; (2) containing the issuer's covenants and obligations with respect to the project and payment of debt service; (3) specifying the events of default; and (4) outlining the trustee's fiduciary responsibilities and bondholders' rights.

trustee—A bank designated by the issuer as the custodian of funds and official representative of bondholders. ''Trustees'' are appointed to insure compliance with the contract and represent bondholders to enforce their contract with the issuers.

underwrite—To purchase a bond or note issue from an issuer to resell it to investors.

underwriting spread—The difference between the offering price to the public by the underwriter and the purchase price the underwriter pays to the issuer. The underwriter's expenses and selling costs are usually paid from this amount.

unit investment trust (municipal)—A fixed portfolio of tax-exempt bonds sold in fractional, undivided interests (usually $1,000).

unlimited tax bond—A bond secured by the pledge of taxes that are not limited by rate or amount.

variable-rate demand obligation (VRDO)—A Bond which bears interest at a variable or floating rate established at specified intervals (*e.g.*, daily, weekly, or monthly) and which contains a put option permitting the bondholder to tender the bond for purchase on the date a new interest rate is established.

yield to maturity—A yield concept based on the assumption that the bond is held to maturity and that all interest received over the life of the bond is reinvested at the coupon rate of interest. The concept is used when a transaction is done at a price other than at par.

zero-coupon bond—A bond that is issued at a deep discount and which bears no stated rate of interest. Like a Series E savings bond, the bond is bought at a discount price which implies a stated rate of return calculated on the basis of the bond being payable at par at maturity.

Bibliography

Advisory Commission on Intergovernmental Relations. ''A Commission Report: Bankruptcies, Defaults and Other Local Government Financial Emergencies.'' Washington, D.C.: ACIR, 1985.

Advisory Commission on Intergovernmental Relations. ''A Commission Report, City Financial Emergencies: The Intergovernmental Dimension.'' Washington, D.C.: ACIR, 1973.

Andrew, John. *Buying Municipal Bonds, The Common Sense Guide to Tax-Free Personal Investing.* New York, N.Y.: The Free Press, A Division of Macmillan, Inc., 1987.

Anthony, Robert N. *Financial Accounting in Nonbusiness Organizations.* Stamford, Conn.: Financial Accounting Standards Board, 1978.

Auletta, Kenneth. *The Streets Were Paved with Gold.* New York, N.Y.: Random House, 1979.

Bahl, Roy, and Bernard Jump, Jr. *Projecting the Fiscal Viability of Cities.* Syracuse, N.Y.: Metropolitan Studies Program, Maxwell School of Citizenship and Public Affairs, Syracuse University, 1977.

The Bond Buyer. *Municipal Finance Statistics,* annually. New York, N.Y.

The Bond Buyer. *Directory of Municipal Bond Dealers of the United States,* semiannually. New York, N.Y.: The Bond Buyer.

Bourgene, Donald D., Robert W. Doty, Ronald W. Forbes, and John E. Petersen. ''Searching for Standards: Disclosure in the Municipal Securities Market.'' *Duke Law Journal* 6 (1976).

Center for Capital Market Research, University of Oregon. *Improving Bidding Rules to Reduce Interest Costs in the Competitive Sale of Municipal Bonds: A Handbook For Municipal Finance Officers.* Eugene, Oreg.: CCMR, 1977 (out of print, library copies only).

Chan, James L., ed. *Research in Governmental and Non-Profit Accounting: A Research Annual.* Chicago, Ill.: Office for Governmental Accounting, Research and Education, vol. 6., University of Illinois, 1985.

Cole, Lisa A., and John A. Vogt. *A Guide To Municipal Leasing.* Chicago, Ill.: Government Finance Officers Association, 1983.

Cooner, James J. *Investing in Municipal Bonds, Balancing Risks and Rewards.* New York, N.Y.: John Wiley & Sons, 1987.

Darst, David M. *The Complete Bond Book.* New York, N.Y.: McGraw-Hill, Inc., 1975.

The Donoghue Organization, Inc. IBC/"Donoghue's Money Fund Report®," Holliston, Mass.: The Donoghue Organization, Inc., 1989.

Doty, Robert W., and John E. Petersen. "The Federal Securities Laws and Transactions in Municipal Securities." *Northwestern University Law Review* 3 (July-August 1976), 283-416.

Fabozzi, Frank J., Sylvan G. Feldstein, Irving M. Pollack, and Frank G. Zarb, eds. *The Municipal Bond Handbook,* vol. 1. Homewood, Ill.: Dow Jones-Irwin, Inc., 1983.

Fabozzi, Frank J., and Irving M. Pollack, eds. *The Handbook of Fixed-Income Securities,* 2d ed. Homewood, Ill: Dow Jones-Irwin, Inc., 1987.

Federal Reserve Board. *Flow of Funds.* Washington, D.C.

Feldstein, Sylvan G., and Frank J. Fabozzi. *The Dow Jones-Irwin Guide to Municipal Bonds.* Homewood, Ill.: Dow Jones-Irwin, Inc., 1987.

Feldstein, Sylvan G., Frank J. Fabozzi, and Irving M. Pollack, eds. *The Municipal Bond Handbook,* vol. 2. Homewood, Ill.: Dow Jones-Irwin, Inc., 1983.

Financial Publishing Company. *Comprehensive Bond Values Tables.* Boston, Mass.

Government Accounting Standards Board and Government Accounting Research Foundation. *Codification of Governmental Accounting and Financial Reporting Standards* as of November 1, 1984. Stamford, Conn. and Chicago, Ill.: GASB and GARF, 1985.

Government Finance Officers Association. *Disclosure Guidelines for State and Local Governments.* Chicago, Ill.: GFOA, 1988.

Government Finance Officers Association. *Official Statements for Offerings of Securities by Local Governments—Examples and Guidelines.* Chicago, Ill.: GFOA, 1981.

Hempel, George H. *The Postwar Quality of State and Local Debt.* New York, N.Y.: National Bureau of Economic Research, 1971.

Homer, Sidney. *History of Interest Rates.* 2d ed., completely revised. New Brunswick, N.J.: Rutgers University Press, 1977.

Homer, Sidney, and Martin L. Liebowitz. *Inside the Yield Book: New Tools for Bond Market Strategy.* Englewood Cliffs, N.J.: Prentice-Hall, Inc., and New York Institute of Finance, 1972.

Hopewell, Michael H., and George G. Kaufman of the Center for Capital Market Research, University of Oregon. "Costs to Municipalities of Selling Bonds by NIC." *National Tax Journal* 27 (March 1974).

Joint Economic Committee, Congress of the United States. *Hard Choices.* U.S. Government Printing Office (S. Prt. 98-164), February 1984.

Kidwell, D., and T. Koch. "Market Segmentation and Term Structure of Municipal Yields." *Journal of Money, Credit, and Banking* (February 1983), 40-55.

Laffey, Martharose F., John E. Petersen, and Catherine L. Spain, eds. *State and Local Government Finance and Financial Management: A Compendium of Current Research.* Washington, D.C.: Government Finance Research Center of the Government Finance Officers Association, 1978.

Lamb, Robert and Stephen P. Rappaport. *Municipal Bonds, The Comprehensive Review of Tax-Exempt Securities and Public Finance.* New York, N.Y.: McGraw-Hill, Inc., 1980.

Lamb, Robert and Stephen P. Rappaport. *Municipal Bonds.* 2d ed. New York, N.Y.: McGraw-Hill, Inc., 1987.

Miller, Girard. *A Public Investor's Guide to Money Market Instruments.* Chicago, Ill.: Government Finance Officers Association, 1982.

Moak, Lennox L. *Municipal Bonds: Planning, Sale, and Administration.* Chicago, Ill.: Government Finance Officers Association, 1982.

Moak, Lennox L. *Administration of Local Government Debt.* Chicago, Ill.: Government Finance Officers Association, 1970.

Moak, Lennox L. and Albert M. Hillhouse. *Concepts and Practices in Local Government Finance.* Chicago, Ill.: Government Finance Officers Association, 1975.

Moody's Investors Service, Inc. *Moody's Bond Record: Corporates, Convertibles, Governments, Municipals and Commercial Paper Ratings, Preferred Stock Ratings,* monthly. New York, N.Y.: Moody's.

Moody's Investors Service, Inc. *Moody's Bond Survey,* weekly. New York, N.Y.: Moody's.

Moody's Investors Service, Inc. *Moody's on Municipals: An Introduction to Issuing Debt.* New York, N.Y.: Moody's, 1987.

Municipal Securities Rulemaking Board, *Glossary of Municipal Securities Terms,* adapted from the State of Florida's *Glossary of Municipal Bond Terms.* Washington, D.C.: MSRB, 1985.

Municipal Securities Rulemaking Board. *MSRB Manual, Laws, Rules and Regulations,* updated semiannually. Chicago, Ill.: Commerce Clearing House, Inc., 1986.

National Council on Governmental Accounting, Government Finance Officers Association. *Governmental Accounting, Auditing, and Financial Reporting.* Chicago, Ill.: GFOA, 1980.

National Council on Public Works Improvement. *The Nation's Public Works: Defining the Issues.* Washington, D.C.: 1986.

Nicholas, James C. *The Changing Structure of Infrastructure Finance.* Lincoln Institute of Land Policy, February 1985.

Petersen, John E., and Wesley C. Hough. *Creative Capital Financing for State and Local Governments.* Chicago, Ill.: Government Finance Officers Association, 1983.

Petersen, John E. *The Rating Game.* New York, N.Y.: The Twentieth Century Fund, 1974. Reprinted by Kraus Reprint Co., Millwood, N.Y., 1977.

Public Securities Association. *An Investor's Guide to Tax-Exempt Securities.* New York, N.Y.: PSA.

Public Securities Association. *An Investor's Guide to Tax-Exempt Unit Investment Trusts.* New York, N.Y.: PSA.

Restoring Credit and Confidence, A Report to the New York State Moreland Act Commission, 1976.

SEC Staff Report on Transactions in Securities of the City of New York, 1977.

Smith, Owen T., ed. *Municipal Finance Journal,* quarterly. Greenvale, N.Y.: Panel Publishers.

Smith, Wade S. *The Appraisal of Municipal Credit Risk.* New York, N.Y.: Moody's Investors Service, Inc., 1979.

Standard & Poor's Corporation. *Municipal Credit Overview.* New York, N.Y.: S&P, 1986.

Standard & Poor's Corporation. *Standard & Poor's Municipal Bond Book.* New York, N.Y.: S&P, 1987.

Stigum, Marcia. *The Money Market,* rev. ed. Homewood, Ill.: Dow Jones-Irwin, Inc., 1983.

White, Wilson. *The Municipal Bond Market: Basics.* Jersey City, N.J.: The Financial Press, 1985.

Index